EBONY and TOPAZ

A COLLECTANEA

EBONY AND TOPAZ

A COLLECTANEA

Edited by

CHARLES S. JOHNSON

The Black Heritage Library Collection

BOOKS FOR LIBRARIES PRESS
FREEPORT, NEW YORK
1971

First Published 1927
Reprinted 1971

Reprinted from a copy in the
Fisk University Library Negro Collection

INTERNATIONAL STANDARD BOOK NUMBER:
0-8369-8823-X

LIBRARY OF CONGRESS CATALOG CARD NUMBER:
70-161264

PRINTED IN THE UNITED STATES OF AMERICA

FOREWORD

※─❦─※

IF "every life has pages vacant still whereon a man may write the thing he will," it is also true that in many little-considered lives there are pages whereon matter of great interest has already been written, if the appraising eye can only reach it.

So with the recently developed discoveries of the wealth of material for artistic and intellectual development in the life, manners, and customs of the Negro and his unique and all-too-frequently unappreciated and unasked contribution to our American self-consciousness.

This challenging collection focuses, as it were, the appraising eyes of white folks on the Negro's life and of Negroes on their own life and development in what seems to me a new and stimulating way.

Great emotional waves may not be stirred by taking cognizance of the performances of Negroes in art and literature, but faithfulness to an ideal of proportion or fair play makes us uneasy lest through ignorance we miss something by straying into the tangles of prejudice.

Most of us claim to recognize Miss Millay's thought that

> *"He whose soul is flat, the sky*
> *Will fall in on him by and by."*

and will follow with zest the explorations of appraising eyes which have been made available to us in attractive form on these pages.

L. HOLLINGSWORTH WOOD.

CONTENTS

FOREWORD..By L. Hollingsworth Wood

INTRODUCTION—By Charles S. Johnson.. 11

JUMBY—A Story by Arthur Huff Fauset.. 15

ON THE ROAD ONE DAY, LORD—By Paul Green.......................... 25

DUSK—A Poem by Mae V. Cowdery 26

DIVINE AFFLATUS—A Poem by Jessie Fauset................................... 27

GENERAL DRUMS—A Story by John Matheus.................................... 29

GULLAH—By Julia Peterkin... 35

REQUIEM—A Poem by Georgia Douglas Johnson............................... 35

FORECLOSURE—A Poem by Sterling A. Brown................................. 36

DREAMER—A Poem by Langston Hughes... 36

THE DUNES—A Poem by E. Merrill Root... 36

EIGHTEENTH STREET—An Anthology in Color by Nathan Ben Young...... 37

JOHN HENRY—A Negro Legend by Guy B. Johnson............................ 47

THINGS SAID WHEN HE WAS GONE—A Poem by Blanche Taylor
    Dickinson 51

APRIL IS ON THE WAY—A Poem by Alice Dunbar Nelson................... 52

THE FIRST ONE— A Play in One Act by Zora Neale Hurston................ 53

THIS PLACE—A Poem by Donald Jeffrey Hayes................................. 57

THREE POEMS—By Countee Cullen.. 58

NEW LIGHT ON AN OLD SONG—By Dorothy Scarborough................. 59

LA PERLA NEGRA—By Edna Worthley Underwood............................. 60

THE NEGRO OF THE JAZZ BAND—Translated from the Spanish of
    Jose M. Salaverria by Dorothy Peterson....................................... 63

IDOLATRY—A Poem by Arna Bontemps.. 66

TO CLARISSA SCOTT DELANY—A poem by Angelina W. Grimke......... 67

JUAN LATINO, MAGISTER LATINUS—By Arthur A. Schomburg......... 69

AND ONE SHALL LIVE IN TWO—A Poem by Jonathan H. Brooks....... 72

A POEM—By Phillis Wheatley.. 78

THE RUNAWAY SLAVE AT PILGRIM'S POINT—By Elizabeth Barrett
    Browning... 78

THE NATURAL HISTORY OF RACE PREJUDICE—By Ellsworth Faris... 89

FACSIMILES of Original Manuscripts of Paul Laurence Dunbar............... 95

SYBIL WARNS HER SISTER—A Poem by Anne Spencer 94

SOME OBSERVATIONS ON THE AMERICAN RACE PROBLEM—
By Eugene Kinckle Jones 96

ARABESQUE—A Poem by Frank Horne 99

PHANTOM COLOR LINE—By T. Arnold Hill 100

THE CHANGING STATUS OF THE MULATTO—By E. B. Reuter 107

SUFFRAGE—By William Pickens 111

CONSECRATION—A Poem by Lois Augusta Cuglar 114

UNDERGRADUATE VERSE—Fisk University 115

OUR LITTLE RENAISSANCE—By Alain Locke 117

MY HEART HAS KNOWN ITS WINTER—A Poem by Arna Bontemps 118

RACIAL SELF-EXPRESSION—By E. Franklin Frazier 119

OUR GREATEST GIFT TO AMERICA—by George S. Schuyler 122

EFFIGY—A Poem by Lewis Alexander 124

THE NEGRO ACTOR'S DEFICIT—By Theophilus Lewis 125

TWO POEMS—By Edward S. Silvera 127

DUNCANSON—By W. P. Dabney 128

YOUTH—A Poem by Frank Horne 129

THE PROSPECTS OF BLACK BOURGEOISIE—By Abram Harris 131

TO A YOUNG POET—A Poem by George Chester Morse 134

A PAGE OF UNDERGRADUATE VERSE—Shaw University, Lincoln
University, Tougaloo College, Howard University 135

VERISIMILITUDE—A Story by John P. Davis 137

MRS. BAILEY PAYS THE RENT—By Ira DeA. Reid 144

A SONNET TO A NEGRO IN HARLEM—A Poem by Helene Johnson 148

TOKENS—A Story by Gwendolyn Bennett 149

A PAGE OF UNDERGRADUATE VERSE—Tougaloo College, Cleveland
College of Western Reserve University 151

THE RETURN—A Poem by Arna Bontemps 153

I—By Brenda Ray Moryck 154

A GLORIOUS COMPANY—By Allison Davis 156

A STUDENT I KNOW—A Poem by Jonathan H. Brooks 157

AND I PASSED BY—By Joseph Maree Andrew 158

WHO'S WHO 163

ILLUSTRATIONS

Half-title page ....By Charles Cullen

Frontispiece..By Charles Cullen

Pen Drawings in Contents..By Richard Bruce

Drawing for *Jumby*—By Aaron Douglas... 14

Drawing for *On the Road One day, Lord*—By Aaron Douglas.................... 22

Drawing for *General Drums*—By Aaron Douglas....................................... 28

Reproduction of African Sculptures from Barnes Foundation....................... 76

A pen drawing of Phillis Wheatley—By W. E. Braxton............................... 78

Illustrations for *Runaway Slave at Pilgrim's Point*—By Charles Cullen........ 80

A drawing—By Baron Von Rucksteschell... 88

A pen drawing of E. K. Jones—By Francis Holbrook................................. 97

Four drawings for Mulattoes—By Richard Bruce....................................... 103

A drawing—By Charles Cullen... 116

A drawing—by Aaron Douglas.. 130

A drawing from *Copper Sun*—By Charles Cullen...................................... 136

Mezzo tint from a painting by P. Van Dyk del... 68

Facsimile of privilege to print and title page of book by Latino................. 71

Four paintings by Sebastian Gomez, the Negro of Spain:

    Jesus Tied to a Column.. 73

    The Sacred Family.. 74

    Immaculate Conception 74

    The Immaculate Conception 75

Facsimile of pamphlet of *An Elegy*—By Phillis Wheatley......................... 77

A mezzo-tint of Ignatius Sancho from a painting by Gainsborough............ 79

Reproduction of a portrait of Francis Barber by Sir Joshua Reynolds........ 79

A Drawing by Charles Cullen

> "It is better to walk
> Than to grow angry with the road."
> An African Proverb.

INTRODUCTION

IT is only fair to rid this volume, at the beginning, of some of the usual pretensions, which have the effect of distorting normal values, most often with results as unfortunate as they are unfair. This volume, strangely enough, does not set forth to prove a thesis, nor to plead a cause, nor, stranger still, to offer a progress report on the state of Negro letters. It is a venture in expression, shared, with the slightest editorial suggestion, by a number of persons who are here much less interested in their audience than in what they are trying to say, and the life they are trying to portray. This measurable freedom from the usual burden of proof has been an aid to spontaneity, and to this quality the collection makes its most serious claim.

It is not improbable that some of our white readers will arch their brows or perhaps knit them soberly at some point before the end. But this is a response not infrequently met with outside the pages of books. There is always an escape of a sort, however, in ignoring that which contradicts one's sense, even though it were the better wisdom to give heed.

Some of our Negro readers will doubtless quarrel with certain of the Negro characters who move in these pages. But it is also true that in life some Negroes are distasteful to other Negroes. Following the familiar patterns, we are accustomed to think of Negroes as one ethnic unit, and of whites as many,—the Nordics, Mediterraneans; or Germans, Irish, Swedes; or brachycephalics and dolichocephalics, depending upon our school of politics or anthropology. The significance of the difference is not so much that Negroes in America actually represent different races among themselves, as that there is the same ground, in dissimilar customs and culture patterns, which are the really valid distinctions between races, for viewing Negroes differently among themselves. The point, if it were important enough, could be proved about as satisfactorily as proofs in this field go, and with the same type of data. Beneath the difference, however, as must be evident, is the cultural factor which distinguishes one group of Negroes from another: the small, articulate group from the more numerous, and, one might even add, more interesting folk group; the unconscious Negro folk contributions to music, folk lore, and the dance, from the conscious contributions of Negroes to art and letters. The sociological confusion here has brought about endless literary debates.

Accepting the materials of Negro life for their own worth, it is impossible to escape certain implications: It is significant that white and Negro writers and artists are finding together the highest expression of their art in this corner of life. And, as Mr. Albert Jay Nock reminds us, an interesting person in literature is just what he is in life. It is evident in many quarters that Negroes are being discovered as "fellow mortals," with complexes of their own to be analyzed. With Julia Peterkin, Paul Green, Dubose Heyward, Guy Johnson, there has been ushered in a refreshing new picture of Negro life in the south. Swinging free from the old and exhausted stereotypes and reading from life, they have created human characters who are capable of living by their own charm and power. There is something here infinitely more real and honest in the atmosphere thus created, than in the stagnant sentimental aura which has hung about their heads for so many years.

The Negro writers, removed by two generations from slavery, are now much less self-conscious, less interested in proving that they are just like white people, and, in their excursions into the fields of letters and art, seem to care less about what white people think, or are likely to think about the race. Relief from the stifling consciousness of being a problem has brought a certain superiority to it. There is more candor, even in discussions of themselves, about weaknesses, and on the very sound reasoning that unless they are truthful about their faults, they will not be believed when they chose to speak about their virtues. A sense of humor is present. The taboos and racial ritual are less strict; there is more overt self-criticism, less of bitterness and appeals to sympathy. The sensitiveness, which a brief decade ago, denied the existence of any but educated Negroes, bitterly opposing Negro dialect, and folk songs, and anything that revived the memory of slavery, is shading off into a sensitiveness to the hidden beauties of this life and a frank joy and pride in it. The return of the Negro writers to folk materials has proved a new emancipation.

It might not seem to go too far afield to refer to the statements offered not infrequently in criticism, that the cultured Negroes are not romanticized in fiction as generously as the folk types. This has a distinctly sociological implication back of which is the feeling that a loftier opinion of all Negroes would follow an emphasis in fiction upon more educated individuals. The attitude is not uncommon in the history of other races and classes. For many years, Americans were affected by the same sensitiveness in relation to Europe, and even in the Southern United States, until very recently, the literature has been defensive and for the most part ineffectual. Aside from the greater color and force of life in those human strata which seem to have struck lightning to the imaginations of our present writers, it might be suggested that the educated Negroes, even if they are not yet being romanticized in fiction, are finding a most effective representation through their own comment upon the extraordinarily interesting patterns of Negro folk life to which they have intimate access. Or, perhaps, they have succeeded only too well in becoming like other people whom writers generally are finding it difficult enough to make interesting.

The most that will be claimed for this collection is that it is a fairly faithful reflection of current interests and observations in Negro life. The arrangement of the materials of this volume follows roughly the implications of significance in the new interests mentioned. The first part is concerned with Negro folk life itself. The vast resources of this field for American literature cannot be escaped even though they are no more than hinted at in this volume. There is here a life full of strong colors, of passions, deep and fierce, of struggle, disillusion,—the whole gamut of life free from the wrappings of intricate sophistication.

The second part sweeps in from a wider radius of time and space some of the rare and curiously interesting fragments of careers and art which constitute that absorbing field of the past now being revealed through the zeal and industry of Negro scholars. The garnering of these long gone figures who flashed like bright comets across a black sky is an amenity which has found root quietly and naturally in Negro life.

A third division is concerned with racial problems and attitudes, and these are rather coldly in the hands of students. In these, there is the implication of a vast drama which the stories and the poetry merely illuminate.

The fourth section might well be set down as the most significant of current tendencies—the direction of Negro attention inward in frank self-appraisal and criticism. The essays touch boldly and with a striking candor some of the ancient racial foibles. At frequent points they violate the orthodoxy, but in a spirit which is neither bitterly hopeless nor resentful. This is perhaps one of the most hopeful signs of life and the will to live. And finally, there is a division which gives a brief glimpse into the intimate self-feeling of articulate Negroes. These lack conspicuously the familiar tears of self-pity and apology.

The classification is not a strict one, but it has a possible usefulness as a guide through the varieties of expression to be found herein. There will be in one an abandonment to the fascination of a new life, in another a critical self searching, in one humor for its own sake, in another humor with a thrust; there will be stoical rebellion, self reliance, beauty. Those seeking set patterns of Negro literature will in all likelihood be disappointed for there is no set pattern of Negro life. If there is anything implicit in the attitude toward life revealing itself, it is acceptance of the fact of race and difference on the same casual gesture that denies that the difference means anything.

This is probably enough about the contributions to this collection to let them take their own course. From the list of contributors are absent many names with as great reason for inclusion as any present. There were, however, physical limits to such a volume, with all that this implies, and, if there is, for those who must pass judgment, less merit in what appears than should be, some measure of this deficiency may be laid to the omissions.

A spirit has been quietly manifest of late which it would be a gentle treason to ignore. Its expression has been a disposition on the part of established writers, scholars, artists and other interested individuals, to offer to Negro writers the practical encouragement of those facilities which they command. To this may be accredited among other things a share in the making of that mood of receptivity among the general public for the literature of Negro life.

CHARLES S. JOHNSON.

If you want to tell anything to Heaven, tell it to the wind.

An African Proverb

A DRAWING FOR JUMBY
By Aaron Douglas

JUMBY

(To Doris)

By Arthur Huff Fauset

Jean-Marie

JEAN-MARIE tossed fitfully upon her bed of straw until a cock, crowing shrilly in the early morn awoke her with jarring suddenness. She raised herself slightly, and fearing to open her eyes, clutched the wall of the thatch-roofed hut, in order to steady her trembling body.

Feverishly she felt of her waist, her temples, her pale brown limbs, and her feet. She was puzzled. Assuredly there was something wrong. But where? She peeled open her eyes timorously. As the delicate brown lids slowly unfolded, she beheld the marvelous blue Caribbean, bobbing gently, playing a child's game, as it were, with the rising sun.

Jean-Marie shivered. Then from her throat came a tiny sound like the cluck of a hen. She stretched out full length on her back, and extending her clasped hands as far as possible from her body, she heaved a sigh of gladness.

Thanks be to Jumby, a dream! Suppose, now, that she had awakened to find herself bitten by a cobra, her limbs swollen double, and her pale amber brownness turned a hideous black! Just suppose Kasongo, the obeah man, *could* really put "nastiness" upon her, and she had awakened with Barbados Big Foot (elephantiasis), and thousands of tiny chiggers building their houses in the seams of her feet!

Ah, the chiggers! They got everywhere, and into everything. You could not move for the chiggers. And how they did bite! She gazed upon a tiny red splotch on her arm, and scratched it ruefully. The more she scratched the more it burned.

But the blacks did not mind the chiggers. Manja, sleeping over there in the corner, her almost naked body exposed to the caprices of brown scorpions, red and green lizards, mosquitoes, huge white ants, and roaches big as fingers . . . she did not mind the chiggers. Why, she had colonies of them, on her elbows, the sides of her hands, of her feet! The tops of her feet were live chigger-hives. But Manja did not mind. . . .

But then, what had she to do with these folk anyway! She did not look like them, she did not think like them. They were black; she was pale brown. Their eyes were constantly red, and the whites spotted with gelatine-like masses which affected their sight. Hers were clear like the Caribbean, and soft and brown like a chewink's feathers. Instead of the brittle, harsh mat of hair which adorned their heads, rough almost to prickliness, her hair was black, and soft like velvet or silk.

Jean-Marie leaped lightly from her bed, and glided to the door of the hut. Her tall slim figure was lithe like a leopard's; her pale brown limbs moved with the grace of a beautiful race horse. She opened wide the door and gazed at the silent wonder of the island on which her home was situated.

Mateka, the sacred mount, towered in the distance, some dark green knight, hiding his crest in a thin white mist. The sun, a streak of white in a pale blue sky, peeked his head over the mountain's top.

Jean-Marie noted the light green patches by the side of the mountain, where the blacks had cultivated their cane and their cotton, and the roads, looking like brown streaks crawling up the great hill. She saw a dozen tiny sail-boats, much like geese-feathers, tossing and bobbing on the Caribbean. Far in the distance, the native huts looked like cattle lying in the grass.

Frogs croaked. Crickets chirped. Tall palms, glistening in the sunlight, and looking like sentinels on the side away from the sun, bended and swayed to the occasional purring of the breezes.

Far off a boy was yodeling. Somewhere a woman was hoeing and spading. Between the pat-pats of her hoe, she sang snatches of lines from hymns taught by Wesleyan missionaries:

"... . that Jesus doied fo' me."

Jean-Marie remained some moments entranced. The spell was broken, however, by a sudden rustling of leaves in front of the hut. Out of the shrubbery, hobbled an old woman. She was black, and she wore a head-dress of red and gold which sparkled in the sunshine. In her mouth was a clay pipe, in her right hand a gnarled stick which she carried for a cane. She wore a simple frock of brown and white, and her feet were bare.

They called her Ganga the Good.

"Hyeh, hyeh," she fairly screamed as she perceived Jean-Marie standing in the doorway. Her cry aroused Manja and two other women who dwelt in the hut.

"Hyeh, hyeh, lookit, lookit," Ganga cried again.

She pointed to a spot on the ground, some distance away from the hut. Everyone rushed to see.

"Da' he," she said. "Jumby comin' dis toime roight hyeh. Sure, Oi knows you be's de one sometoime, Miss Jean-Marie. Hyeh be's it, roight where's Jumby's put it."

Breathlessly, they crowded about the speaker who gazed intently upon an object on the ground. There lay the head of a white cock, its beak pointing to the corner of the hut where Jean-Marie slept.

"Bukra," shouted Manja, as she turned to Jean-Marie, a malicious look in her red eyes, "nas'iness shor' git you dis toime. Laf' on an' hop skippity-skip, but you kitch de chigger foot yit."

Blood mounted to Jean-Marie's cheeks.

"So!" she exclaimed. "Maybe if I have chigger foot, Babu trade my brown leg for your ugly black leg of an elephant!"

"E-yah, e-yah," screamed Manja, the whites of her eyes glistening with rage. "You bukra bitch. You no say nas'iness come ovah you. . . . You see . . . mebbe *you* leg swell like banyan; mebbe breasts look like jellies (cocoanuts); mebbe you guts rot an' grow snakes . . .wait an' see . . . e-yah, e-yah."

Manja spat on the ground. She turned her back on Jean-Marie and rushed back to the hut, dragging her "big foot" behind her.

Ganga looked at Jean-Marie and pointed to the cock's beak. Then directing a warning finger towards the young girl she said, "Keerful, white chile . . . white cock mean badness . . . trouble pointin' yo' way."

Kasongo

MANJA hobbled away from the *ajoupa* (thatched hut) of Kasongo the obeah man. Kasongo lived far back in the island, away from the village, away from the road, away from the sea. He had to hide himself. Were not the police everlastingly on his heels, trying to send him to Antigua for a good ten years' stretch, with twenty lashings a week?

But he had been too clever for the stupid police. Anyway, they were afraid of him, afraid of his charms. Was it not a common saying that when Kasongo looked at a man thru his dead eye (the other eye was like fire), he was sure to be caught in a squall and die by drowning? or if you caught him whistling thru his hare-lip it meant loss of a dear one?

When Flonza, the half-Indian wife of Francois died suddenly, even the police knew that Kasongo had baked a tarantula, beaten it into powder, and secreted it in Flonza's food. And why? . . . So that Francois might marry another woman.

There was Mariel. He was secretly hated by Kasongo, because he had gone to the States and learned powerful obeah. Fool! Mariel should have known better than to drink whiskey out of Kasongo's glasses. Everyone knew that Kasongo had a habit of slipping powders made from maggots, roaches and crickets in his whiskey. No wonder Mariel developed swelling in his right arm. What might have happened if he had not gone over to Martinique and consulted the most powerful obeah man on the island? There they slit open his arm with a knife. His hand was alive with small black worms! Only the powerful medicine of the obeah man prevented them from eating him up alive. Instead, they came jumping out of his flesh like skippers from a piece of rotten ham. . . .

Manja hurried to a sequestered spot under some tall banyan trees. She emptied the pocket of her dress of some charms she had received from Kasongo. There were strands of hair taken from the dead body of a man who had died from "bad man's" disease (syphilis), some huge yellow-stained toe-nails, a clot of human blood, a dried chicken gizzard, and a rabbit's paw. All had been dipped in a peculiar black powder.

She bound these together in a piece of cloth torn from an old dress worn by Jean-Marie. Standing with her back to the sun, she held the bag over her left shoulder and mumbled these words:

> Be some Peter
> Be some Paul
> An' be de Gahd dat mek us all,
> Spin ball,
> Spin jack,
> An' ef she don' do whut you says
> May I neber come back.

Then she hastened to the hut where Jean-Marie lived. No one was about. She walked rapidly to the little plot of earth behind the hut, where every evening just before sun-down Jean-Marie tended her tiny garden. Near a favorite rose-bush Manja placed the charm on the ground, saying softly,

> Not for Manja,
> Not for Adova,
> Not for Merve,
> But only for Jean-Marie.

Then she strode briskly into the hut and prepared for evening.

Jumby

IN the heart of the night Jean-Marie woke suddenly. Her eyes felt like blazing coals.

Feverishly she gazed out on the starry firmament. The heavens were a curtain of soft velvet studded with diamonds. Moonbeams, the molten music of star-elfs, streamed into the hut, and played weird tunes in the sunken depths of her eyes.

Night, the black obeah man who sprinkles star dust in lovers' potions, drugged her with his lures, and before she was able to recover from the magic spell of soft loveliness, her body was aflame with madness and longing.

(Oh, Jungle Girl, with amber face, why do you struggle against a foe who draws you tight with bands like steel, and will not let you go?

Oh, Jungle Girl, with eyes so pure, would you be a jungle lover and scoff at jungle charms?

Oh, Jungle Girl, with limbs pale brown, fly, fly to your destiny!)

She looked in the direction of Manja and saw a dark bundle, half clear in the moonlight. Manja was asleep.

Fever mounted in her body. The spell of love added to its flame until the pallet on which she lay burned like a bed of fire.

She tried to cool the flame which was her body by crooning soft words to her lover:

> Babu, my Babuji, you will come to me.
> Say, Babuji, that you will come.
> Oh, my Babuji, come to me . . . come.

Quietly, so that Manja should not hear, she murmured the words of a lovesong taught her in Trinidad by her African grandmother who had learned it from a wandering Zulu:

> U-ye-ze, u-ye-ze,
> Ma-me! U-ye-ze U-mo-ya!
> U-ye-ze, u-ye-ze,
> Ma-me! U-ye-ze U-mo-ya!
> Nakuba
> Se-ku-li—
> Ba-nchi la-ke ngo—
> Sha-da na-lo
>   Ngomte-to!
> He cometh, he cometh,
> Rapture! Cometh the Strong Wind!
> He cometh, he cometh,
> Rapture! Cometh the Strong Wind!
> Let me have
> But his robe,
> And the marriage vows
> I will utter,
>   By the law!

Her body moved in rapturous rhythm with each note. She imagined herself in the arms of her lover, and that she was perishing in a fire of passion.

Abruptly she ceased her chanting. Somewhere in the distance, she heard the faint din of beating. Gradually it swelled, then as gradually died away, only to swell again. Jean-Marie listened intently. She heard. E-yah! Jumby!

> Dum-a-lum-a-lum (pom-pom)
> Dum-a-lum-a-lum (pom-pom)
> a-Dum-a-lum-a-lum
> a-Dum-a-lum-a-lum
> Dum-a-lum-a-lum (pom-pom)

E-yah! Jumby!

Eh! eh! Bomba, hen, hen!
Canga bafio te,
Canga moune de le,
Canga do ki la,
Canga li.

All of her body was aflame. Her eyes, her ears, her hands, and those pale brown limbs were like live coals of fire. Her bed had become a pyre.

Like a panther pierced by the hunter's spear, she leaped from her cot, and gliding across the floor of the hut, rushed out into the moonlight. Louder and louder the drums beat. Swifter the pale creature sped along her path.

The way was tortuous and long. The Jumby Dance must not be within hailing distance of the police, and beside, members of the village would never have it said that they believed in Jumby.

Jean-Marie sped over the dense underbrush. Her tiny feet tripped over the brambles and thorns with the lightness of a hare. Her brown body moved forward with the speed of a gazelle.

Over hills tracked with sharp-pointed stones she traveled; down into valleys where the tangled grass lay hidden neath the waters of the swamp she trod. The gray mongoose darted from beneath her feet, and occasionally a huge field rat; but these she never saw.

She came nearer the spot from whence sounded the monotonous call of the drum. Its tones sank louder into the depths of her heart.

Dum-a-lum-a-lum
Dum-a-lum-a-lum

As she came out of a clump of forest, she suddenly espied a hut in a small open space close by the ocean. Tall cocoanut palms, and mango trees heavy ladened with fruit, sheltered it from the moon's beams.

The drumming stopped abruptly, as Jean-Marie appeared like some elfin sprite under the shadowed moon-light.

She approached the hut.

There, squatting on the ground, she perceived dimly the forms of nearly a score of men and women, many of them old. They were barefooted, and naked except for loin-cloths. All of them wore amulets, made from sharks' teeth, dried frogs, and mummified rats.

As she came near to them, they rose, then bowing almost to the ground, they murmured, "Welcome, fair daughter of the kings. Welcome."

The door of the bamboo hut opened. A tall dark man appeared. He was bedecked in leopard skins, and with charms which rattled all over his body like many sea-shells. His body was smeared with the blood and brain of fowls, and his eyelids were daubed with white paint.

Extending his arms towards Jean-Marie, he greeted her.

"Welcome, oh daughter of the kings," he said. "Many days and nights we have been waiting for you. At last Jumby has sent you forth. Enter with me, for this night we feast to Jumby, and celebrate with the dance of the leopard."

Jean-Marie clasped her hand in his, murmuring, "Babuji, my Babuji. . . . I have come at last . . . to you Babuji . . . at last I have come."

The head-man beckoned to the others to follow. Slowly they filed in couples into the hut.

The room was nearly bare except for a small table which was alight with the unsteady gleam of ten candles placed around its edges. The flickering flames cast eerie shadows on the walls of the hut.

In the center of the table was the body of a two-footed creature, half beast, half fowl, made from carcasses of small animals sewed together, into which had been stuffed the entrails of a cow.   Mounted on its neck was the head of a white cock.   A roasted pig, squatting with its fore-paws extended was to the left, and to the right was the roast carcass of a huge gray rat.

These were the gifts to the Jumby.

Jean-Marie and the company bowed in silence before the objects on the table, and formed around them in a circle.   Soon the sputtering candles mixed their vapors with the stench of sweat and unwashed bodies.

"Daughter of the kings," intoned the head-man, "soon Jumby will appear. You are his daughter, and the mother of the children of men.   Pray guard your children well."

He bowed and disappeared silently into the darkness.

As the door closed upon him, a drum suddenly sounded a warning note.   Almost hidden, it stood with the drummer in a corner of the room.

"E-yah!" shouted the drummer.   "E-yah!   It is Jumby."

He commenced to beat slowly and gently, accompanied by the sound of rattles and castanets which another tall figure played upon.   Softly the drummer began chanting an African melody as if imploring Jumby to enter the hut and partake of the feast prepared for him. . . .

But Jumby does not appear.   The drummer as if to coax him, quickens his beat, and raises his voice; then permits the song to die down to a low sob, while the measures of his beating become long and sustained.

Very slowly, almost imperceptibly, the door opens.   In the diminishing candle light it is difficult to make out the head-man, who clad in his leopard skins, silently enters the hut.   But the drummer has seen the door open.   He beats madly upon his instrument and sings:

Mbwero! Mbwero! Mbwero!
Beware! Beware! Beware!

Jean-Marie steps out from the group and prepares to save her children from the ravages of the leopard, who by this time is seen almost creeping on all fours.   Meanwhile the crowd of dancers move slightly, now forward, now backward, keeping time with the drummer, and shouting.

Mbwero! Mbwero! Mbwero!

Jean-Marie dances nearer the leopard.   She sings:

Be careful, children.
It is Jumby in the form of a leopard.
Be careful! Mbwero! Mbwero! Mbwero!

Her "children" scream and sing, all the while stepping backward and forward to the drum accompaniment.

Slowly the leopard advances, sniffing the air, but at first ignoring the dancers and proceeding to the feast prepared for him on the table.   He bows before the central figure, then proceeds to eat portions of the roast pig and roast rat.   Suddenly he turns upon the crowd, and with his tongue extended and emitting terrible growlings, he throws them into convulsions of fear.

Madder beats the drum.   Wilder the hissing of the snares and rattles.   More hideous the screams of the participants to whom the intoxicating effect of sweat, burnt tallow, and palm oil which is poured on the candles to make them sputter, bring a strange reality to the dance.

Jean-Marie in the role of protector, steps in front of her children, and attempts to keep off the onslaught of the leopard.   Her steps grow quicker, now forward, now backward. As she moves backward she motions to the children behind her to flee, calling out to them, "My children, Mbwero!"

The participants imitate her steps, her motions, her calls.

The leopard, swaying and measuring his step to the music of the drummer, dashes forward suddenly, and catches one of Jean-Marie's children, whom he sets aside. Jean-Marie screams defiance, but he brushes her aside and snatches another child from her protecting embrace.

One after another of her children he captures, until only a single child remains. Jean-Marie has become exhausted. Her steps become slower and feebler. She clings to the remaining child with fingers that are numbed with weakness and exhaustation. No use . . . the leopard seizes it also, and casts it aside to be devoured.

Once more the drum beats wildly. Jean-Marie the mother has become a furious tigress. Her children are all dead. Must she die also?

The leopard slowly approaches her. Jean Marie rushes to attack him, then retreats with backward steps. With claws protruding, the leopard rushes again, but the snarling Jean-Marie holds her ground, forcing him to turn back. The leopard prepares to leap. Jean-Marie seizes a club which rests on the table for the purpose, and lifts it high over her head in order to strike the leopard and slay him. . . .

Behold . . . a silver gleam from the thatched roof-top. It is the flash of a cobra's fang, which darts like an arrow straight into the pale brown arm of Jean-Marie. One shrill scream she utters, and falls in a heap on the floor.

Now she seems to be swimming against an overpowering current. Her arms and limbs become numb and heavy. She feels a terrible swelling in her breasts. Her eyes are balls of fire burning, burning, burning. There is a putrid smell in her nostrils, as of flesh rotting . . . and the sensation of myriads of swarming creatures. . . .

Jean-Marie awoke from an age of slumber. Startled, she looked into the loving eyes of Ganga the Good.

"But—but—the cobra—" she gasped, feeling her arms and limbs.

"Po' chile," whispered Ganga, "dat was mighty close call. All de jumbies sho' dancin' in you."

"But Ganga . . . my children . . . where are they?"

"Da now, Bukra chile, you mus' a seed all dat de night we fin' you tearin' t'roo de bush. Fever mos' burn you to def!"

She held Jean-Marie close in her arms.

"Bukra chile," she said softly, "ma po' Bukra chile."

"Babuji," whispered Jean-Marie, "my Babu-ji."

Drawing for ON THE ROAD ONE DAY, LORD
by AARON DOUGLAS

On The Road One Day, Lord

BY PAUL GREEN

SIX striped figures on a blazing road, swinging their picks, and four behind piling out the dirt with shovels. The white dust hides the blackberries in the hedge and the willow clumps are bent under its weight. The heat of July shimmers across the wide land as far as the eye can see. The sweat pours down. It is the only dampness in the world for the ten mourners on the road. On a stump to the left a guard squats, drowsy, vapid, like a toad. The rifle in the crook of his arms keep alert, it watches, its muzzle watches like an eye, it threatens. Fall, picks, and heave arms! On the bankside to the right, another guard sits. He also is sleepy, drowsy. His rifle also keeps alert and watches, its muzzle threatens. The convicts dig with their backs to the guards, their faces set down the infinite stretch of road that disappears in a point on the horizon. Like so many soulless puppets, they lift their hands towards the sky and bring them down, never any slower, never any faster. And as the picks strike against the earth with a thud, a husky desperate groan bursts from their baked lips. As rhythmic as the beating of their hearts the "hanh" accompanies the falling of the picks, carrying over long maddening hours of pain, carrying over until the sun sinks cooling in the west and the guard stirs and croaks, "Call it a day." At times their voices are raised in a chant, level, patient, eternal and tough as the earth in which they dig. They don't talk much, not so much. Talk breaks up the rhythm of labor, and that's what they're there for—labor, labor, working on the roads. Ninety days on the roads, Tom Sterling, and sixty days for you, Bantam Wilson. The judge dropped his tobacco by his foot, rose and gave sentence. Disturbance of the peace. Assault with intent to kill. These niggers, these everlasting niggers, always fighting, always shooting. They've got no sense, they'll never have no sense. Give 'em the law, let 'em feel it. Obedience, peace, peace. This is the republic, these are the institooshuns. Land of our fathers. This shall be a lesson. Sixty days. Ninety days. Dig, dig. Side by side they dig—Bantam Wilson and Tom Sterling. Misery has made them friends, sorrow companions. Bantam's spirit walks unbroken, Sterling is crushed and under. The feel of iron and abuse of tongues have broken him. His great shoulders are bent, his legs hardly sustain his weight, and his arms fling up the pick and let it fall hour after hour, day after day, with slowly decreasing power. See, his face now bends above the lightless earth beneath. These are the children—hanh. These are the brethren marching to Canaan Land. The guard on the right stirs in his sleepiness and beats at the flies with his hat.

First Guard. Rain or shine the old dog flies stay with you.

Second Guard. (Lighting cigarette and passing the package on to the first.) And the dam' muskeeters allus drilling for water.

First Guard. Heigh you, Sterling, raise up that pick and let 'er come down. (The convicts dig on, accompanying every blow with their everlasting "hanh", saying never a word.) You hear me? I say put some **pep** into that digging.

Bantam. (After a moment—without looking around). He sick. Ain't able to work.

Second Guard. You bastard monkey runt, who's talking?

First Guard. Hell 'll be frozen 'fore you git this little digging done. (They lapse into silence again. The second guard stretches his arms in a yawn.)

Second Guard. Lord, I'm sleepy—sleepy.

First Guard. Better leave her off a few nights. (The convicts with the shovels burst into a snicker.

Second Guard. (Brutally, his voice sharp with hate.) Somebody begging for the little rawhide. (The four convicts terrified push their shovels deeper into the loose earth and pile it out).

First Guard. I want water.

Second Guard. The goddamned water boy's fell in and drownded. (Standing up and calling). Water boy! Water boy! Heigh, water jack! Could a-been there and half way back! (The diggers begin a low working chant, pitiful and pleading. "Mercy, mercy," it calls. "Water, water, give us some water. Where is it? Where is he? Where is the Great I Am, the Almighty God! Listen now, Jesus, while us gi' you de call. Eigh Lawd, come wid de 'sponse'!"

Convicts.

> I called my people—hanh,
> I said my people—hanh,
> I mean my people—hanh,
>   Eigh, Lawd!

First Guard. That's right, sing him out'n the bushes.

Second Guard. If it ain't water it's grub, ain't that it's something else. Bear down on them picks! Jesus Christ! (Sterling suddenly tumbles over and falls with his face flat in the dirt. A convulsive shudder runs through the other convicts, but they carry on their digging, never any slower, never any faster.)

Convicts.

> I called my friends—hanh,
> I said my friends—hanh,
> I mean my friends—hanh,
>   Eigh, Lawd!

First Guard. (Springing up as he glances at Sterling). Heigh now, none o' that, none o' that!

Bantam. (His voice rising in a whine). He sick, bad sick!

First Guard. Better got cured fore he come here. (Marching up to the prostrate body). Git that face out'n the dirt! Git it out. (Whirling towards Bantam.) Nobody asked for your jowing. (Eyeing him). Want the little cat-tails?

Bantam. (Slinging his pick). Jesus, Jesus!

First Guard. Snap out'n it, Sterling.

Second Guard. (Getting a leather thong from his coat). Put a fire-coal on his tail and rise him.

First Guard. Gonna step to it, Sterling? (But Sterling makes no answer).

First Guard. He's a stall boy. Hell, he's stalling!

Second Guard. Damn right, he's stalling.

First Guard. This ain't no party.

Second Guard. Hell it ain't no party! (He smoothes the thong with his hand and looks at the first guard).

First Guard. Make 'em work, make 'em work—that's right.

Second Guard. Work, work—that's what they're here for—work!

First Guard. Work—work—let him taste it.

Second Guard. (Raising the strap above his head). Thirty-nine, thirty-nine. We got our orders. (His voice coming out stronger now, more sharply). The law, the law, it's wrote in a book. (But still he holds the leather poised without bringing it down. A low murmur of horror rises among the convicts, growing into their chant, full of hate now, full of begging, but hopeless withal).
   Convicts.

> I called my sister—hanh,
> I said my sister—hanh,
> I mean my sister—hanh,
>   Eigh, Lawd!

First Guard. Hold her a minute, we'll see, we'll see. (He goes up to Sterling and pokes him gently in the ribs with the muzzle of his rifle, but only the twitching back makes answer).
   Second Guard. Stick him in the collar. (He cuffs him gently in the collar, then with more insistence, at last with vehement roughness. A low whine is heard). He's saying something.
   First Guard. (Bending down). Goddamn it we'll see!
   Second Guard. And what song is he singing now?
   First Guard. Don't say nothing. Moans and whines. He don't say nothing.
   Second Guard. By God we'll see. Oh yes, he'll talk. He'll tell us a mouthful! (The chant grows fuller, the rhythm begins to shape the picks, to hold the rising and falling arms to their labor. The prayer for help, for peace, grows stronger—and with it the baffled will, the confused soul sends forth its cry).
   Convicts.

> I called my brother—hanh,
> I said my brother—hanh,
> I mean my brother—hanh,
>   Eigh, Lawd!

First Guard. Let him have it. (The second guard hands his rifle to the first and then looking around the world as if for a witness of justification, begins to beat the prostrate figure. Again a shudder and the gust of a groan sweep the convicts. They drive their picks deeper in the ground, but never any faster, never any slower).
   Convicts.

> I called my mother—hanh,
> I said my mother—hanh—

Second Guard. Six—seven—eight—nine—ten—
   First Guard. And now you'll work—and I reckon you'll work.
   Second Guard. Eleven—twelve—thirteen—fourteen—(And the watchers in the skies cry blood, blood—earth, earth, sweet earth receive it. Keep it, or save it till the next harvest).
   First Guard. Oh yes he'll work, and I reckon he'll work. (The water boy bursts through the hedge at the left, stands terror-stricken a moment, and then dropping his bucket with a clatter tears down the road. The precious water sinks into the dried earth. Now they chant in hopelessness and the four with shovels wag their heads, their parching tongues protrude through baked lips. Ah, hope is no more—life is no more—death—death all around us. Grave, grave, swallow us up, hide us away, keep us).
   Second Guard. Fifteen—sixteen—seventeen—eighteen. (Now Tom Sterling has reached the end. In a last burst of life he staggers to his feet, his eyes glazed with madness).
   First Guard. Go to work. Look out—(The second guard turns to grab his rifle but Sterling is upon him. He strikes him in the face and beats him to earth, crushing

the stems of the early golden rod by the ditch and tearing the clumps of knotted lady-thumb).

Sterling. (His voice coming out in a great animal scream). Hah—hah—hah— (He beats the guard's upturned face with his fists).

Second Guard. Kill him! Kill him! (The convicts sing on, now their chant rises louder, fresher. Revenge! Revenge! Hope he is not perished from us. Our arms are still strong).

Convicts.

> I called my father—hanh,
> I said my father—hanh,
> I mean my father—hanh,
> Eigh, Lawd!

Second Guard. Kill him! Kill him! (The first guard stands stupefied. Then as if suddenly awakening he steps back, raises his rifle, and shoots Sterling through the back. He rolls over and lies with face upturned in the burning sun. The second guard crawls over to the bank and lies stretched out in the grass, his body heaving and jerking with angry strident sobs. The first guard stands looking foolishly down at the dead Negro. The four convicts drop their shovels and hover together in a shuddering group, the six sing on, beaten—darkness, night—God sits high in heaven, his face from the Negro, his hand towards the white man. The poor and needy stretch their weak hands and the iron palings divide them).

First Guard. The goddamned fool, he's dead, dead!

Second Guard. (Sitting up with a high laugh as he wipes the blood from his face). Had to kill him, we had to kill! (Peering forward). Dead as a fly. (With a sort of wild sob). This ain't right. They's something wrong—something wrong here.

First Guard. Sing, you bastards. Dig, you sons of bitches! (And the body lies still. Once it knew swiftness, legs that ran by the cabin, played in the cornfield. Eyes that knew starlight, knew moonlight, as was said in the song. Tongue that knew singing! And I lay this body down. In the cool hedge the fly says "zoom." And a buzzard wheels by the flat disc of the sun. And they dig and they sing. O earth, give us answer! Jesus hear us!)

Convicts.

> I called my Jesus—hanh,
> I said my Jesus—hanh,
> I mean my Jesus—hanh,
> Eigh, Lawd!

DUSK

By MAE V. COWDERY

Like you
Letting down your
Purpled shadowed hair
To hide the rose and gold
Of your loveliness
And your eyes peeping thru
Like beacon lights
In the gathering darkness.

DIVINE AFFLATUS

By JESSIE FAUSET

Tell me, swart children of the Southland
Chopping at cotton
In the sandy soil,
What do ye dream?
What deeds, what words of heroes
Leaven and lighten up
Your toil?
Know ye of L'Ouverture who freed a nation?
Heard ye of Crispus Attucks,
Or of Young?
Does fiery Vesey
Stir the spark within ye,
Or Douglass
Of the rare and matchless tongue?
That Washington
Who moulded a Tuskegee—
Does he inspire ye?
Does brave Moton thrill?
Mark ye Du Bois
That proud, unyielding eagle,
Beckoning ye higher than the highest hill?

But the swart children
Of the Southland
Stopping to dash the sweatbeads
From dull brows,
Answer: "These names
Mean nothing to us,
They, nor the unheard causes they espouse.
Only we know meek Jesus,
Thorn-encircled,
Broken and bleeding
In his Passion's toils;
And Lazarus
Sharing crumbs with dogs;
And Job,
Potsherd in hand, a-scraping at his boils!"

A drawing for GENERAL DRUM
by Aaron Dougla

GENERAL DRUMS

By John Matheus

THE drums were beating incantation over the tops of the pines, through the witching moss festoons of oily-leaved magnolias. The throbbing tones hugged the low earth, too, like the sultry heat beneath the Southern moon, beguiling men from normal ways of thinking. Little fears lurked in hallucinating shadows, unnamed trepidations and bold, brazen dread. Memories came thumping, drubbing, rubbing the soft, somnolent night.

The drums caught Charles Pringle in their tentacles, as he stumbled along Yazoo road, his wide-toed army shoes kicking up yellow flakes of dust. War came to engulf him in all the menace of its terror. Again the boom of 75's, the tatoo of machine guns, the shriek and whine of shells. Startled in him was that latent impulse to flatten his trim form into the earth, color of khaki, color of him.

The silence and the loneliness coveted his composure, envied his anticipated happiness. Out from them leaped the sullen drumming. The weird opalescence was filled with ghostly armies. They came even though he shut his eyes, transcending material vision. So many things he remembered and Jimmy Spiles, handsome, yellow Jimmie Spiles, white teeth flashing, curly hair awry.

But Jimmie was dead in France. He knew that.

The moon was a golden chandelier and its light was argent, silvering the memories of the many times he had dreamed of just this hour, when he should be walking down Yazoo Road to Malissy's house, alone, the only suitor now for her olive brown hand.

Up from the shadows of tall trees and fronded shrubs, loomed faint, familiar outlines—picket fence, shining white, triangle of rambling roses, pyramid of japonica bush, the high, flat-roofed porch and ancient house with wide weather-boarding, planed by slaves with their hands. Time by way of wage for that unrequited labor had swept away the old master and his clan, had left the heritage in plebian black hands emancipated.

That reckoning had been settled long ago; two wars had devastated since then, spreading the oblivion of changing interests over rancorous feelings. And now Charles Pringle was coming back on an August night, when the moon was full.

He was not the same trifling, unsophisticated plow boy of the Yazoo bottoms. He had seen much of the world in eighteen months and the vision had made him wise and cunning. Inoculated with the virus of murder by hard-boiled second lieutenants in bustling cantonments, where healthy, human animals were trained to kill, then thrown on the firing line, the very fibre of his being had been branded by it all. One torturing, inerasable memory, standing out in bold relief, had sensitized chords of his nature which the echoes of the drum beats touched to responsive vibrations—wild drum beats, pounding in the night!

Malissy, herself, came to the door when he knocked, standing before him, graceful as a magnolia, with its ivory-petaled flowers blooming.

"Charlie Pringle! Charlie Pringle!" she cried, giving vent to the demonstrative quality of her African blood.

He remained on the threshold, twirling his over-sea cap in his big hands, grinning and joyous to hear her mocking bird voice echoing *his* name.

Then she burst into tears, into hysterical weeping, summoning forth her gray-haired squaw-faced grandma.

"Laws a-mussy, what *is* agwine on hyah," she spluttered.

Seeing the familiar face of Charlie Pringle in unfamiliar clothes, she stopped, surveying him from head to foot.

"Howdy, chile. Yo' back heah! De Lawd allus teks de righteous an' leabs debils tuh repent. How yo', son? Come in. What yo', ca'in' on fo' dat away, Malissy?"

"But—but—granny, yo'—Ah can't help it. Po' Jimmie. To think he might be here too an' we—we—jes' married."

"'Twas de Lawd's way, honey," soothed the old-woman soberly. "Yo' aint been home yit, Charlie?"

"Naw. Don't spose pap's special anxious 'bout seein' me, sence ah knocked him out the night 'fo' we all lef' fo' camp."

"Yo' ought to been ashamed, strikin' yo' own pappy."

"It were de licker that made me done it," said Charlie, hanging his head, hypocritically.

"Charlie, what did he say? What did he do? How did it happen?" questioned Malissy, eyes swollen with weeping.

"Dey say ol' man Spiles don' gone nummy in de haid, sence he got dat ar deespatch fum Washington, tellin' him 'bout Jimmie bein' kilt. He was br'r Spiles onliest daughter's son. Po' chile! Po' chile! Hit's turrible—lostin' he's girl when Jimmie was bo'n, dough what evah buckra man war Jimmie's daddy, don' gi' de ol' man a pow'ful heap o' money. Didn't he done built him a new cabin? Wha' he git de dollahs to do 'at?"

The gossipy reminiscence of old age would have wandered on and on, if Malissy's sharp voice had not broken in.
"Granny, let him talk, let him tell me."

Charlie Pringle began his story with the sneaking satisfaction that he could command attention *now,* that *he* was important because he held a secret and no one should ever know that secret, unless he willed to tell it.

"We all lef' No'folk sudden one night 'bout ten o'clock. Come 'roun' woke us all up an' down tuh de wharf we went. Jimmy jokin' an' laughin' lak he always was."

Malissy sighed and sobbed afresh.

"We was sick pretty near all de time goin' across de watah. Sich waves and hearin' shootin' at submarines.

"When we all landed we stood around half a day—pourin' down rain, waitin' to git somein' t'eat. Then they took us tuh de woods whar we camped and drilled some mo'. In about two weeks we broke camp, took freight cars. We rid all night. De nex' day say we wasn't in them trenches!

"Jimmy sho' war skeert," he eyed Malissy covertly.

"Then one mo'nin' dey tol' us tuh get ready—we was goin' ovah de top."

He went into the details of the military manoeuvers while the two women listened, trying to comprehend the technique of the art of killing.

"Dat white man blew his whistle an' ovah we went, yellin', screamin'. I disremember anything mo' ontell ah saw Jimmy fall—bullet hit him in de haid. He never said nary a word, jes' lay there a-jerkin' and—"

He stopped short. A breeze from the woods bore the beating of the drums.

"Tha' 'tis. Jes' ez Ah was sayin', ol' man Spiles beatin' fo' Jimmy, gone nummy in de haid."

"Hunh!" ejaculated Charlie, rolling his eyes, "Ah mus' be goin' now. Guess pappy may be glad tuh see me aftah so long. Ah'll be back tuh tell you' mo', 'bout tuh-morrow night."

Malissy was too weak to move. Her grandmother escorted their visitor to the door. The moonlight shadowed his form, doggedly treading towards town.

The returned soldiers were all heroes in the eyes of Negro town. The bravado and loquacity of Charlie Pringle even found favor in the sight of his grieved and mistreated parent. He forgave the prodigal and enjoyed basking in the glow of his son's present greatness.

Overgrown black boys from all sides flocked into town, strutting in khaki and putees, never to look upon life again as in the old days.

There was a mass meeting in honor of the soldiers' return in Ebenezer Baptist Church, where speeches were made and ice cream was served. Then until wee hours of the morning a dance swayed in K. of P. Hall with raucous blare of string and wind instruments.

Charlie Pringle did not go to the church, but he was present at the dance, that is he was, until an old man entered, shuffling his big feet over the smooth floor, peering and peeping into people's faces with queer, bloodshot eyes, filmed with watery scum of weakness. He was an eccentric old man, with the face of a black Punch, long, beaked nose and under lip projecting. He apologetically elbowed through the crowd, showing toothless, blue black gums.

The older Negroes addressed him in skirting, awesome tones, "Howdy, Gen'ral Spiles."

The younger folk, with their passions mounting in the dance's revelry, paid him little thought.

He began to talk loudly in a cracked, squeaking voice:

"Any yo' all seen Jimmie. Yo' know Jimmie, mah po' gran'son, Jimmie Spiles. He done aint come back. Wha's 'at Cha'lie Pringle. Ah wants tuh ax him 'bout Jimmie. Yes, Ah was a gen'ral in de Union A'my, fit in de battle o' Vicksburg, beatin' drums, beatin' drums—callin' up speerits tuh hep us—beatin' drums—"

This was why Charlie Pringle went out the back door and some minutes later entered Negro town pool room, with its sawdust box spittoons and cabbage smelling "eatin' house" across the hall.

September passed and October came. Charlie Pringle found himself on many nights sitting on Malissy's porch. She, with sad brown eyes; he, with cunning in his gaze.

"Yo' nevah wan' tuh lissen tuh me," he was protesting one night, "less A'hm talkin' 'bout Jimmie Spiles. Always Jimmie."

"Well wasn't he my husban'?"

"An' ain't he dead, too?"

"Not in mah heart," said Malissy rising.

"But, but Malissy, Ah—Ah laks yo'."

"Go 'way, Charlie, an' yo' his frien' too."

He grabbed the girl in fierce desire and kissed her.

The sting of her strong, brown hand still burned on his cheek, when he bolted away, muttering, "Always Jimmy. Jimmy livin' an' Jimmie dead!"

The first armistice day celebration provoked great excitement in town. Preparations were made to observe the anniversary of the occasion with fitting aplomb. The local leaders began to spread advertisments and work up spirit from the first of November. The editor of the town paper wrote patriotic editorials urging one hundred percent participation.

Then came the question that always caused trouble. The colored ex-soldiers had asked to be allowed to march in the parade. They had also asked for the privilege of allowing some one to represent their only dead member, Jimmy Spiles, that he might march in memory of the departed.

Much discussion followed among the whites. There was some talk of allowing the Negro ex-soldiers and ex-stevedores to march in the rear. Some such request or suggestion had been made, but no answer was ever sent back.

Charlie Pringle had been picked out by the colored committee to represent his dead buddie. He turned quite ashy and vowed he never could do it, because, because.—

So the colored people compromised and voted to celebrate at the K. of P. Hall with a monstrous Armistice Night Ball.

When the eleventh of November came the public schools were closed, the stores and workshops. Main street, with its ramshackled line of one and two story buildings put on decoration of bunting and American flags.

Promptly at ten o'clock the parade appeared. At the head marched the local band. The strident notes of Dixie floated in the morning breeze. The crowd rushed to the curb. Black faces peered as best as they could behind the barrage of their white fellow townsmen.

Down the street marched the pride of the home town, dressed in their old doughboy uniforms and cheered enthusiastically by the patriotic watchers.

Ten paraded for the boys who had not come back. They bore banners with the names of the martyrs written in gold stars.

Then when everyone thought the parade had passed and the excited people were pushing toward the Court House Square where Lawyer Chester was to give the oration of the day, who should appear, togged in all the faded, ragged splendor of an old blue Union Army uniform, the trousers bagging down over the brogans, the coat buckled tightly around the middle, crowned by a bespangled hat with gold cords—who should appear but old man Spiles.

He marched with a strange erectness and alacrity. His old beaked nose seemed to beget a subtle fierceness as some smouldering ember trying to flare up once more before going out entirely.

He was beating a drum, making it reverberate with martial briskness and exuding a dignity worthy of all the faded tinsel.

There rose a great shout of hilarious laughter.

"Ha! Ha! Ha! Ho! Ho! Ho! He! He! He!"

"Old man Spiles."

"Howdy, uncle. Howdy, General Drums."

But on he went.

"Ah'm marchin', yessah, Ah'm marchin'," he quacked. "Ah'm marchin' fo' Jimmie, Jimmie Spiles. He war in de wah. Yessay, mah gran'chile ain't come back."

General Drums was the crowning excitement of the morning. The Negro spectators looked with popping eyes. Charlie Pringle saw and dodged around the corner.

"A Yankee uniform," someone shouted.

It was like waving a red flag before a bull.

The jests became menacing. Somebody threw a stone, but the old man never wavered.

The tone of the crowd became more and more hostile.

"Let that old darkey alone," shouted a stentorian voice at the threatening crowd.

It was Lawyer Chester himself, jumping from his Cadillac, his wavy brown hair brushed back from his high forehead, bearing his middle years with fresh vigor of early manhood.

"Gentlemen, yo' all wouldn't harm a crazy old uncle, would you?"

A chorus of laughter greeted his query, good nature prevailed and the crowd drew back shouting, "General Drums, General Drums, where'd you learn to beat them there drums?"

"Jes' bo'n dat away, chilluns. Yessah, bo'n wif a caul I was."

"What do yo' mean, what are yo' doing this for, uncle?" the lawyer turned to the old man.

"Ah'm marchin' fo' Jimmy Spiles," he answered simply, peering at his questioner.

He seemed then to recognize him, for he took off his hat and standing, gave the military salute.

Lawyer Chester turned pale under his coat of tan.

He reached in his pocket and put something in the old man's right hand, encumbered with drum sticks.

"Take this and go home," he commanded sharply.

Schooled long in obeisance to the white man's will, old General Drums doffed his hat again, but quickly put it back, and beginning to beat quite lustily, marched on, tramping in the dust a twenty dollar bill.

"Ah'm marchin' fo' Jimmie Spiles," he quacked over and over again.

Then Lawyer Chester reached for the money, swearing softly, and mopped his fine, high forehead and went away to the Court House Square to deliver his oration.

Dusty Main Street was deserted and only the red, white and blue bunting glared and the flags of the United States of America fluttered in the near noonday sun.

Charlie Pringle showed up at Malissy's house, with his wheedling air and lecherous gaze, begging the girl to come to the Armistice Ball with him. She refused.

"Go on, chile," encouraged her grandmother. "Yo' don't do nothin' but set 'roun' here a-moppin' and a-drizzlin' roun'. Go out and enjoy yo'self one ebenin'."

So Fate played into Charlie Pringle's hand.

"Why don't you fix up in your best, Malissy?" said he.

"If yo' don't wan' to go with me as Ah am, yo' don't need to tek me *atall,*" said the girl.

He dared not say more.

Malissy found the dance not at all in keeping with her sombre thoughts. In the first place she had come against her better judgment to a public dance when she innately shrank from the raw promiscuity of the males who presumed a familiarity she resented. Jimmie had been of a different sort. In the second place she mistrusted this persistent and audacious pursuit of Charlie Pringle and regretted yielding in this instance, for he might construe her acquiescence as privilege for irrefutable concessions. Then she had a general misgiving of his motives and reliability.

But once in the Negro town and inside the crowded hall the intimate contact with the hilarity of the crowd and intoxication of the semi-barbaric music began to weave their subtle web around her.

She had purposely refused to dress her best, fearing the consequences of attracting too much attention, holding back under the leash of her self imposed restraint. But the fact that she had been a war bride and was now a war widow, gave her unwittingly in the eyes of admiring beaux the advantage of prestige.

Thus she was lead to dance with many partners, defying the furious scowls of Charlie Pringle and thereby asserting her none too complete surrender to his wishes.

He chafed under the gnawing fire of jealousy.

Always a creature of sudden caprice Malissy became smitten with inexplicable remorse. A desire to leave at once urged her to the act. There was nothing for her escort to do save follow.

It was nearing midnight. The moon had come up late and was shedding its magic opalescence over the metamorphosed country. The road was deserted. The air felt refreshing after the crowded heat of the dance hall. Clumps of pines became visible by and by and the sweetly fragrant magnolias.

"Malissy," suddenly blurted out her moody partner, "are yo' goin' tuh marry me?"

"No," snapped Malissy. "How many times must Ah tell yo'. Yo' posin' as po' Jimmie's best frien'."

"Oh, damn Jimmie," snarled Pringle, wild, steaming fury rising in him.

Malissy turned with heaving bosom, "Don't ever come near me again, yo' dirty viper."

"Yo're goin' to be sorry fo' that, Miss Uppity," was the hot rejoinder.

He grappled with the woman.

"Yo're mine an' Ah'll have yo' or Ah'll know the reason why. Ah've done too much tuh git yo'. Yo'—Ah shan't be outdid."

Malissy became calm and quiet in her terror. Interpreting her change as submission he was melting from his fiery mood, when noises came loping out of the night, a vague whirring, indicating distance but no sense of direction. With increasing intensity it was closing in upon them.

Neither stirred. Malissy felt a coldness clutching at her heart. Her fear of the man merged into the greater apprehension of the unknown. She felt the strong, lithe body pressed against her go limp.

The approaching sound grew intelligible. It was the drums, that ungodly rhythm was the drums. And that shrill, cracked quavering was saying, "Jimmy Spiles."

And while the drums beat on there came a popping as of guns and Charlie Pringle saw the glare of the battle again and heard the roar of musketry. And behind them all loomed that inerasable memory which made him gaze ahead with glassy stare and point with trembling finger.

As Malissy turned, a cloud passed over the moon, but she could see a form in the shadows and a face, her husband's face, dead Jimmy Spile's face, pale, curly hair awry.

Then Charlie Pringle's courage snapped.

"Save me, Malissy," he screamed. Tell him to go away. Ah thought that bullet in the back killed him. It might a been a German bullet, but Ah couldn't wait. I did it fo' yo'. I swear tuh Gawd, Ah did it fo' yo'. Ah'm leavin'. Tell him Ah'm leavin'."

Footsteps approached and the drums.

A voice cried, "Stop that damn beating, Spiles. What's the matter with yo'."

The grey cloud drifted from the pallid moon. They saw the form of Lawyer Chester, hat in hand.

Charlie Pringle's face was working like an epileptic's in a fit.

"Beatin' fo' Jimmy Spiles. Bof us been in de ahmy."

"You skunk," shouted Lawyer Chester, pushing Charlie Pringle from Malissy's side, "I'll give you three hours to be on your way out of Yazoo bottom. If I ever catch sight of your sneaking hulk yo'll hang for murder."

Charlie Pringle stood rooted to the spot, abashed by the shadow of the hangman's noose, speechless, more terrified than if he had seen the accusing wraith of Jimmie Spiles.

"General, I'm going to take you home."

"Yessah," and the old man doffed his hat.

"Come here, girl," he commanded and guided the prostrated girl with the gesture of a gentleman.

He put her in his car.

"No back firing," he soliloquized, looking at his engine, "because I want to take you to your grandmother, girl, without any more disturbance."

And old man Spiles sat in the rear, hugging his drums.

GULLAH

By JULIA PETERKIN

T is surprising to find that outside of the South, there is scarcely any acquaintance with the word "Gullah" although it stands not only for a large number of Negroes who make up most of the population along our lower coasts but also for the quaint and charming patois which they speak.

There are many theories concerning the original home of these people, almost as many as there are ways of trying to reduce their odd speech into written words. Although some of them still have a distinct pride of race they know nothing of where they came from. I have heard people living in the Quarters here on Lang Syne Plantation boast that they who are Gullahs were bound to be better in every way than the people on a neighboring plantation who are Guineas. This belief was probably being handed down prior to the earliest days of slavery.

These Gullahs may have been brought from Angola on the west coast of Africa by the traders who took them to market along with the gold and ivory transported from that rich country, and the word "Angola" shortened to "Gullah." Or they may have been brought from Gallah on the African east coast along with cargoes of salt which was so valuable it was once used as money currency. But this question will never be settled.

The human cargoes were brought to the rice and cotton plantations, and since they often out-numbered the white people in the ratio of hundreds to one, none but the house servants or body servants came into close contact with their owners, the rest having to learn to speak English from the white overseers or other white servants.

A strange mixture of old English and French resulted, many of the words being utterly changed in tone and cadence and grammar. Harsh sounds were eliminated and this new speech slid easily, musically off the lips of the people who used it.

After the Civil War and Freedom, most of the plantation owners moved away and the Negroes were left to shift for themselves the best they could, in the deserted rice and cotton fields. Generations have succeeded each other in the same isolated environment. The same old customs, superstitions, religion, tradition and language have been faithfully handed down. And this language which is not easily understood except by a trained ear, is not only beautiful, but its whimsical words and phrases, its quaint similes and shrewd sayings are undoubtedly a permanent enrichment of American language and literature.

REQUIEM

By GEORGIA DOUGLAS JOHNSON

I weep these tears upon my bier
Another may not shed,
For there is none save I alone
Who knows that I am dead.

FORECLOSURE

By Sterling A. Brown

Father Missouri takes his own.
These are the fields he loaned them,
Out of hearts' fullness; gratuitously;
Here are the banks he built up for his children—
Here are the fields; rich, fertile silt.

Father Missouri, in his dotage
Whimsical and drunkenly turbulent,
Cuts away the banks; steals away the loam;
Washes the ground from under wire fences,
Leaves fenceposts grotesquely dangling in the air;
And with doddering steps approaches the shanties.

Father Missouri; far too old to be so evil.

Uncle Dan, seeing his garden lopped away,
Seeing his manured earth topple slowly in the stream,
Seeing his cows knee-deep in yellow water,
His pig-sties flooded, his flower beds drowned,
Seeing his white leghorns swept down the stream—

Curses Father Missouri, impotently shakes
His fist at the forecloser, the treacherous skinflint;
Who takes what was loaned so very long-ago,
And leaves puddles in his parlor, and useless lakes
In his fine pasture land.
Sees years of work turned to nothing—
Curses, and shouts in his hoarse old voice,
"Aint got no right to act dat way at all"
And the old river rolls on, slowly to the gulf.

DREAMER

By Langston Hughes

I take my dreams
And make of them a bronze vase,
And a wide round fountain
With a beautiful statue in its center,
And a song with a broken heart,
And I ask you:
Do you understand my dreams?
Sometimes you say you do
And sometimes you say you don't.
Either way
It doesn't matter.
I continue to dream.

THE DUNES

By E. Merrill Root

LET earth have her ancient way—
  Sun and sand and wind and spray—
On the lonely dunes today.
Trampling silver dust of spumes
Strides the wind: he wears the glooms
Of vast purple clouds for plumes.
Mightily Lake Michigan
Hurls his white diluvian
Wolves across the narrow span.
Mournful grass like huddled sheep
Cowers from the roar and sweep
Of the waves and winds that leap.
And the sand (that once was proud
Rock) lies desolate and cowed,
Broken to a level crowd.
And one tree, a twisted gnome,
Rises from the monochrome
Leprous silver of his home.

There in primal joy I lie
Underneath a savage sky
Where the pluméd clouds go by.
Joyful on the trampled verge
Of two worlds, I lie and urge
In my soul their shock and surge.
For my spirit wins elation
And majestic affirmation
Best from stormy desolation.
There in primal loneliness
Let me lie amid the stress
Of the cosmic emphasis.
Let me hear forevermore
Life, of which I am the shore,
On my body's beaches roar!
Not for me earth's plenilune
But the wild white crescent moon
Of the beach that ends the dune!

EIGHTEENTH STREET

(BIRMINGHAM)

An Anthology in Color

By NATHAN BEN YOUNG

STROLLING MUSICIANS

EIGHTEENTH Street hath music of its own. Some of it harks back to the far away Continental Africa, some of it is the new American music.

Like strolling minstrels of old these rag-tag fellows appear on the Street from nowhere and depart as they come. One night it is the Kitchen Mechanics Quartet in the Bon Ton Drug Store in an impromptu progrom of bearded medleys and ballads in which the first tenor switches to baritone and the basso to lead ad. lib. But even in their rendition of "Sweet Ando-line" there is a quaint touch of something three hundred years or more old.

Oh yes, "Kitchen Mechanics" because they cook, wait table, and chauffeur for the rich "white folks" on the Highlands.

Another night it is a strolling string band: a three string weather-beaten bass fiddle upon which a stumpy fellow of ginger-cake complexion plays, singing a "mean" tenor to boot; a red-brown guitar lashed to its 'framer' by a red ribbon attached to neck and tail piece; a small fiddle handled like a tender baby by a fat black man. A block from them and they sound like a suppressed orchestra, a half block and you get the rhythm more pronounced, a choice place in the standing circle and you are a-tingle to a rondo of metallic harmony.

Still another night and The Street is tuneless except for the rattle of the electric piano in the entrance of the Dreamland Theater. Along this thoroughfare of rustling mixtures for once music is absent. Then you walk into a crowd; in the center is a solitary black boy of wild eyes. In his hand is an ordinary piece of fishing pole bamboo about two feet long.

"Play 'When the Saints Go Marching In'," someone requests; and without emotion the bamboo is raised to his lips and a tune flows like golden honey. It is crude, here and there a flattened note or lack of accidental, but that only makes it more seducing. And you stand by until this solitary Mozart of the street responds with "The Yellow Dog Blues," "Da-da Strain" and "Maggie."

"Where'd he come from?" the person next to you asks.

"Wetumka," comes the answer. "Been looking for a job but can't find one."

"Why don't you see Hopkins—he's always atta good musicians," suggests the bystander.

"I ain't no musician," grunts the boy. "Jes' toots my flute for fun. It's one I made—bored the holes with a hot iron and learnt to play it myself."

"Play the 'Star Spangled Banner'," comes out of the crowd.

"What for?" challenges the man already talking to the flute player. "Ain't we all standing already—and furthermore, I done heard too much of that tune in camps and over in France. An' what good we get from fighting in the war? Play 'Sweet Mama'."

But most common are the blind beggars with guitars or accordions, attended to by half-naked boys, and even girls in some instances. These children lift the collection in tin cups, asking everyone and even visiting the nearby places of business.

Chief among these beggar boys is Fat Boy. He wears his job like a veteran and is the most difficult to get rid of without dropping a coin in his cup. His tactics never vary; just a dogged presentation without loss of words of poor-mouth.

Where the other boys chided, "please help the blind," Fat Boy simply said, "mister—mister—mister—" a hundred times if need be until you did something.

"Mister—mister—mister" and in a soft yet persistent voice Fat Boy plagued and plainted until he caught your eye. One look into those round expectant eyes of a wary child and if you gave only a rebuff you would surely think about it later and regret. And the time he approached you fall a victim of Fat Boy's tenacious subtlety, maybe saying to yourself that you gave to get rid of the nuisance.

HENRY RUNROUND—18th Street Dandy

IT'S Henry Somebody—but no one knows what that Somebody is.   Everybody knows Henry Somebody as Henry Runround.   That last name is purely descriptive. Simply that for years Henry has been running around with the girls.

Henry's specialty is mid-night butterflies, ice cream fillies and baby vamps, to use by force those effete, commonplace labels.   But that's just what they are and that's Henry's main purpose in life.   With his dapper self, with his smile and chivalrous air, with his affable voice and everreadiness to do the slightest favor, he finds much to keep him busy between the Peoples Cafe, Dreamland theater, Bon Ton Drug Store and intervening points.

Henry always arranges to have a new sartorial touch about him, either a low cut sport shirt, or kitty-bow jazz tie, or hanging monocle, or flare-open vest, or any fad that's not been overdone by the numerous lesser dandies.   And don't leave unmentioned Henry's two gold teeth that he lets at you through intermittent smiles.

Besides being an automatic, endless chain lover, Henry has an ambition.   His ambition takes various shoots: News reporter, fireman on the railroad, soda jerker, and injuree minuteman.

He may be all these things in a single week. He writes sporting items and acts as official scorer for the Palmetto Giants baseball games; the very next day you encounter him in blue striped overalls, blue cap and red bandana handkerchief swashed around his throat, with a trimmed lantern in one hand and a pair of gloves in the other.

"What's the dress-up mean, Henry?" a friend greets him.

"Firing for the Frisco—going out on Number 26," coldly replies Henry.

"Henry's lying," another fellow breaks in. "Henry wouldn't carry the fireman's dinner on salary.

"Well, mister Know-all, come go and see. See if I don't fire No. 26 out this evening. Come on!" Henry has started off, beckoning his accosters.

"Oh, I get you Henry," announced the first fellow, "you're putting on a stunt for the masquerade ball at the Palm Garden to-night. We've got you Runround Henry!" And they laughed as the probable fireman ambled on through the crowded street.

Nevertheless, they were not sure that Henry Runround or Runround Henry, which is just as good, was really firing or not. No one knew; Henry did so many things and had so much time to do anything, so why not a fireman?

Well, when Henry wasn't on his beat attracting the female and wasn't writing up a ball game or serving in a rush as extra soda jerker at the Bon Ton, and wasn't dressed up as a fireman, then there was a chance of him being in another role. The chance didn't come often but always Henry accepted it. Accident orphan or expert injuree. On the first news of a street car accident or public disaster, Runround Henry made it there and made good use of a couple of handkerchiefs, his pen knife and his lugubrious look. A cash settlement was his favorite way out.

Henry Runround—what an apt name for him to live up to!

MADAM ANTOINETTE SANDAL

PARVENU—Eighteenth Street does not know of the word but it knows Madam Antoinette Sandal, it knows her cherry colored sedan, her Woman's Crowning Glory Beauty Parlors, her beribboned Pekingese, her seven diamond rings on one hand and even talks of her bank balance in two down-town banks as running in five figures.

The gold rush and the oil booms—to the Americans of color, hair and beauty culture is the mild equivalent. Washer-woman yesterday, maker of home-made hair grower today, and the Growmo Company, Inc. to-morrow.

However, not all of the many hundred 'entrepreneurs' strike wealth in such quickness; only the lucky few. Madam Antoinette Sandal was lucky—except in the matter of husbands! Recently her third husband departed with his handbag of belongings to parts unknown. His two forerunners had set the precedent. In fine, the Madam gets husbands with the same ease she gets dollars, and gets rid of them both in like manner.

But her unpardonable shortcomings according to the high circles of gossip is her inability to get the washboard out of her makeup, to dispel the atmosphere of suds in her social bearing. However, money spent freely will make a difference—and so, Madam Antoinette Sandal is paid homage by the upper crust.

"My hair and beauty preparations work for me, my social secretary writes for me, my money talks for me and I should worry, indeed," out of the Madam's own gold-rimmed mouth.

LAWYER HARREL—The Old Tiger

NOW, Gentlemen of the Jury. Remember the law says it is better to turn loose ninety-nine guilty men than convict one innocent man, and from the evidence submitted the defendant is only surrounded by the megrest circumstances. . . ."

"Your Honor," interrupted the District Attorney, "such mathematical calculations are not in the law of Alabama as the attorney would have the jury believe."

"Well, Your Honor, I didn't say it was in the law of Alabama; but Your Honor and Gentlemen of the Jury, it is in the *moral law!* Now, coming back to this defendant whom the State's case would have you believe is a murderess, you all remember the parable of the Master which He told about the woman at the well. You have a picture of it . . . the scorners, the accusers, the woman with her face in her hands, and the Master standing over her. He stooped and wrote in the sand; what He wrote no man knows, and then he charged them, ' He that is without sin among you, let him first cast a stone at her.'

"And what did those scoundrels do? *What did they do?* They slunk away one by one. . . ."

"Your Honor," the District Attorney again to his feet, "is this Court to understand that the lawyer is actually intimidating the jury and insulting this Court? Sounds like that to me."

"Now, Your Honor, I did not interrupt the good attorney for the State when he was speaking, when he stood flatfooted and berated this jury with his scornful forefinger, arousing them with, 'who are you going to believe? Who are you going to believe? White man or niggers?' If that isn't intimidating their prejudices, then. . . ."

"The defense may proceed with the speech; too much time has been spent on this case as it is," ordered the Court eyeing the wall clock.

That was a bit of the case of "State of Alabama vs. Dolly Jones," charged with murdering her husband. Dolly got ten years and Dolly's attorney got ten dollars for defending her. Sometimes he doesn't get anything. But he's used to that now; fifteen years in the courts, and seventy-one years old, he has long before set up for himself a philosophy of life. Never in a Law School, read it and passed the Bar orally, Lawyer Harrell was in the manner born to the profession. His mind wrapped intuitively around legal knots and softened them; he always seemed to have the right angle of things. He hangs around the criminal courts out of pure love, as a youngster broods over a puzzle or a dime detective story. It was play to him, counting in the odds of his swarthy face. The court bailiff summed it up unknowingly when he remarked: "That old nigger lawyer Harrell must carry a rabbit foot—he never misses the point."

HAPPY TRAMP

HAPPY Tramp has a real name but only Verge Deems, the undertaker, knows it. Yet everybody in the downtown section knows Happy Tramp. He is a guttersnipe. He is no tramp now for he never gets a mile away from Eighteenth Street. But he was a tramp once.

Talk? Shut your eyes and hear him; with little imagination you could feel that a professor of English was speaking. What a contrast! a statue of brown humanity, chest-sunken, matted hair and draped in a pair of patched overalls and a jumper coat, straw hat with aspects of a wreck victim, and shoes a stevedore would sneer at. Those shoes: well, hear Happy Tramp:

"On my feet again, gentlemen. You see I've been off them for two months, but I'm on my feet again." And he hoists up a leg, one after the other, showing his bare foot through a completely worn sole.

"And you smoking a Portina, with another in your pocket," someone comments.

"Gentlemen, you see the aroma from a good cigar lifts me to ephemeral heights and allows me to transcend my ransomed body. Listen to Browning: 'Poor vaunt of life indeed, were man but formed to feed on joy, to solely seek and find a feast. . . .'"

"You see, I've told you Happy Tramp's been to school," a lounger remarks to another. And it was true. Somewhere back a decade or more this same floating piece of humanity stood high in his classes. He was a genius of his day and a coming light for his Race, but Time worked a slipknot and the 'coming leader' was blown to the four corners of the earth, returning with what is now known to Eighteenth Street as Happy Tramp.

T. FAIRFAX LEROUX

GENTLEMAN of leisure, minister of the Gospel, economist, editor, social worker, and general jumping-jack is this fellow. And all those things easily in the course of one twelve months.

But nothing short of a picture of him suffices. Not a measly word picture, not even a real photograph. Nothing but an eyeful picture of him gets over to you the amount of dignity and eminence that can be covered under so little a stretch of brown skin. Dapper would weakly describe him, only he's no young man. Grey headed, prematurely so he pompously claims, but there's too much of the old grafty world in his bloodshot eyes to prove youth in the thirties even.

Some more words of him: a snaggle-tooth bombast, a gospel ballyhooer, a misogynist, a brass paper weight. This last needs explanation. Living in a district where his people are needed as laborers, he reaches the height of his power, both egotistically and dollarly, when they, his people, are floating Northward. Brass paper weight— for the corporations depending on black hands he is a sort of sinker to hold down those with a tendency to flitter away to other fields. Brass because it takes that for such a job.

There are so many sides to him, so many facets, until it is difficile to know just when you are getting him right. Perhaps his anti-feministic affectation is worth while. To him ladies are merely breakable china for men not busy with the thought burden of the world. They never entered his life—at least, not now, since his hair was beginning to turn grey. "Young man, when you've reached my stately age and grandeur of thought," he explained to a youngster on the street, "you'll know not to mix women and toil. Let me but remind you of honest history: Antony, snuffed out of the noonday light of Rome by artful Cleopatra, biblical Sampson shorn of his hair and resistive powers, Alexander the Great sunk in ribaldry with his hundred generals by a Persian female, Napoleon millstoned with Josephine around his neck. Young man, go to your history."

But this was just a preamble to one of his street harangues. And with a voice that warmed in on a good pitch, his set jaw and sloping forehead, topped by a wiry pompadour of streaked grey, were charms that gathered him an audience.

Yet, when all was said and done by him, his hearers walked away still unconvinced, they walked away as if somebody had hit them in the face with a handful of confetti.

Another favorite theme of his that must not be omitted is: My past glories, me, and the future. He seldom got past the middle—me. Incidental to his past were his French and Negro ancestors, as you see from his name; Creole by common usage, but he negates this cleavage vehemently.

The sweet meat of his past was his foreign training—"two years in Glasgow, one in Leipzig, and then four years under the English flag on the seven seas," he puts it. "But," he concludes eloquently, "never have I felt the pangs at my heart cockles so gripping as when I came under the gracious outstretched hand of Miss Liberty to land in that great cosmopolitan monolith, New York, then to wend my way to this glorious Southland, where God and men, black and white, are working out a great destiny. How but can my last and eternal rest be sweet in this land of magnolias and corn, how. . . ."

And then some roughneck breaks loose with, "Hurrah, he's stumping for corn. *Corn*—bottled in bond!"

And that was the switch that threw his verbal train into a siding, wrecking the impromptu speech.

TWO-GUN HART

THERE are all kinds of fools: natural born, self-made, sick fools, half-wits, love-lorn and plain. Two-gun Hart is different and perhaps an appropriate title would be Strutting Phool. He ranges from Third Avenue along Eighteenth Street down to Fourth Avenue and back, touching all the four theaters. He doesn't miss a single show but he does miss several meals. A western thriller is his best diet, and on them he lives, longs and thrives. And it is this imitating of the two-gun movie heroes that has turned him a dunce. Yet his imitating is original.

Talk to him. He is incoherent and rattle-tongued, but you can catch some of his atmosphere.

"Adius, Senor," he greets you in foreign. He culled these from the screen, not by reading them himself but by hearing someone repeat them.

"Howdy Hart," you say for the sake of getting him to talk. "What's on at the Star to-day?" as if you were planning to go to the theater.

"What's on? Me. Fight ind'uns and they shoot my hat off, but I get's 'em. Bookety, bookety, bookety—that's the way I makes my get-way," and this with a kicking up of his heels to give you the scene. There are spurs on his high-heel shoes, and from the spurs up he is dressed like a cow boy. Two-gun Hart stays that way, sleeps that way for that matter.

"Hart, can *you* ride a horse?" you jostle him.

"Umph. What you take me for? Me ride? I bust broncoes for Ringling Brothers three years." And again he gives you a pantomime of a rider on a bucking horse. Remember, this is on the street, people are passing, those few who have not stopped for the show. Hart sees his audience thickening and puts on other western antics, lassoing a boy out of the crowd with an imaginary rope or flashing a gun from his empty holster—the gun being imaginary, but the technic he displays making it rather real.

Then a lady has paused to see what the excitement is and the Phool sees her. That breaks up the show, for he suddenly turns Don Quixotic and bows graciously to her feet, after which he arms through the crowd, mumbling, "no act the fool for squaw; will fight for her."

His expression has changed and no one attempts to stop him; his jaw is set and shoulders held straight. He has flashed from the simpleton to the sane, apparently.

CLEOMANTHA

BEAUTY in a woman is both a triumph and a tragedy on a fifty-fifty basis; it is like glistening gold in the eyes of mad men. And stronger, beauty in a swarthy skin in Dixie is ten percent triumph and ninety percent tragedy. They are increasing two-fold with every generation. "High yellows, whipped-creams, yellow-hammers, Egyptian olives, velvet browns," are just a few of the sobriquets.

Cleomantha, ticket girl at the Dreamland Theater, was born to a bewitching golden brown complexion. There was nothing sharp about her features or form and then there was nothing coarse or ponderous about her either. Her perfection points were her big expressive brown eyes, an unblemished complexion and a melting voice.

Cleomantha now belonged to Eighteenth Street. For five years she has been selling tickets from the various theater booths, and who was it who did not know Cleomantha, who was it who could pass, catch a glimpse of her face and not turn for a second look?

She came from Demopolis, a farming town barely out of the echo of the guns of Shiloh and Vicksburg; most of the good looking colored girls come from these small towns. In the city one never knows anything of their back-home ties; there is only that general rumor that colored men are not tolerated on the streets with these creamy-skinned girls back home, that their white paramours will first warn and then do violence. Such was the rumor that haloed itself around Cleomantha. But Cleomantha treaded her way along the Street composedly and without stopping. She seemed to bend herself to dressing and reading lightsome books and magazines. How she wards off the wolves and whether she does, are still riddles for Eighteenth Street.

THE REVE'ND BUNN

SOLVING the race question, solving it in a 'Jim-swinger' and a pair of heavy tortoise shell spectacles is the job-in-chief of the Rev'end G. W. Bunn, D.D., Ph.D. With such a herculean task upon him he takes it calmly. He is a pacifist without the "fist", and to certain members of his Race little more than a baby's rattle.

However, the evening dailies give space to his articles. Here is a sample:

"When one considers the army of good white people here one must be fair and say a word about them. Notwithstanding those who would drive us to other fields of labor there are those good men and women of the Caucasian Race who understand us and our needs, who loved and harbored our forebears, who will give us a square deal, and it is with these folks that the American Negro had best stay in touch with. Each day they are voicing his part more and more, and in time will see that right here in the South will be a place of desire, and happiness.

Then too, there is no overlooking the rigor of the Northern climate, the coldness of the Northern white man, the competition of the Northern foreigner. The South is the only place for the Negro. . . ."

That is about as good as any of the others he submits. It is what the editors want and there is where the Rev'end's headwork comes in. The world pays for what it wants as a rule, and each one of these epistles is a foundation for the Rev'end to solicit and collect funds for the Welfare Southern Home League, which he officers and headquarters in his ante-room office in the Washington Building.

Where is the corporation employing colored workmen who would not contribute to such an asset? "The South is the best place for the Negro" is a text that anyone can cash in on. Say it louder and longer enough and silver will clink mysteriously into your pockets.

Notwithstanding the sneer that the Rev'end is a cat's paw, me-too-boss Negro, in truth he is a good business man, or in the slang, a jack-getter and a seducer of dollars.

"Selling your birthright," somebody chunked at him. "Hurting your Race," another.

"Wrong," he came back aplomb, "my Race is yet a child, and who is it but knows that when you tell a child *not* to do a thing, he does it. Why, I'm responsible for several train loads going North. May I hint that I'm simply killing two birds with one stone. Ah, brothers, you must learn to look beyond your nose."

LAWYER HARRELL

OLD man Harrell had another murder case to-day. Didn't free his man, but says he will. Jury gave his client six years, which is a lot for a jury to admit in some of his cases.

Leaving the Court room the Court Clerk stopped him. "Harrell, you know more Bible than you do law."

"Glad I do," replied the old man.

"You ought to get a brick church and preach to the niggers," suggested the clerk.

"It's you folks who need preaching to," answered Harrell.

"You'd be a great help to your people," insisted the official.

"My people? Who do you mean? My people?"

They looked at each other fiercely and said no more. Harrell's father owned twenty slaves, among which was Harrell's mother, a mulatto.

MADAM ANTOINETTE SANDAL

AGAIN Madam Sandal has compelled social acknowledgement. This time she extended herself by presenting a fete entitled "The Nile Queen's Garden." Among the citizens of color nothing like it had ever been given. It was a masquerade with a ban on all costumes not foreign. "Only Oriental costumed guests admitted" read the invitations and enclosed separately was the program, to wit:

Costume Reception   (Ten till Eleven)
Madam Angel Bradshaw, Receptress
Dansante Generale
Sampson's Jazz Serpents—Music

Danseuse de specialty
Damsel Juliet Moore
One O'Clock—Demasque et Luncheon
Two O'Clock—The Sheik of the Night

It was an affair of creation and a surprise ending. To have seen the Crowning Glory Ball Room where the fete was given would have been a long remembered scene. But for the French doors and adjustable windows it was a roof garden. However, it is for all-year use and the fete was in March, no time for outdoor effect. For orientation all the window panes were colored alternately green, red and amber; in addition strange new scents from concealed incense burners were released.

At one end of the ball room was draped a purple curtain. Reams of rhythm and impelling tunes from Sampson's Jazz Serpents came through its royal folds and likewise was issued forth Damsel Juliet Moore in a Nile River terpsichorean conception. At one o'clock with the ball room darkened the curtain parted and appeared a huge face of a clock, the hour marks and hands illuminated. A single penetrating gong stroke told the hour and the lights came on by degrees like day-break. One hour later the illuminated clock appeared again telling the hour. This time the lights came on quickly. Ensemble music was played by the orchestra; a hush of expectancy seized the guests. A shiny black cat emerged from the curtain slit and literally sailed down the middle of the ball room. Its body was the anchor for two balloons, one red and one white. Midway the room the balloons were freed and floated lazily towards the ceiling while the inky feline made a good escape through the door. No single guest dared move across the imaginary path of the midnight creature until the door through which the cat left shut with a bang.

The balloons now held everybody's attention. On the white balloon was the letter S and on the red balloon was the letter H. Comment broke from all lips—what was the significance? The lights were softening, finally leaving the doubtful green glow from the stained windows.

"The—hour—has—come," measured a rounded baritone behind the curtain. Strange music as if from a distance was heard again. "Hear ye—all. The—hour—has —come—when—the—Sheik—of—the—Night—will—appear!"

Slowly parted the curtain; gradually came on the amber lights; nearer the music seemed and in solemn carriage stepped forth the "Sheik of the Night," a tall masked figure, clothed in silk and velvet such as no sultan could ever despise. To the center of the room he strode arrogantly and then and there he deliberately unmasked.

Sheik of the Night—none other than Dozier Horn, paragon of bootleggers along Eighteenth Street.

"The balloons, the balloons," someone exclaimed. "I have it—S stands for Sandal and H stands for Horn. They're engaged!"

Chatter, laughter and congratulations were showered upon the Sheik of the Night and the hostess, who suddenly appeared in the midst of the party as the Queen of the Nile.

THE REV'END BUNN

THE Rev'end Bunn has been conspicuous by his absence from Eighteenth Street for a month. His long coat and wilted panama, his loping walk and twisted walking cane, his horned glasses and tar-tinted face, are marks of distinction he has carried elsewhere. Just before he left it was announced that he would take a vacation, swinging through the North and East. Now, tri-weekly his letters are published in the local dailies. Here is one from Youngstown:

Since I have arrived in this busy city I have been overwhelmed with acquaintances from the South, and every one of them makes it known in some way his desire to once more see the good old Southland, where there is consideration of his methods of living and where the grind is not that of a tread mill.

One man told me that if he doesn't save enough money to buy a ticket to Andalusia, he'd walk back. . . .
And one from Cleveland:

. . . Nothwithstanding the high wages and many jobs, the Southern migrants don't seem to be able to get their bearings here at all—the herding into cramped quarters, the eternal rushing, the lack of time to fraternalize, makes them wish and long for their old Southern surroundings.

It makes me tremble to think what a terrible thing would happen to my wayward people in the event the industrial bottom should drop out of things here. . . .
And a letter from New York:

This great city has already far too many colored Americans. I solemnly advise my fellow Racemen not to think of coming to this gigantic place. . . . The South has more to offer them. . . .

And one of the dailies had an editorial comment on the Rev'end Bunn's great trip of revelation, stating that it "should open the eyes of the Southern Negroes to the fact that undisputably the South is the only and best place for them."

HAPPY TRAMP

HAPPY Tramp has just passed along. He does not look one whit different than he always has. Same threadbare trousers completely faded, a jumper coat that was once somebody else's, trash pile shoes topped by bare brown ankles, a two-season straw hat and it is now October.

Six months ago he began selling corn and synthetic rye for Dozier Horn; he has not missed a day and is the best known bootlegger along the Avenue.

"Can't understand Happy Tramp," said Dozier Horn. "I have in keeping for him over two thousand dollars and he won't let me buy him a decent pair of shoes."

Others had wrenched ready dollars from their illicit game; they either gambled and dressed it away, or lost it in paying fines and lawyer fees, or as a few attempted, quit and lived on what they had saved until in need again. Happy Tramp alone remained unaffected.

Then one day Happy Tramp came to Dozier Horn and said:

"I want you to put that money of mine in the bank in the name of Temple Scott. And next, I'm going to have a will drawn up. Early in my life I was sent to Tuskegee to school; in my final year I ran away. I'm going to keep on working and what money I save I'm going to will to Tuskegee."

"But Tuskegee doesn't want blood money," suggested Dozier Horn.

"Many an honorable institution has been built on what you call blood money," Happy Tramp came back. "I pick up a coin from the filth of the gutter; I rub it and it shines. The money's clean and good. Must it be bad if put to a worthy use? That's just the trouble with religion—it's too afraid of the gutter."

"All right, Happy," spoke up Horn. "I'll fix it as you say. But since you're going to be one of those 'philanthepers' I wish you'd put on some decent clothes and look like one. Tuskagee'll be ashamed of you."

"But they don't know me—Happy Tramp. They know Temple Scott." And he strode out to Eighteenth Street and away.

THE REV'END BUNN

Eighteenth Street has lost another habitue. The Rev'end Bunn, D.D., Ph.D. (this latter by correspondence) left to-day for Detroit, where he will take up the pastorate of the Mt. Sinai Baptist Church. In accepting the call he gave out the following statement:

I am not leaving my people in the South, I am following them. Too long have I been sidetracked from preaching the word of God, and it is with His Grace I come back into the work.

So it has come to pass that I go to Detroit to do His will. . . .

But this did not get in the white dailies. The Rev'end Bunn, go-between and trumpeter, found the current of migration too strong to resist. When he was on his tour for the Southern Labor Syndicate, Detroit had impressed him with its possibilities and problems. Then had come the clincher, the offer to minister the Mt. Sinai flock at three thousand per year.

JOHN HENRY
A Negro Legend

By GUY B. JOHNSON

NEGRO folk have produced so many interesting characters that it is difficult to choose one from among them who stands above the others. However, I believe that most of those who know anything about John Henry will agree with me that he deserves a very high rank, not only in Negro folklore, but in American folklore in general. In the sixty years since this legend originated it has grown tremendously. In song and story John Henry is celebrated in every part of the country where Negro working men are to be found.

John Henry, so the legend goes, was a steel driver. He lived in a day when steam drills and compressed air drills were just beginning to be used in tunnelling, mining, and the like. It is said that John Henry was a superior steel driver and that he enjoyed quite a reputation for his strength and endurance. He felt resentful when he heard steam drills were becoming practicable, and he said that he believed he could out-drill the things. He soon got his chance to make good. One day a representative of a mechanical drill company came to the tunnel where John Henry was working and tried to sell the contractor a steam drill. The contractor was skeptical—said that he believed the drill was no faster than a good hand driver. The agent protested this statement, so the contractor retorted that he had a man whom he was willing to put against the drill. John Henry was called in, and he agreed to compete. As the story goes,

> John Henry said to his Captain,
> "Well, a man ain't nothin' but a man,
> An' befo' I'd be beaten by that old steam drill,
> I'll die with the hammer in my han'
> Lawd, I'll die with the hammer in my han'."

According to some versions of the story, a wager was made between John Henry's "Captain" and the steam drill agent. Some say that in case John Henry lost, his "Captain" was to buy the drill; but if John Henry won, the agent was to give his drill away. At any rate, the legend has it that the contest took place. John Henry drove the required depth before the steam drill did, but the poor man had put too much into the contest. He had barely taken his last stroke when he fell over in a faint and died "with hammer in his hand."

That, I believe, is about as dramatic an episode as one could ask for. I do not wonder that John Henry is regarded almost reverently by thousands of the Negro common folk, or that the tale has a fascination for all who have only recently heard if for the first time.

The John Henry tradition exists in several forms. First, there are the stories, opinions and reminiscences of people who know something about John Henry. There are any number of people living, by the way, who claim to have known John Henry intimately. Of these I shall speak later. Then there are innumerable songs about John Henry. These may be divided into the ballad of narrative type and the work-song type. The former tells a story and is usually sung as a solo with guitar or banjo accompaniment, while the latter is rarely consistently narrative and is most often sung by groups of workmen swinging picks or hammers in unison.

An expert "musicianer" singing a John Henry ballad, picking his "box," patting his foot, swaying his body, is a picturesque sight. The following version is brief, but it gives the essential elements of the story. It was transcribed from the singing of a Negro workman at Chapel Hill, North Carolina.

John Henry was a steel-drivin' man,
Carried his hammer all the time,
An' befo' he'd let the steam drill beat him down,
He'd die with the hammer in his han',
Die with the hammer in his han'.

John Henry went to the mountain,
Beat that steam drill down;
Rock was high, po' John was small,
Well, he laid down his hammer an' he died,
Laid down his hammer an' he died.

John Henry was a little babe
Sittin' on his daddy's knee,
Said "Big Ben" Tunnel on C. & O. road
Gonna be the death o' me,
Gonna be the death o' me."

John Henry had a little girl,
Her name was Polly Ann.
John was on his bed so low,
She drove with his hammer like a man,
Drove with his hammer like a man.

But a group of dusky workmen singing and swinging in perfect rhythm is a still more picturesque sight. There is little substance and much repetition in their song, nevertheless it is enchanting. Here is a good example of a John Henry work song.

This old hammer—huh!
Hammer killed John Henry—huh!
This old hammer—huh!
Hammer killed John Henry—huh
Can't kill me—huh!
Lawd, Lawd, can't kill me—huh!

The variations of ballads, work songs, and stories about John Henry which exist among the Negro folk would fill an enormous volume, so I can only sketch briefly here the ramifications of the legend.

Take, for example, the varying ideas as to the situation in which John Henry met his death. The usual opinion is that he was working in a tunnel when he had his great contest with the steam drill. But steel driving is a term applied not only to the drilling operations used in mining, tunneling, and other work in which explosives are used, but also to the driving of spikes into railroad cross-ties. Therefore, we find John Henry driving steel in tunnels, in mines, in quarries, and on railroads. Practically every Southern state claims John Henry, the legend varying according to local conditions. Sometimes, in fact most often, he is said to have died at "Big Bend Tunnel on the C. and O. Road." Sometimes it is "Tunnel No. Nine" on the Southern Railroad. Again it is a tunnel which railway engineers say does not exist. Sometimes John Henry is represented as dying immediately after the contest, sometimes it is said that he was taken to his shanty where he died later. And I have come across such beliefs as that expressed in the following stanza:

John Henry was killed on the railroad
A mile and a half from town,
His head cut off in the driving wheel
And his body ain't never been found.

Or take the ideas about John Henry's surname. Of course, his full name might have been just John Henry, for that was once a very popular name among Negroes, both slave and free. There were about a dozen free Negro heads of families who bore the name of John Henry even as far back as 1830. But I often ask this question as to John Henry's full name when I am talking to some one about John Henry, and the replies are interesting. One man who claimed to have worked with John Henry said that his name was John Henry Dula. Another who claimed to have been with John Henry when he died, said that his surname was Dabney. Other names I have encountered are John Henry Brown, John Henry Martin, John Henry Jones, John Henry Whitsett.

Some say that John Henry was a North Carolinian, others say he was from South Carolina, or Tennessee, or Alabama, or Virginia. Some Negroes feel very strongly on this matter. In fact, I once heard of a fight arising between two men because one of them said that John Henry was born somewhere other than Virginia. Some admirer of John Henry was so eager to give Virginia the credit that he put a stanza like this in one of the John Henry ballads.

Some said he came from England,
Some said he came from Spain,
But it's no such thing, he was an East Virginia man,
And he died with the hammer in his hand,
He died with the hammer in his hand.

Similar variations of other aspects of the legend might be pointed out, but these will suffice to show the trend. No two persons tell the story of John Henry alike, yet on the whole there is among the Negro folk a firm conviction that John Henry really lived, really beat the steam drill and really "died with the hammer in his hand."

And this leads to the question of how it all got started. Is this John Henry tradition true? I do not consider this question of any great importance, but it is usually the first one which one asks on hearing about John Henry for the first time, so I want to touch upon it briefly.

There are quite a few people living who claim to have known John Henry. I have talked or corresponded with several such persons, and their testimony is an important part of the evidence on this question of John Henry's reality. For example, one old Negro man in western North Carolina told me that he knew John Henry and that he was certain that John Henry really beat a steam drill at Big Bend Tunnel. Another man, a Negro minister from Kentucky, said that as a boy he "packed" water in Big Bend Tunnel and that he saw John Henry beat the steam drill. A young man from Cleveland, Ohio, wrote me that his father worked with the "original John Henry" in Kentucky in 1886. A man from South Carolina wrote that his father once worked with John Henry in Tennessee, but he does not know where John Henry's death occurred. A white man of Orange County, Virginia, stated that he was once employed by one of the contractors who built the Big Ben Tunnel and that he has heard the contractor say time and again that the story of John Henry is true. Three different persons, one from Alabama, one from Michigan, and one from Utah, have written me about the John Henry story, vouching for its authenticity, and giving the time and place of the contest as northeastern Alabama about 1882. There are various other reminiscences, but these are typical of the ones most frequently found.

Thus, when we consider the testimony of old timers who claim to have personal knowledge of John Henry, we find that, while there were inconsistencies and impossibilities in the details, there is a convergence of opinion pointing toward only one or two places as possible locations of the original steel-driving contest. Practically all of the clues which are worth following point either toward the Big Bend Tunnel on the C. and O. Railroad in West Virginia, or toward some such place as Cursey (or Cruzee) Mountain Tunnel in Alabama. The Big Bend Tunnel was built in 1870-72, and, since it antedates the alleged Alabama tunnel by ten years, it is the more likely place.

Last year I made a personal investigation at Big Bend Tunnel, interviewing the residents, especially the old timers who worked on the tunnel when it was being built. I might summarize the situation as follows: There is a pretty general disposition around the Big Bend region to take the John Henry story for granted, but there are several people who firmly believe that John Henry is a myth, and there are only three or four who will say that they actually saw John Henry or saw the famous contest. One man gave me a detailed description of the steam drill and of the contest, which he said he saw as he went back and forth carrying water and drills for the gang on which John Henry worked. Yet his testimony is disputed by other residents who apparently were in as good position as he to know what was going on, as well as by railroad officials and mechanical engineers who say that no steam drill was ever taken to Big Bend Tunnel.

What, then, is the answer to the question? It is entirely possible that the whole thing is purely legendary and that certain men have heard the legend so long that they have actually come to believe that they knew this man John Henry. On the other hand, it is just as possible that the legend is based on an actual occurrence. Indeed, it is possible that more than one John Henry competed with a steam drill and "died with the hammer in his hand" or came so near dying that it was not difficult for his admirers to say that he died. An investigation of the Alabama claims noted above might bring out the same sort of evidence of authenticity as has been found at Big Bend.

At any rate, one who goes out to look for the answer to the mystery of John Henry's origin will not have easy sledding. He will find personal testimony galore, but it is fallible and contradictory and not the sort of proof which scientists demand. Personally, I am pretty well convinced that John Henry existed in the flesh and beat a steam drill at Big Bend Tunnel, but I confess that my belief is based on a sort of common-sense logic and not on what the historians call documentary evidence.

But the question of the origin and truth of the legend does not matter greatly. The legend is here, as vigorous and as fascinating as ever. The great thing, after all, is that thousands of Negro folk believe in John Henry and think of him reverently. To them he is a hero, an epic figure, a martyr who died defending the dignity of common labor and its superiority over that symbol of the white man's civilization—the machine.

I marvel that some poet among the "New Negro" generation does not sing John Henry's praises, that some playwright does not dramatize him, that some painter does not picture him as he battles with the steam drill, or that some sculptor does not fulfil the wishful phantasy of that Negro pick-and-shovel man who said to me, "Cap'n, they tells me that they got John Henry's statue carved out o' solid rock at the head o' Big Ben' Tunnel. Yes, sir, there he stan' with the hammer in his han'."

THINGS SAID WHEN HE WAS GONE

By BLANCHE TAYLOR DICKINSON

My branch of thoughts is frail tonight
As one lone wind-whipped weed.
Little I care if a rain drop laughs
Or cries; I cannot heed

Such trifles now as a twinkling star,
Or catch a night-bird's tune.
My whole life is you, to-night,
And you, a cool distant moon.

With a few soft words to nurture my heart
And brighter beams following love's cool shower
Who knows but this frail wind-whipped weed
Might bear you a gorgeous flower!

APRIL IS ON THE WAY

By Alice Dunbar Nelson

April is on the way!
I saw the scarlet flash of a blackbird's wing
As he sang in the cold, brown February trees;
And children said that they caught a glimpse of the
sky on a bird's wing from the far South.
(Dear God, was that a stark figure outstretched in
the bare branches
Etched brown against the amethyst sky?)

April is on the way!
The ice crashed in the brown mud-pool under my
tread,
The warning earth clutched my bloody feet with
great fecund fingers.
I saw a boy rolling a hoop up the road,
His little bare hands were red with cold,
But his brown hair blew backward in the southwest
wind.
(Dear God! He screamed when he saw my awful
woe-spent eyes.)

April is on the way!
I met a woman in the lane;
Her burden was heavy as it is always, but today
her step was light,
And a smile drenched the tired look away from her
eyes.
(Dear God, she had dreams of vengeance for her
slain mate,
Perhaps the west wind has blown the mist of hate
from her heart,
The dead man was cruel to her, you know that,
God.)

April is on the way!
My feet spurn the ground now, instead of dragging
on the bitter road.
I laugh in my throat as I see the grass greening be-
side the patches of snow
(Dear God, those were wild fears. Can there be
hate when the southwest wind is blowing?)

April is on the way!
The crisp brown hedges stir with the bustle of bird
wings.
There is business of building, and songs from brown
thrush throats
As the bird-carpenters make homes against Valen-
tine Day.

(Dear God, could they build me a shelter in the
hedge from the icy winds that will come
with the dark?)

April is on the way!
I sped through the town this morning. The florist
shops have put yellow flowers in the win-
dows,
Daffodils and tulips and primroses, pale yellow
flowers
Like the tips of her fingers when she waved me that
frightened farewell.
And the women in the market have stuck pussy wil-
lows in long necked bottles on their stands.
(Willow trees are kind, Dear God. They will not
bear a body on their limbs.)

April is on the way!
The soul within me cried that all the husk of in-
difference to sorrow was but the crust of ice
with which winter disguises life;
It will melt, and reality will burgeon forth like the
crocuses in the glen.
(Dear God! Those thoughts were from long ago.
When we read poetry after the day's toil,
and got religion together at the revival
meeting.)

April is on the way!
The infinite miracle of unfolding life in the brown
February fields.
(Dear God, the hounds are baying!)
Murder and wasted love, lust and weariness, deceit
and vainglory—what are they but the spent
breath of the runner?
(God, you know he laid hairy red hands on the
golden loveliness of her little daffodil body)
Hate may destroy me, but from my brown limbs
will bloom the golden buds with which we
once spelled love.
(Dear God! How their light eyes glow into black
pin points of hate!)

April is on the way!
Wars are made in April, and they sing at Easter
time of the Resurrection.
Therefore I laugh in their faces.
(Dear God, give her strength to join me before her
golden petals are fouled in the slime!)
April is on the way!

"THE FIRST ONE"

A Play in One Act

By ZORA NEALE HURSTON

Time: Three Years After the Flood
Place: Valley of Ararat
Persons: Noah, His Wife, Their Sons: Shem, Japheth, Ham;
Eve, Ham's Wife; The Sons' wives and children (6 or 7).

Setting:

Morning in the Valley of Ararat. The Mountain is in the near distance. Its lower slopes grassy with grazing herds. The very blue sky beyond that. These together form the back-ground. On the left downstage is a brown tent. A few shrubs are scattered here and there over the stage indicating the temporary camp. A rude altar is built center stage. A Shepherd's crook, a goat skin water bottle, a staff and other evidences of nomadic life lie about the entrance to the tent. To the right stretches a plain clad with bright flowers. Several sheep or goat skins are spread about on the ground upon which the people kneel or sit whenever necessary.

Action:

Curtain rises on an empty stage. It is dawn. A great stillness, but immediately Noah enters from the tent and ties back the flap. He is clad in loose fitting dingy robe tied about the waist with a strip of goat hide. Stooped shoulders, flowing beard. He gazes about him. His gaze takes in the entire stage.

Noah (fervently): Thou hast restored the Earth, Jehovah, it is good. (Turns to the tent.) My sons! Come, deck the altar for the sacrifices to Jehovah. It is the third year of our coming to this valley to give thanks offering to Jehovah that he spared us.

(Enter Japheth bearing a haunch of meat and Shem with another. The wife of Noah and those of Shem and Japheth follow laying on sheaves of grain and fruit (dates and figs). They are all middle-aged and clad in dingy garments.

Noah: And where is Ham—son of my old age? Why does he not come with his wife and son to the sacrifice?

Mrs. Noah: He arose before the light and went. (She shades her eyes with one hand and points toward the plain with the other.) His wife, as ever, went with him.

Shem (impatiently): This is the third year that we have come here to this Valley to commemorate our delivery from the flood. Ham knows the sacrifice is made always at sunrise. See! (He points to rising sun.) He should be here.

Noah (lifts his hand in a gesture of reproval): We shall wait. The sweet singer, the child of my loins after old age had come upon me is warm to my heart—let us wait.

(There is off-stage, right, the twanging of a rude stringed instrument and laughter. Ham, his wife and son come dancing on down-stage right. He is in his early twenties. He is dressed in a very white goat-skin with a wreath of shiny green leaves about his head. He has the rude instrument in his hands and strikes it. His wife is clad in a short blue garment with a girdle of shells. She has a wreath of scarlet flowers about her head. She has black hair, is small, young and lithe. She wears anklets and wristlets of the same red flowers. Their son about three years old wears nothing but a broad band of leaves and flowers about his middle. They caper and prance to the altar. Ham's wife and son bear flowers. A bird is perched on Ham's shoulder.

Noah (extends his arms in greeting): My son, thou art late. But the sunlight comes with thee. (Ham gives bird to Mrs. Noah, then embraces Noah.)

Ham (rests his head for a moment on Noah's shoulder): We arose early and went out on the plain to make ready for the burnt offering before Jehovah.

Mrs. Shem (tersely): But you bring nothing.

Ham: See thou! We bring flowers and music to offer up. I shall dance before Jehovah and sing joyfully upon the harp that I made of the thews of rams. (He proudly displays the instrument and strums once or twice.)

Mrs. Shem (clapping her hands to her ears): Oh, Peace! Have we not enough of thy bawling and prancing all during the year? Shem and Japheth work always in the fields and vineyards, while you do naught but tend the flock and sing!

Mrs. Japheth (looks contemptuously at both Ham and Noah): Still, thou art beloved of thy father . . . he gives thee all his vineyards for thy singing, but Japheth must work hard for his fields.

Mrs. Shem: And Shem—

Noah (angrily): Peace! Peace! Are lust and strife *again* loose upon the Earth? Jehovah might have destroyed us all. Am I not Lord of the world? May I not bestow where I will? Besides, the world is great. Did I not give food, and plenty to the thousands upon thousands that the waters licked up? Surely there is abundance for us and our seed forever. Peace! Let us to the sacrifice.

(Noah goes to the heaped up altar. Ham exits to the tent hurriedly and returns with a torch and hands it to Noah who applies it to the altar. He kneels at the altar and the others kneel in a semi-circle behind him at a little distance. Noah makes certain ritualistic gestures and chants):
"O Mighty Jehovah, who created the Heaven and the firmaments thereof, the Sun and Moon, the stars, the Earth and all else besides—

Others: I am here
I am here, O, Jehovah
I am here
This is thy Kingdom, and I am here.
(A deep silence falls for a moment.)

Noah: Jehovah, who saw evil in the hearts of men, who opened upon them the windows of Heaven and loosed the rain upon them—And the fountains of the great deep were broken up—

Others (repeat chant)

Noah: Jehovah who dried up the floods and drove the waters of the sea again to the deeps—who met Noah in the Vale of Ararat and made covenant with Noah, His servant, that no more would he smite the Earth—And Seed time and Harvest, Cold and Heat, Summer and Winter, day and night shall not cease forever, and set His rainbow as a sign.

Noah and Others: We are here O Jehovah
We are here
We are here
This is Thy Kingdom
And we are here.
(Noah arises, makes obeisance to the smoking altar, then turns and blesses the others.)

Noah: Noah alone, whom the Lord found worthy; Noah whom He made lord of the Earth, blesses you and your seed forever.
(At a gesture from him all arise. The women take the meat from the altar and carry it into the tent.) Eat, drink and make a joyful noise before Him. For He destroyed the Earth, but spared us. (Women re-enter with bits of roast meat—all take some and eat. All are seated on the skins.)

Mrs. Noah (feelingly): Yes, three years ago, all was water, *water*, WATER! The deeps howled as one beast to another. (She shudders.) In my sleep, even now, I am in that Ark again being borne here, there on the great bosom.

Mrs. Ham (wide-eyed): And the dead! Floating, floating all about us—We were one little speck of life in a world of death! (The bone slips from her hand.) And there, close beside the Ark, close with her face upturned as if begging for shelter —my *mother!* (She weeps, Ham comforts her.)

Mrs. Shem (eating vigorously): She would not repent. Thou art as thy mother was—a seeker after beauty of raiment and laughter. God is just. She would not repent.

Mrs. Ham: But the unrepentant are no less loved. And why must Jehovah hate beauty?

Noah: Speak no more of the waters. Oh, the strength of the waters! The voices and the death of it! Let us have the juice of the grape to make us forget. Where once was death in this Valley there is now life abundant of beast and herbs. (He waves towards the scenery.) Jehovah meets us here. Dance! Be glad! Bring wine! Ham smite thy harp of ram's thews and sing!
(Mrs. Noah gathers all the children and exits to the tent. Shem, Japheth, their wives and children eat vigorously. Mrs. Ham exits, left. Ham plays on his harp and capers about singing. Mrs. Ham re-enters with goatskin of wine and a bone cup. She crosses to where Noah reclines on a large skin. She kneels and offers it to him. He takes the cup—she pours for him. Ham sings—)

Ham:
"I am as a young ram in the Spring
Or a young male goat.
The hills are beneath my feet
And the young grass.
Love rises in me like the flood
And ewes gather round me for food."
His wife joins in the dancing. Noah cries "Pour" and Mrs. Ham hurries to fill his cup again. Ham joins others on the skins. The others have horns suspended from their girdles. Mrs. Ham fills them all. Noah cries "pour" again and she returns to him. She turns to fill the others' cups.

Noah (rising drunkenly): Pour again, Eve, and Ham sing on and dance and drink—drown out the waters of the flood if you can. (His tongue grows thick. Eve fills his cup again. He reels drunkenly toward the tent door, slopping the liquor out of the cup as he walks.) Drink wine, forget water—it means death, *death!* And bodies floating, face up! (He stares horrified about himself and creeps stealthily into the tent, but sprawls just inside the door so that his feet are visible. There is silence for a moment, the others are still eating. They snatch tid-bits from each other.)

Japheth (shoves his wife): Fruit and herbs, woman! (He thrusts her impatiently forward with his foot.) She exits left.

Shem (to his wife): More wine!

Mrs. Shem (irritated): See you not that there is plenty still in the bottle? (He seizes it and pours. Ham snatches it away and pours. Shem tries to get it back but Ham prevents him. Re-enter Mrs. Japheth with figs and apples. Everybody grabs. Ham and Shem grab for the same one, Ham gets it).

Mrs. Shem (significantly): Thus he seizes all else that he desires. Noah would make him lord of the Earth because he sings and capers. (Ham is laughing drunkenly and pelting Mrs. Shem with fruit skins and withered flowers that litter the ground. This infuriates her.)

Noah (calls from inside the tent): Eve, wine, quickly! I'm sinking down in the WATER! Come drown the WATER with wine.

(Eve exits to him with the bottle. Ham arises drunkenly and starts toward the tent door.)

Ham (thickly): I go to pull our father out of the water, or to drown with him in it. (Ham is trying to sing and dance.) "I am as a young goat in the sp-sp-sp-. (He exits to the tent laughing. Shem and Japheth sprawl out in the skins. The wives are showing signs of surfeit. Ham is heard laughing raucously inside the tent. He re-enters still laughing.)

Ham (in the tent door): Our Father has stripped himself, showing all his wrinkles. Ha! Ha! He's as no young goat in the spring. Ha! Ha! (Still laughing, he reels over to the altar and sinks down behind it still laughing.) The old Ram, Ha! Ha! Ha! He has had no spring for years! Ha! Ha! (He subsides into slumber. Mrs. Shem looks about her exultantly.)

Mrs. Shem: Ha! The young goat has fallen into a pit! (She shakes her husband.) Shem! Shem! Rise up and become owner of Noah's vineyards as well as his flocks! (Shem kicks weakly at her.) Shem! Fool! Arise! Thou art thy father's first born. (She pulls him protesting to his feet.) Do stand up and regain thy birthright from (she points to the altar) that dancer who plays on his harp of ram thews, and decks his brow with bay leaves. Come!

Shem (brightens): How?

His wife: Did he not go into the tent and come away laughing at thy father's nakedness? Oh (she beats her breast) that I should live to see a father so mocked and shamed by his son to whom he has given all his vineyards! (She seizes a large skin from the ground.) Take this and cover him and tell him of the wickedness of thy brother.

Mrs. Japheth (arising takes hold of the skin also): No, my husband shall also help to cover Noah, our father. Did I not also hear? Think your Shem and his seed shall possess both flocks and vineyard while Japheth and his seed have only the fields? (She arouses Japheth, he stands.)

Shem: He shall share—

Mrs. Shem (impatiently): Then go in (the women release the skin to the men) quickly, lest he wake sober, then will he not believe one word against Ham who needs only to smile to please him. (The men lay the skin across their shoulders and back over to the tent and cover Noah. They motion to leave him.)

Mrs. Shem: Go back, fools, and wake him. You have done but half.

(They turn and enter the tent and both shake Noah. He sits up and rubs his eyes. Mrs. Shem and Mrs. Japheth commence to weep ostentatiously).

Noah (peevishly): Why do you disturb me, and why do the women weep? I thought all sorrow and all cause for weeping was washed away by the flood. (He is about to lie down again but the men hold him up.)

Shem: Hear, father, thy age has been scoffed, and thy nakedness made a thing of shame here in the midst of the feasting where all might know—thou the Lord of all under Heaven, hast been mocked.

Mrs. Shem: And we weep in shame, that thou our father should have thy nakedness uncovered before us.

Noah (struggling drunkenly to his feet): Who, *who* has done this thing?

Mrs. Shem (timidly crosses and kneels before Noah): We fear to tell thee, lord, lest thy love for the doer of this iniquity should be so much greater than the shame, that thou should slay us for telling thee.

Noah (swaying drunkenly): Say it, woman, shall the lord of the Earth be mocked? Shall his nakedness be uncovered and he be shamed before his family?

Shem: Shall the one who has done this thing hold part of thy goods after thee? How wilt thou deal with them? Thou hast been wickedly shamed.

Noah: No, he shall have no part in my goods—his goods shall be parcelled out among the others.

Mrs. Shem: Thou art wise, father, thou art just!

Noah: He shall be accursed. His skin shall be black! Black as the nights, when the waters brooded over the Earth!

(Enter Mrs. Noah from tent, pauses by Noah.)

Mrs. Noah (catches him by the arm): Cease! Whom dost thou curse?

Noah (shaking his arm free. The others also look awed and terrified and also move to stop him. All rush to him. Mrs. Noah attempts to stop his mouth with her hand. He shakes his head to free his lips and goes in a drunken fury): Black! He and his seed forever. He shall serve his brothers and they shall rule over him— Ah—Ah—. (He sinks again to the ground.

There is a loud burst of drunken laughter from behind the altar.)

Ham: Ha! Ha! I am as a young ram—Ha! Ha!

Mrs. Noah (to Mrs. Shem): Whom cursed Noah?

Mrs. Shem: Ham—Ham mocked his age. Ham uncovered his nakedness, and Noah grew wrathful and cursed him. Black! He could not mean *black*. It is enough that he should lose his vineyards. (There is absolute silence for a while. Then realization comes to all. Mrs. Noah rushes in the tent to her husband, shaking him violently.)

Mrs. Noah (voice from out of the tent): Noah! Arise! Thou art no lord of the Earth, but a drunkard. Thou hast cursed my son. Oh water, Shem! Japheth! Cold water to drive out the wine. Noah! (She sobs.) Thou must awake and unsay thy curse. Thou must! (She is sobbing and rousing him. Shem and Japheth seize a skin bottle from the ground by the skin door and dash off right. Mrs. Noah wails and the other women join in. They beat their breasts. Enter Eve through the tent. She looks puzzled.)

Mrs. Ham: Why do you wail? Are all not happy today?

Mrs. Noah (pityingly): Come, Eve. Thou art but a child, a heavy load awaits thee. (Eve turns and squats beside her mother-in-law.)

Eve (carressing Mrs. Noah): Perhaps the wine is too new. Why do you shake our father?

Mrs. Noah: Not the wine of grapes, but the wine of sorrow bestirs me thus. Turn thy comely face to the wall, Eve. Noah has cursed thy husband and his seed forever to be black, and to serve his brothers and they shall rule over him.

(Re-enter the men with the water bottle running. Mrs. Noah seizes it and pours it in his face. He stirs.) See, I must awaken him that he may unspeak the curse before it be too late.

Eve: But Noah is drunk—surely Jehovah hears not a drunken curse. Noah would not curse Ham if he knew. Jehovah knows Noah loves Ham more than all. (She rushes upon Noah and shakes him violently.) Oh, awake thou (she shrieks) and uncurse thy curse. (All are trying to rouse Noah. He sits, opens his eyes wide and looks about him. Mrs. Noah carresses him.)

Mrs. Noah: Awake, my lord, and unsay thy curse.

Noah: I am awake, but I know of no curse. Whom did I curse?

Mrs. Noah and Eve: Ham, lord of the Earth. (He rises quickly to his feet and looks bewildered about.)

Japheth (falls at his feet): Our father, and lord of all under Heaven, you cursed away his vineyards, but we do not desire them. You cursed him to be black—he and his seed forever, and that his seed shall be our servants forever, but we desire not their service. Unsay it all.

Noah (rushes down stage to the footlights, center. He beats his breast and bows his head to the ground.) Oh, that I had come alive out of my mother's loins! Why did not the waters of the flood bear me back to the deeps! Oh Ham, my son!

Eve (rushing down to him): Unspeak the Curse! Unspeak the Curse!

Noah (in prayerful attitude): Jehovah, by our covenant in this Valley, record not my curses on my beloved Ham. Show me once again the sign of covenant—the rainbow over the Vale of Ararat.

Shem (strikes his wife): It was thou, covetous woman, that has brought this upon us.

Mrs. Shem (weeping): Yes, I wanted the vineyards for thee, Shem, because at night as thou slept on my breast I heard thee sob for them. I heard thee murmur "Vineyards" in thy dreams.

Noah: Shem's wife is but a woman.

Mrs. Noah: How rash thou art, to curse unknowing in thy cups the son of thy loins.

Noah: Did not Jehovah repent after he had destroyed the world? Did He not make all flesh? Their evils as well as their good? Why did He not with His flood of waters wash out the evil from men's hearts, and spare the creatures He had made, or else destroy us all, *all*? For in sparing one, He has preserved all the wickedness that He creates abundantly, but punishes terribly. No, He destroyed them because vile as they were it was His handiwork, and it shamed and reproached Him night and day. He could not bear to look upon the thing He had done, so He destroyed them.

Mrs. Noah: Thou canst not question.

Noah (weeping): Where is my son?

Shem (pointing): Asleep behind the altar.

Noah: If Jehovah keeps not the covenant this time, if He spare not my weakness, then I pray that Ham's heart remains asleep forever.

Mrs. Shem (beseeching): O Lord of the Earth, let his punishment be mine. We coveted his vineyards, but the curse is too awful for him. He is drunk like you—save him, Father Noah.

Noah (exultantly): Ah, the rainbow! The promise! Jehovah will meet me! He will set His sign in the Heavens! Shem hold thou my right hand and Japheth bear up my left arm.

(Noah approaches the altar and kneels. The two men raise his hands aloft.)

Our Jehovah who carried us into the ark—

Sons: Victory, O Jehovah! The Sign.

Others (beating their breasts): This is Thy Kingdom and we are here.

Noah: Who saved us from the Man of the Waters.

Sons: Victory, O Jehovah! The Sign.

Others: We belong to Thee, Jehovah, we belong to Thee.

(There is a sudden, loud raucous laugh from behind the altar. Ham sings brokenly, "I am a young ram in the Spring.")

Noah (hopefully): Look! Look! To the mountain—do ye see colors appear?

Mrs. Noah: None but what our hearts paint for us—ah, false hope.

Noah: Does the sign appear, I seem to see a faint color just above the mountain. (Another laugh from Ham.)

Eve: None, none yet. (Beats her breast violently, speaks rapidly.) Jehovah, we belong to *Thee,* we belong to *Thee.*

Mrs. Noah and Eve: Great Jehovah! Hear us. We are here in Thy Valley. We who belong to Thee!

(Ham slowly rises. He stands and walks around the altar to join the others, and they see that he is black. They shrink back terrified. He is laughing happily. Eve approaches him timidly as he advances around the end of the altar. She touches his hand, then his face. She begins kissing him.)

Ham: Why do you all pray and weep?

Eve: Look at thy hands, thy feet. Thou art cursed black by thy Father. (She exits weeping left.)

Ham (gazing horrified at his hands): Black! (He appears stupified. All shrink away from him as if they feared his touch. He approaches each in turn. He is amazed. He lays his hand upon Shem.

Shem (shrinking): Away! Touch me not!

Ham (approaches his mother. She does not repel him, but averts her face.) Why does my mother turn away?

Mrs. Noah: So that my baby may not see the flood that hath broken the windows of my soul and loosed the fountains of my heart.

(There is a great clamor off stage and Eve re-enters left with her boy in her arms weeping and all the other children in pursuit jeering and pelting him with things. The child is also black. Ham looks at his child and falls at Noah's feet.

Ham (beseeching in agony): Why Noah, my father and lord of the Earth, why?

Noah (sternly): Arise, Ham. Thou art black. Arise and go out from among us that we may see thy face no more, lest by lingering the curse of thy blackness come upon all my seed forever.

Ham (grasps his father's knees. Noah repels him sternly, pointing away right. Eve steps up to Ham and raises him with her hand. She displays both anger and scorn.)

Eve: Ham, my husband, Noah is right. Let us go before you awake and learn to despise your father and your God. Come away Ham, beloved, come with me, where thou canst never see these faces again, where never thy soft eyes can harden by looking too oft upon the fruit of their error, where never thy happy voice can learn to weep. Come with me to where the sun shines forever, to the end of the Earth, beloved the sunlight of all my years. (She kisses his mouth and forehead. She crosses to door of tent and picks up a water bottle. Ham looks dazedly about him. His eyes light on the harp and he smilingly picks it up and takes his place beside Eve.

Ham (lightly cynical to all): Oh, remain with your flocks and fields and vineyards, to covet, to sweat, to die and know no peace. I go to the sun. (He exits right across the plain with his wife and child trudging beside him. After he is off-stage comes the strumming of the harp and Ham's voice happily singing: "I am as a young ram in the Spring." It grows fainter and fainter until it is heard no more. The sun is low in the west. Noah sits looking tragically stern. All are ghastly calm. Mrs. Noah kneels upon the altar facing the mountain and she sobs continually.

We belong to Thee, O Jehovah
We belong to Thee.
She keeps repeating this to a slow curtain).

CURTAIN

THIS PLACE

By DONALD JEFFREY HAYES

This is the place where strangers meet
And break a friendly bread
This is the place where the wanderer
May rest his weary head . . .

This is the place where songs are sung
Where winter's tales are told
This is the place for broken dreams
When they grow worn and old . . .

This is the place of As-You-Will
Come in—abide—depart
This is the place I offer you
This place—my heart. . . .

THREE POEMS

By COUNTEE CULLEN

SELF CRITICISM

Shall I go all my bright days singing,
  (A little pallid, a trifle wan)
The failing note still vainly clinging
  To the throat of the stricken swan?

Shall I never feel and meet the urge
  To bugle out beyond my sense
That the fittest song of earth is a dirge,
  And only fools trust Providence?

Than this better the reed never turned flute,
  Better than this no song,
Better a stony silence, better a mute
  Mouth and a cloven **tongue.**

A SONG NO GENTLEMAN WOULD SING TO ANY LADY

There are some things I might not know
Had you not pedagogued me so;
  And these I thank you for;
Now never shall a piquant face
Cause my tutored heart a trace
  Of anguish any more.

Before your pleasure made me wise,
A simulacrum of disguise
  Masked the serpent and the dove;
That I discern now hiss from coo,
My heart's full gratitude to you,
  Lady I had learned to love.

Before I knew love well I sang
Many a polished pain and pang,
  With proper bardic zeal;
But now I know hearts do not break
So easily, and though a snake
  Has made them wounds may heal.

EXTENUATION TO CERTAIN CRITICS

Cry Shame upon me if you must,
Shout Treason and Default,
Say I betray a sacred trust
Aching beyond this vault.
I'll bear your censure as your praise,
Yet never shall a clan
Confine my singing to its ways
Beyond the ways of man.

No racial option narrows grief;
Pain is no patriot;
And sorrow braids her dismal leaf
For all as lief as not.
With blind sheep groping every hill
Seeking an oriflamme,
What shepherd heart would keep its fill
For only the darker lamb?

NEW LIGHTS ON AN OLD SONG

By Dorothy Scarborough

I WAS giving a lecture on Negro Folk Songs in Denison, Texas, and was speaking of my fondness for one which is my favorite among the spirituals. At the conclusion of the lecture, I boarded an inter-urban car to return to Dallas, when a young girl who had been sent from Sherman to interview me sat down beside me. In the course of our conversation she reported to me something that her brother, a missionary in Africa, had casually told her while he was at home on a recent furlough. It interested me so much that I asked her to write me a letter about it, in order that I might be sure of having the facts correctly fixed in my memory.

Here is her letter:

*Sherman, Texas,
November 30, 1927.*

Dear Dr. Scarborough:

Below is a brief account of the origin of "Swing Low, Sweet Chariot," for which you asked last evening on the Inter-urban.

My brother, who is a missionary in the Bokuba Kingdom, Couge Belge, Africa, relates that as he was "on the trail" one day in his hammock, the hammock boys began singing a song (in other language, of course, the tune of which was strangely familiar.)

He inquired of one of them, "Who taught you that song?"

"No one, chief. That song is as old as our tribe. It is a funeral dirge."

The tune was unmistakably that of "Swing Low, Sweet Chariot." It did not vary from the old Southern air in the slightest.

Under separate cover I am sending you a copy of my brother's little book "The Leopard Hunts Alone" of which I spoke. It is all too brief and contains only the suggestions of things he would have liked to say had he the opportunity. But maybe you will find in it a few facts of interest.

Sincerely yours,

(Signed) Catherine Wharton.

I mean to write to Mr. Wharton in the hope of finding out if he got the words of the dirge. I should like to know if the parallelism extends . . . to actual language, as well as to theme and melody.

Miss Wharton said that her brother told her that the Bokuba language had not been written down before the missionaries undertook the task, but that it is musical and well inflected. He has discovered in the tribal folk-lore a collection of fables which are almost identical with those of Aesop, and many stories similar to old Testament accounts.

Some skilled musician, trained in Negro folk-song, should go to Africa and make a study of native songs, with the thought of discovering how much relation there is between specific Negro folk-songs found in America and African music. The results of such research would be extremely valuable.

On the day after the letter reached me I visited the Booker T. Washington High School in Dallas, to hear the trained chorus of more than eight hundred voices sing a number of spirituals. Portia Washington Pittman is doing an admirable work in developing the musical talents of these young people, and in teaching them the value of their heritage of racial songs. I read the letter to the audience, and this daughter of Booker T. Washington expressed keen interest in this bit of information concerning the immemorial history of a song that everyone loves. I thought that others might like to know of it too.

LA PERLA NEGRA

By Edna Worthley Underwood

I SAW her first in *El Teatro Nacional,* the splendid building which the Cubans erected in honor of their love of music and art, just as similarly luxurious buildings—equally sumptuous and satisfying to the eye—have been erected throughout the cities of South America.

It was in May and a night of grand opera. A new tenor of Mexican blood was going to try to initiate a lasting rivalry with Caruso, by his singing of the song of tears in "Pagliacci."

In that audience of beautiful women, whose jewelled *decolletage* was heightened by white shoulders that shone like satin, by the piled up splendor of curls that were blacker than ebony, I found her. She arose upon my field of vision slowly almost imperceptibly, as a great slow-sailing ship swings into sight upon the disconcerting levels of the sea. Or better, perhaps, I did not really *see* her, as that phrase is commonly understood, but instead I *became aware* of her, in the same way as in an art gallery a piece of silent marble impresses itself upon the senses.

She sat a few seats in front of me, swathed in dull, white, dotted lace. On this night of heat she wore a high collar that reached in points behind her ears. She wore long sleeves of the same material, whose points partly covered her hands. For the rest the dress was old-fashioned—a basque, tightly gripped at the waist, and a long draped skirt,flowing into a train; in fact the sort of dress that the great portrait painters of France were painting in 1860. Not a jewel, not a flower did she wear, and on this night of heat she did not use a fan. But what astonishing splendor of line! She represented *form* such as Fantin Latour loved.

A round, superbly poised head, whose short, waving hair was hidden in order not to cloud the outline. And she possessed the motionlessness, the nerveless repose of an animal.

In the intermission, when the audience arose—in friendly Spanish fashion—to go below to the club room for an ice, I saw her face. She was a pale, grey Negress, with the faultless body of an Attic marble, and eyes in which there was no mind, no soul, eyes that were the misty, mellow-green of absinthe. And those astonishing eyes were framed in lashes that made me think of black palm-plumes, when the pulse of the sea shakes them.

Her companion was as unusual as herself, an old, old man—a white man—well over seventy, and not a Spaniard. He was tall, faultlessly attired, evidently a great gentleman, upon whom the salon life of a polished people had set its seal. The only thing a trifle bizarre, perhaps, was the matched emeralds of extraordinary size that fastened his shirt.

During the first part of the opera I did not see her speak, nor pay the slightest attention to what he said to her. Down below in the clubroom where the world was enjoying wines and ices, she was equally silent and impassive. Even when distinguished friends of the old man gathered about them, not once did I see her speak. She merely looked with eyes limpid and green, green as degenerate emeralds are green, or sea-water in the cold north. But she was by far the most distinguished figure in this elegant and aristocratic assembly. She represented majesty of line, and the insolence of indolent youth.

Some nights later, in the crowded midnight parade upon the Prado, where all the races of the islands of the earth are mingled, under the languorous, yellow moon that hangs over seas, I saw them again. The old gentleman was making a pitiful attempt to hold himself erect, with the proud, easy exactness of youth. Beside him she walked—*La Perla Negra*—supple and sullen, walked like a panther. Tonight she wore grey lace the hue of her skin, and about her neck, ropes of pale green jade.

I wondered what she thought, what she busied herself with in her mind, she who not only never spoke, but who seemed not even to listen. Forgetful of proud Spanish etiquette, I addressed my nearest neighbor.

"Do you know who they are—that man and woman?"

"Why yes—of course! He is Monsieur X—," mentioning the name of a painter of Europe to whom the world had accorded honors for his art. "The woman is a Negress. He worships her for her beauty. He says that in the old days of his youth— in Paris—he created art. Now he is doing something different. He is living it. He spends his time in designing clothes for her. He dresses and redresses her like a doll. Day-long he feasts his eyes upon her, this living statue of grey marble. They live in that faded violet-tinted palace—in the great garden—not far from the Malecon."

Then this trembling old man was a modern Paris, still going on, on the ancient quest—Beauty. For it he had left home, country, fame, companionship, in his old age. What an artist was he who could feast upon it as upon a miraculous food, and live.

But what was all this for her? Was she happy? Was she contented? Had she any interests, any pleasures, any personality. Did she ever think? And if she did, of what? The great genius, the incredibly sensitive artist who lived beside her, what was he to her? Within her was there anything superior to the instinct for trickery of the savage?

In the early morning when I drove out to that surprising curve of blue water, which is called the Malecon, I passed their faded palace. She was walking in the garden and she wore apple-green and black. A figure in white linen was on the veranda. What subtlety of poetry, what penciled persistence of art was it, that made him dress her in coarse tinted laces, gauzes, and never in satin or silk? And what harmonies he achieved in these gowns he so busily planned! I drove on and forgot them, in looking at the old buildings that border the white, curving Malecon, buildings which, when super-imposed by distance, recalled to me vaguely Turner's "Palace of the Caesars."

The next morning, I drove to a beach outside the city, while yet the hour was early, and the tropic sun was kindly and not bitter. When I reached the beach and the blue haze of the ocean, I saw another car. The old artist, immaculate in white linen, was lounging in his limousine, while *La Perla Negra,* in a bathing suit of dull surfaced white silk, was in the water. Upon the wet, moulded silk the blue sea sent its shivers. She was a statue of the dead, antique world come back to life. Her body, however, was not that of the Greeks and Romans. Its racial heritage was different, but it was of a fineness equally great. The astonishing grey-whiteness of her skin was one that might not belong to a Caucasian race. By blending and interbreeding it had come up for slow generations from ancestors scattered among all the islands of these blue, disconcerting, magic seas.

I watched her swim far out, out where sailing vessels were, which black, greasy Negroes were loading. Sometimes their boat-songs the wind swept over to our ears. Their huge, brutal, semi-naked bodies were within eye-shot—and their gestures. At length he called to her to come back, somewhat impatiently it seemed, explaining that the sun was getting high, and that it was time to go within. As she stepped out of the water to walk toward the limousine, and came straight toward us, I saw a change in her.   The usually dull, cold eyes were blazing like the burnished levels of the sea. She moved with a great vigor, a great joy, as if in the depths of her soul, the fire of the morning burned.   A waiting maid wrapped her hastily in a white robe of rough wool. As they started to drive away, she looked back again, toward the sea, threw her head back with a savage gesture as if freeing herself from something, and for the first time, I saw her laugh.   Her laugh was unpleasant.   It was cruel and wild.

Some weeks later I saw the old artist promenading alone at night upon the Prado. Again my curiosity got the better of me.

"Why is he alone?" I asked.   "What has become of *La Perla Negra?*"

"Haven't you heard?"

"No.   How could I?"

"It was in the paper."

"What paper?"

"La Prensa."

"I did not see it," I admitted regretfully.

"She ran away with a black Negro boatman—a regular Senegambian—to Haiti, the black man's paradise.   She did not take any of her beautiful and expensive clothes. She was tired of them.   She left them all.   She went away bare footed, in a long, white, cotton shirt, just such as island Negresses wear.

"He was inconsolable for a while.   Now he is picking up and declared that he is going to create again—paint again—become again the great artist that he was.   He says, you can not live art and create art at the same time.   He ought to know.   He has given it a trial."

She had gone back to the wild undisciplined life of her race.   She must have different things.   She must have the heated dance under the stars—at night—and the fight that followed.   She must feel hunger, discomfort and weariness.   She must feel upon her faultless, grey-marble shoulders, the overseer's lash.   She must burn up her youth, her beauty in a frenzy of feverish life; in toil, in the brittle dawn, by the edge of the cane fields.   She must have the fierce things of her blood.

Not yet was the white man's life, with its weakening trivialities, for her.

She had escaped from that consuming disease which we call *civilization.*

THE NEGRO OF THE JAZZ BAND

(Translated from the Spanish of José M. Salaverría)

BY DOROTHY R. PETERSON

I DO not know thru what strange vagaries I was first induced into becoming an habitueé of that particular tea room, as with polite exaggeration it was called, and which, in reality, was no more than a modest eating place foundering along the extreme end of a cosmopolitan beach resort. The tea that they served there was tasteless. The only thing worthy of admiration was the name of the establishment, emblazoned in red letters on a large sign over the arched doorway: *At the Charm of Russia.*

Perhaps I responded to the call of the name or perhaps I had been attracted by the singularity of that deserted corner on the open coast. The fact is, however, that I began to repeat my visits to that motley and scantily furnished eating house, which did indeed display in a quite picturesque manner, a series of promising symbols: flags, colored lanterns, huge crayon posters, cubist pictures and other like accessories. Everything tended to show that on that one spot there had been concentrated a small bit of modern Russia. The lure of advertising is so great that there were always to be found a few benevolent tourists who attended the "thé-dansants" which were held every afternoon in that paint daubed hall of *At the Charm of Russia.*

The charm reduced itself to a handful of girls who performed the duties of waitresses, attired in the costumes of Spanish peasant girls, and to a Jazz Band. This jazz band was far from thrilling. It was hardly more than mediocre. But it was sufficiently tuneful to lure some Spanish and French couples and a few stray Americans into the abandon of a fox trot or Charleston. As I never dance at all, I was limited merely to listening to the music of the jazz band which at times, does not fail to interest me. I was also entertained by the rhythmic and clownish gestures which the poor devils who made up the orchestra executed while playing. Particularly the Negro!

He was an authentic and magnificent Negro. That is, he was a completely black Negro, of an unmistakable and unredeemable black. He might have come forth from the very depths of the Guinea jungle. But no, his home was in the United States of North America, because at moments, when the tempo of the music so required, the Negro would utter some words in English, as a sort of refrain, while he manipulated the complicated hardware of which his instruments consisted, a bass drum, a kettle drum, a triangle, cymbals and even, I believe, a fog horn. And with his enormous mouth and thick red lips, the Negro knew how to intercalate at the proper and opportune moment, a series of delirious guffaws completely Negroesque in sound, and which to me, (why should I deny it?) were extremely pleasing. And the truth is that after repeatedly staring at him and studying him, I confess that I became completely fascinated by the Negro of the jazz band.

One night I happened to go for supper to a chop house nearby, where, altho nothing else seemed worthy of recommendation, they served a common variety of very delicious fish soup. Some foreigners, who had also discovered the secret of that marvellous soup á la Marseille, used to frequent the same chop house, which indeed offered few other comforts. On this night at a table next to mine sat a heavily built man. Suddenly the man turned and faced me, and I could not suppress a cry of surprise. The Negro from the jazz band!

But he was no longer a Negro. He was as white as you or I or anyone else. So great was my surprise that I exclaimed with incomprehensive naiveté:

"But, weren't you black this afternoon?"

This discovery of mine produced no pleasure on the other man. I realized it by his expression, the play of the muscles around his mouth, the whole gesture of repugnance. He repressed his annoyance, however, and made haste to answer me courteously:

"It is true that I was black this very afternoon, and now I am completely white. But the surprising part is your discovery of it. I flattered myself that I played my part better...."

"And the flattery is well deserved. You may continue to believe that your dissembling is well done. You make up marvellously well as a Negro. But I am a writer and my habit of close observation has enabled me to pierce your disguise. My interest in writing has caused me to study your physique and your unusual gestures. You, yourself must realize that my curiosity is not difficult to understand, because after all, a man who disguises himself deliberately and intentionally as a Negro is not an everyday occurrence. It is easily comprehensive that one may wish to change his personality, but it is always in the sense of improvement, rather than in a debasing or lowering sense.

I could understand your pretending to the social status of a bankrupt Russian prince, but it is past my comprehension that you should be content to be black."

Then the man who wanted to be a Negro opened his heart to me, as they say, and began to unwind a skein of reflections that stupefied me.

Then listen, sir. At one time in my life I thought as you do. I believed that it was a man's duty to continue striving along an upward path in the pursuit of human perfection, continually striving to become more respected, more renowned and more powerful. It is that for which the majority of people strive, and that, in short, is what explains the progress of the human race. I, like others, aspired to become more. I also proposed to lift myself a few steps in the social scale and raise myself in rank and position. Here, where you see me, I have had conferred upon me the degree of Doctor of Laws; I prepared myself for the position of a political orator; I made my entry into politics; I was on the point of becoming an office-holder, a representative of the people; I even aspired for diplomatic appointment. No one can say that I did not do all that was humanly possible to further that ambition, which in its natural states, inspires man to the improvement and enhancement of his personality; but Luck seemed always against me! Finally, one day while I was smoking innumerable cigarettes close to a formidable Negro in a jazz band, (that one was undeniably a Negro) I conceived this unheard of idea. Why not? I could make as good a Negro as anyone else."

"And did you become easily resigned to this tragedy?"

"Of what tragedy are you speaking to me? There is no tragedy. On the contrary, as soon as I had converted myself into a Negro, I discovered that Life had assumed an aspect of ineffable facility. I was paid well and punctually, and the owners of the business, as well as the leaders of orchestras found it easier to get along with an intelligent Negro than with the ordinary Negro of the jazz band type. My disguise amused them. But no one has ever discovered my greatest disguise."

"Will you permit me to ask you?"

"Why certainly. You have made a certain sympathetic appeal to me and I am going to disclose to you my greatest secret. But do not imagine it to be any complicated nor prodigous mystery. It consists of reversing the whole tide of effort so that while everyone else is straining with all his might towards rising in the scale of Life, you, pretending unawareness, employ your strength, your intelligence and your entire resources in just "holding on." Do you understand? If, instead of "holding on", one wishes to lower his position, then the success is even more complete. Then Life becomes converted into perfect ease. Nothing upsets one, nothing presents difficulties. In a single word, one finds himself *dominating* Life, instead of, as in the case of most men, being dominated by Life. Life in its usual aspect is an overwhelming force! You, who are a writer, will have to confess that you find yourself inferior before your Art, and that the enormity of the difficulties in your Art grind you down, just as tho' the whole world were bearing all its weight upon your life. Imagine, if you can, the sense of liberty and of ease which you would feel, if, with all your present knowledge and experience, you should decide to engage in a very humble trade. The world would say that you had "lowered" yourself, descended in the social scale. But no—you would then be master of your life and of your work, just as now you are the servant of your life and of your Art. But I fear that I have not given you sufficiently convincing arguments. . . ."

"Frankly,—I do not enthuse greatly over the gift of the secret which you have disclosed to me. The disguise of one's own personality somewhat disgusts me."

"Why? since everyone disguises his own personality—since everything is a lie. The point is that other people disguise themselves under a mask of superiority—they falsify in order to be something more. And so their lies are more blameworthy than mine. The world is a marketplace of falsefaces. The rabble pretend to be noble, the fools wise, the blackguards honest, and so on. For a few months I lived surrounded by circus people, people who practiced deliberate pretense, and I look upon that period as perhaps the best of my life. My side partner, a pretty blond girl, both young and sweet dispositioned, did the part of "wild woman" in one of the side shows of the circus. There was nothing at all wild about her, not even in her character. An intimate friend of mine, whom I loved as a brother, did the "strongest man in the world" stunt and made a great deal of money by lifting bodily—weights of 100 kilos, which in point of fact weighed scarcely 12 pounds. I myself was made up as a Negro. And I assure you that behind our disguises and our reversed personalities we lived extremely well; not only happy but with an interest in Life.

"And how did that little partnership of 'pretenders' dissolve?"

"In a quite natural manner. My friend, the one whom I loved as a brother, ran away with the girl who was my partner and that ended our happy little partnership."

On hearing such a humorous ending to this sentimental episode, I could not refrain from bursting out laughing and then I exclaimed:

"You see, your system sometimes fails."

The counterfeit Negro hastened to interrupt me.

"No, the system has not failed. It was I who had failed to apply the system. I was to blame for everything. And my mistake lay precisely in the fact that I had forgotten for the moment the essential nature of the system. I became too ambitious. I wished to possess for myself alone a lovely, young and charming woman—which plan would coincide with the scheme of aspiring to something better. I had aspired to be loved alone—loved for myself—and that was already too much. Cured finally by self-chastisement, I have not again been negligent. Since then, in love as in everything else, I practice my disguise, my pretence, by abasing myself, and I go off to look for those humbler caresses which are within reach of the whole community. . . ."

I was thoroughly stunned, when confronted by that intelligent man who was constructing for his own use and mortification, so strange and dispiriting a philosophy of life. But he gave no signs of being discouraged. The following afternoon I went to take tea again at the picturesque salon of *At the Charm of Russia,* and there stood my Negro. He seemed blacker than ever in the midst of his horrible set of instruments; and his guttural guffaws, I might say, were still more Senegalese and raucous than on other afternoons. He crossed a wink of understanding with me, and then made a valiant attack on the cymbals. . . .I left the tea room almost immediately and since then I have never seen him again. Who knows in what obscure corners of our planet, the tide of his extravagant destiny may have swept him!

IDOLATRY

By ARNA BONTEMPS

You have been good to me, I give you this:
The arms of lovers empty as our own,
Marble lips sustaining one long kiss
And the hard sound of hammers breaking stone.

For I will build a chapel in the place
Where our love died and I will journey there
To make a sign and kneel before your face
And set an old bell tolling on the air.

To
CLARISSA SCOTT DELANY

By Angelina W. Grimké

1

She has not found herself a hard pillow
  And a long hard bed,
A chilling cypress, a wan willow
  For her gay young head . . .
    These are for the dead.

2

Does the violet-lidded twilight die
  And the piercing dawn
And the white clear moon and the night-blue sky. . .
  When they are gone?

3

Does the shimmering note
In the shy, shy throat
Of the swaying bird?

4

O, does children's laughter
Live not after
It is heard?

5

Does the dear, dear shine upon dear, dear things,
In the eyes, on the hair,
On waters, on wings . . .
Live no more anywhere?

6

Does the tang of the sea, the breath of frail flowers,
  Of fern crushed, of clover,
Of grasses at dark, of the earth after showers
  Not linger, not hover?

7

Does the beryl in tarns, the soft orchid in haze,
The primrose through tree-tops, the unclouded jade
Of the north sky, all earth's flamings and russets and grays
  Simply smudge out and fade?

8

And all loveliness, all sweetness, all grace,
All the gay questing, all wonder, all dreaming,
They that cup beauty that veiled opaled vase,
Are they only the soul of a seeming?

9

O, hasn't she found just a little, thin door
And passed through and closed it between?
O, aren't those her light feet upon that light floor,
. . . That her laughter? . . . O, doesn't she lean
As we do to listen? . . . O, doesn't it mean
  She is only unseen, unseen?

"The lynx says, 'I am fleet of foot,'
But the plains say, 'We are wide'."
 —*An African Proverb.*

A Mezzo-Tint from a Painting by
P. VAN DYK DEL
 —*Courtesy of Arthur A. Schomburg.*

JUAN LATINO, MAGISTER LATINUS

(From the Journal of the search in Spain for fragments of Negro Life.)

By ARTHUR A. SCHOMBURG

OR several hours the snow capped mountain top of the Sierra Nevada was plainly visible as we journeyed onward and upward on the Rosinante express toward the city of Granada. The train came to a full stop. We landed, passed through a veritable bedlam and picked from the hotel agents a resting place more for the name than for its known comforts. After resting we walked to the University grounds, saw the closed gates and walls kalsomined so often that the layers in sections were peeling off. It was dusk and there was a pastoral quiet. We retraced our steps through narrow highways and alleys to the Cathedral. Some form of religious ceremony was on. The voices and the silvery tones from the organ filled the vaulted edifice with a vast religious fervor. People here and there prayed to their favorite saints; others like myself curiously contemplated the solemnity and grandeur of the place. Through the warm colors of the stained and figured glasses light poured in like a flood. We walked up the threadbare steps to the great organ, passing a small urchin pumping air into the bellows as many others have done year on year.

Here in a grilled enclosure were the sarcophagi of Ferdinand and Isabella, who aided Columbus' discovery of America. There they were, amid their pomp and circumstance, seemingly enjoying the perfect even if endless night. And finally, again to the University. I was seeking facts and information on the life of Juan Latino, the Negro who held a professorship at the University as early as 1550. The secretary informed me that Professor Ocete had written a thesis on his life as partial fulfilment for his doctorate degree in philosophy and that he would be glad to introduce me to this man, the holder of the chair of paleontology. Meantime the secretary introduced me to the librarian and I had the great joy of seeing a copy of Juan Latino's own book on the library shelf of his alma mater.

An attendant brought me before Catedratico Ocete and I was invited into his study, where I explained my mission to Granada. I recited the hearsay of my school days when persons remarked that so and so wasn't as *Lati*—taken from the verse that alludes to Latino in Cervantes' "Don Quijote de la Mancha." I had crossed the Atlantic because I was personally satisfied that there was no better place to uncover this information than in Latino's own home and under his own vine and figtree. After my recital, the learned Professor pulled open the drawer of his desk and brought forth a small quarto volume which on inspection was the brochure already alluded to by the secretary of the University. It was an exhaustive research, gathered from fragmentary facts, and buttressed with trustworthy references.

Later he produced an early copy of Latino's work from the Granada University Library, a copy similar to the one in the series which the Ticknor collection of Spanish Literature possessed, but vastly more beautiful in comparison.

What a wonderful city, the Moors called it Paradise Valley, rich with a mellow history and hidden far away up in the foothills of the Sierra Nevada mountains.

Here in Granada during those stormy days when the Abderraman kings were lords of all they surveyed, there were among the people many undiluted black men. It was my pleasure to walk leisurely through and admire the spacious avenue named after the *Gran Capitan* and recall that he was the father of the master of Juan Latino, to pass by the street where his slave lived, the school house and Royal College where he was a tutor, the church where he knelt in humility to his real Master, where he was married to Dona Ana de Carlobar, where his children were baptized, and where eventually after life's task, he was buried in St. Ann's Church.

It is a pleasure to refer to Professor Ocete's monograph *"El Negro Juan Latino Biographical and Critical Essay"* (Granada 1925, 4 to 94 pp.). I view it with a keen desire to see the booklet translated into the English language to help stimulate our own men by the life and services this eminent man has left to posterity.

Catedratico Antonio Marin Ocete of the faculty of the University of Granada is a very charming young man, whose indefatigable knowledge is highly reflected by this work. If we accept, as we cannot otherwise do, the full explanation of our author, it is not illogical to suppose that the docks of Sevilla one day received Catino with his mother, and surely when he was of tender age. To affirm this Ocete begins by denying as notoriously false the affirmation of Salazar that he came to Spain when in his twelfth year. When we study him at close range, what is strange to his personality is the complete adaptation to so distinctly different an environment, the perfect formation of his character and intelligence in plain civilization to reach the height not only of a cultured man but a sage, having a perfect knowledge of languages and classical literature. An eminent master and above all a Latin poet extraordinarily fruitful. Only by his living there from birth under most promising circumstances can we explain it and yet admire such surprising results. Thus it must have been when mother and son were bought by a trafficker who sold them at Baena at the castle owned by the Count de Cabra, Don Luis Fernando de Cordoba and his wife Dona Elvira, only daughter of the Grand Capitan where he played during his infancy with the son of the Duke Don Gonzalo. He was known when a boy by the name of Juan de Sesa, a musician of ability, singer, organist, a player of the lute and the harp. As he grew to manhood his silence and strict application to details were noted; he helped his master's son both with his personal duties and in his studies. The son found in his black companion an apt and intelligent fellow. In time the master rewarded his charge and sent him to the same University where his son won his academic degree. Juan Sesa was afterwards known as Latino who has written his thanks "cum ipso a rudibus omnibus liberaribus artibus institutos et doctus."

Charles V, the instigator and founder of the University of Granada afterward opened by the Archbishop Hernando de Talavera by Bull and Pastoral Letter from Pope Clement VII was received on July 14th, 1531, conferring the same rights and privileges granted previously to the universities of Bologna, Paris and Salamanoa. In the *MSS* book of sermons of Rector Nicholas de la Rosa, it is stated Juan Latino received his B. A. during the year 1546, before the Archbishop, the Chancellor, the Count of Tendilla and many other gentlemen. His age was about twenty-eight. It is grateful to commend Ocete for having successfully located the minutes having the entry of the thirty-nine candidates who received their degree in "artium et philosphie facultate sub disciplina Rvdi. Dmi magistri Benedicte peco" it was duly signed by the learned dignitaries who were empowered by Royal Decree to examine candidates, and attested by the notary Johan de Frias and entered in Book No. 1 de Claustros folio 110.

The year Latino graduated (1546) from the University Archbishop Pedro Guerrero had taken possession of the See, and gave him decided protection, influenced his page, Carlobal, to desist from opposing the Negro for having married his sister, and contrived through his friend the Duke of Sesa that the servitude of the Negro should terminate. When the chair of Latin of the Sacred Cathedral Church School was vacant due to the death of the master Mota, he decided to place his candidate in the person of Juan Latino. As soon as the vacancy became known there was no end of learned men who were aspirants for the honor. On the 8th of August, 1556, while the Cathedral canons were in session licentiate Villanueva entered and said he knew there was a vacancy in the Royal College and it was not proper to let Juan Latino have it when there were so many priests who could fill the position. The Archbishop was inflexible to the undercurrents of opposition and at the beginning of the year the very reverend Pedro de Vivero, Dean of the Sacred Church and Rector of the University named Juan Latino for the chair of Latin Grammar. Professor Ocete states that notwithstanding the fact noted in the printed work of Latino where he is put down as holding a chair in the University, the item is wrong because no such office existed. An exhaustive examination of the documents available only shows him to have filled the office noted in the Royal College. Opposition continued because Latino was only an ordinary bachelor of arts, but when on November 31st, 1556 he was granted his Master of Arts, all seemed to be smooth sailing. The Royal College was a building erected beside the University and next to the Archepiscopal palace. Here was to be seen in those days familiar faces of well known students, ecclesiastical dignitaries, acolytes, Moorish persons, grave and lettered young men, attracted by the fame of a foreign master— a Negro who graced his chair—the equal of the best of his epoch.

The celebration of the feast of St. Lucar was one of the three principal events of Granada—the Rector, the Chancillor, doctors, licentiates of the University and the students from all the colleges were present on this occasion to hear the address "quam principium appellare solent" from the lips of Juan Latino, *Magister Latinus.* "It is to be regretted, says Ocete, "that this Latin oration delivered this day, unforgetable, when all Granda turned out spontaneously to hear him and tender a charming demonstration of respect and admiration, has not reached us, for I believe this example of his prose promised a free style more elegant than his verses."

The learned Ocete in a comparative illustration on letters and philosophy of Europe through the humanists F. A. Wolf of Cottigen and C. O. Muller of Berlin says "After three centuries the minds of these men reached the same conclusion of the Spanish grammarians, with which in some way or other Juan Latino was much concerned."

Latino was a most remarkable individual. Through his own efforts against all prejudice—during his period of servitude in the ducal home of his master until his marriage with a lady of quality—he became a distinguished person in Granada. When he finished his studies he climbed to the first and highest professorship in the Royal College. His further studies brought him to higher esteem since he was, in his day, the best versed in the knowledge of classical antiquity and ancient languages, which he knew perfectly well. During his famous lifetime he published three tomes of Latin verses. Through his influence a generation of original authors and translators were developed that gave birth to the Poetical School of Granada.

Don Juan de Austria the natural son of Philip II upon his triumphal entry into the city of Granada was carried away with the epigrammatic inscriptions that adorned the arches erected to commemorate the defeat of the Turks at the battle of Lepanto. The poems were the work of Juan Latino the *Magister Latinus.* It is noted that frequently

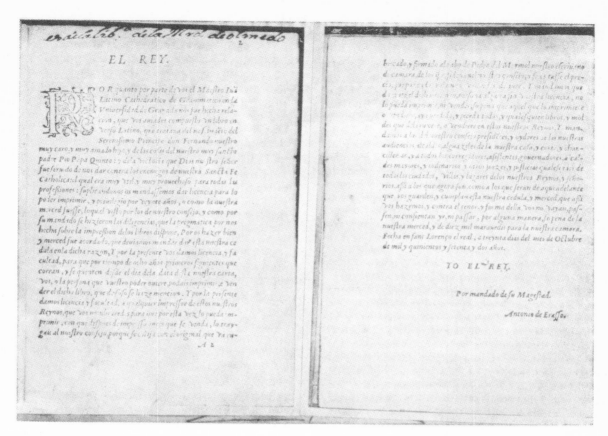

Facsimile

Privilege to print the first book of poetry by a Negro granted by the King of Spain at San Lorenzo the 30th day of October, 1572.

Facsimile

Title page of Juan Latino's epigrammatic book on Philip, King of Spain, Pius V., Don Juan of Austria, the naval battle of Lepanto, printed at Granada, 1573.

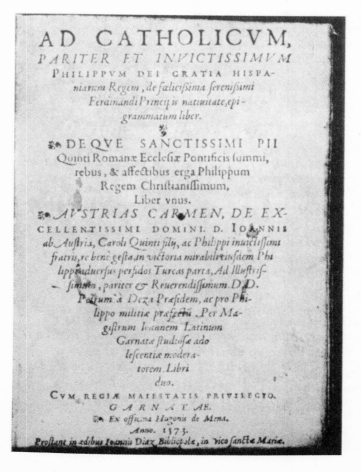

at the table of the Prince were seated two Negroes, Juan Latino was one and priest Christopher de Meneses of the Order of Santo Domingo stationed at Granada, was the other. It is said Don Juan de Austria found great pleasure in the company of these two men whose witticism and literature made them welcome guests at his festive board.

I had the pleasure of examining Latino's other two books of Latin verses at the National Library at Madrid through the courtesy of the Director. The poetical works of this writer and scholar are represented by three tomes. The first was printed by Hugo de Mena in Granada during the year 1573, is eulogistic and deals with the birth of the Prince, with the marriage of Philip II to Mary of Portugal, and with their son who was born in the year 1571, the presumptive heir to the throne named Fernando, whose birth Granada celebrated with joy. Juan Latino who was the local poet, wrote epigrammatic verses for the occasion. The poems on the Pope and the city during his times are also included in this tome.

His poem on the "Austradis libri duo" is an epic poem on the battle of Lepanto and it is the first printed work of the kind to commemorate the naval victory. It is pleasing to read the critical judgment of Ocete on the poetical merit of this obscure writer. "The arduous task has given ample proof of the author's facility to express himself, not a defective verse nor an incorrect description, when the inspiration does not shine the interest lags, yet the form is impeccable. Without doubt, from among his works this is worthy of modern re-printing. Perhaps this may be premature but when our humane culture is more elevated, a discreet selection

from among his poems, if not all, will be read with pleasure and delight. Not a word more nor an idea less, the verses are exact and precise, like fine steel with all the strength yet with all ductibility and often with inspiration without artifices to give exact tone, measure and softness, but awfully real, the idea of death. The whole book can be summed up as the work of a historian who was also a poet."

His second volume of Latin verses was written to lament in panegyrics the re-burial services on the occasion of the transmittal of the royal bodies to the Pantheon erected by Philip II and known as the Monastery of the Escorial. In this work our author included the epitaphs composed for the tablets and other objects used to convey the remains in pomp from Granada. This work was printed during the year 1576.

In his third and last volume, he devoted his pen exclusively to sing the praises of the ducal house of Sesa Don Gonzalo Fernandez de Cordoba. It was his personal tribute to the house that gave him all he received. He wished to let the world know his benefactors. The imprint bears the year 1585 and the only known copy is at Madrid.

There is pleasant satisfaction to know that in the pages of Spanish literature the name of Juan Latino will be further enhanced and remembered through the excellent work of Antonio Marin Ocete, quite unlike Sir William Maxwell-Stirling who in his life of Don Juan de Austria and George Ticknor, who in his "History of Spanish Literature" (Vol. III, p. 492, N. Y. 1869) have delegated the volumes of the Latin scholar to a foot-note in their respective monumental works.

AND ONE SHALL LIVE IN TWO

By JONATHAN H. BROOKS

Though he hung dumb upon her wall
And was so very still and small—
A miniature, a counterpart,
Yet did she press him to her heart
On countless, little loving trips,
And six times pressed him to her lips!
As surely as she kissed him six,
As sure as sand and water mix,
Sure as canaries sweetly sing,
And lilies come when comes the spring,
The two have hopes for days of bliss
When four warm lips shall meet in kiss;
Four eyes shall blend to see as one,
Four hands shall do what two have done,
Two sorrow-drops will be one tear—
And one shall live in two each year.

Sebastian Gomez was known as the "Mulatto de Murillo." During his earlier life, he was a slave purchased to grind the pigments for the colors used by the great master. His talent was discovered by Murillo and he was freed to become a pupil. For nearly a hundred years certain of the paintings of this Negro of Spain were mistaken for those of Murillo.

"JESUS TIED TO A COLUMN"   *By Sebastian Gomez*

This picture came from the Convent of the Cupuchinos. Brother Fray Angel de Leon claims it is this painter's work in his first historical book where most notable events in the convent of San Francisco of Sevilla are noted.

179   Catedral de Sevilla   La Virgen del Mulato   Garzón

"THE SACRED FAMILY"

By Sebastian Gomez

In the Treasury Room of the Basilica of Sevilla.

"IMMACULATE CONCEPTION"

By Sebastian Gomez

In the possession of an antiquarian in the city of Sevilla.

SEB. GOMEZ (le mulâtre de Murillo). 1114. La Conception de la Vierge (au Musée de Séville)

"THE IMMACULATE CONCEPTION"   *By Sebastian Gomez*

In the Museo Provincial de Sevilla, Spain.

TEMPLE DOOR

ZOUENOULA MASK, 14TH CENTURY

From the Barnes
Foundation Collection
of African Art

Courtesy of Dr. Albert C. Barnes

An

ELEGY,

To Miss. Mary Moorhead,

On the DEATH of her Father,

The Rev. Mr. JOHN MOORHEAD·

INVOLV'D in Clouds of Wo, *Maria* mourns,
  And various Anguish wracks her Soul by turns;
See thy lov'd Parent languishing in Death,
His Exit watch, and catch his flying Breath;
"Stay happy Shade," distress'd *Maria* cries;   5
"Stay happy Shade," the hapless Church replies;
"Suspend a while, suspend thy rapid flight,
"Still with thy Friendship, chear our sullen Night,
"The sullen Night of Error, Sin, and Pain;
"See Earth astonish'd at the Loss, complain;"   10
Thine, and the Church's Sorrows I deplore;
Moorhead is dead, and Friendship is no more;
From Earth she flies, nor mingles with our Wo,
Since cold the Breast, where once she deign'd to glow;
Here shone the heavenly Virtue, there confin'd,   15
Celestial Love, reign'd joyous in his Breast;
Till Death grown jealous for his drear Domain,
Sent his dread Offspring, unrelenting Pain,
With hasty Wing, the Son of Terror flies,
Lest *Moorhead* find the Portal of the Skies;   20
Without a Passage through the Shades below,
Like great *Elijah*, Death's triumphant Foe;
Death follows soon, nor leaves the Prophet long,
His Eyes are seal'd, and every Nerve unstrung;
Forever silent is the thrilling Clay,   25
While the rapt Soul, explores the Realms of Day.
Oft has he strove to raise the Soul from Earth,
Oft has he travail'd in the heavenly Birth;
Till Jesus took possession of the Soul,
Till the new Creature liv'd throughout the whole.   30
  When fierce conviction seiz'd the Sinner's Mind,
The Law-loud thundering he to Death consign'd;
Jehovah's Wrath revolving, he surveys,
The Fancy's terror, and the Soul's amaze.
Say, what is Death? The Gloom of endless Night,   35
Which from the Sinner, bars the Gates of Light;
Say, what is Hell? In Horrors passing strange,
His Vengeance views, who feels his final Change;
The winged Hours, the final Judgment brings,
Decides his Fate, and that of Gods and Kings;   40
Tremendous Doom! And dreadful to be told,

To dwell in Tophet 'stead of shrines of Gold.
"Gods! Ye shall die like Men," the Herald cries,
"And fill'd no more the Children of the Skies."
  Trembling he sees the horrid Gulf appear,   45
Creation quakes, and no Deliverer near;
With Heart relenting to his Feelings kind,
See *Moorhead* hasten to relieve his Mind,
See him the Gospel's healing Balm impart,
To sooth the Anguish of his tortur'd Heart;
He points the trembling Mountain, and the Tree,   50
Which bent beneath th' incarnate Deity,
How God descended, wonderous to relate,
To bear our Crimes, a dread enormous Weight;
Seraphic Strains too feeble to repeat,
Half the dread Punishment the GOD-HEAD meet;   55
Suspended there, (till Heaven was reconcil'd,)
Like *Mos'es* Serpent in the Desert wild.
The Mind appeas'd what new Devotion glows,
With Joy unknown, the raptur'd Soul o'erflows;
While on his God-like Savior's Glory bent,   60
His Life proves witness of his Heart's intent.
Lament ye indigent the Friendly Mind,
Which oft relieved, to your Miss'ry kind.
  With humble Gratitude he render'd Praise,
To Him whose Spirit had inspir'd his Lays;   65
To Him whose Goodness gave his Words to flow,
Divine Instruction, and the Balm of Wo;
To you his Offspring, and his Church, be given,
A triple Portion of his Thirst for Heaven;
Such was the Prophet, we the Stroke deplore,   70
Which lets us hear his warning Voice no more.
But cease complaining, hush each murm'ring Tongue,
Pursue the Example which inspires my Song.
Let his Example in your Conduct shine;
Own the afflicting Providence, divine;   75
So shall 'bright Periods grace your joyful Days,
And heavenly Anthems swell your Songs of Praise.

Boston, Decem.
15 1773.

Phillis Wheatley.

Printed from the Original Manuscript, and Sold by WILLIAM M'ALPINE, at his Shop in *Marlborough-Street*, 1773.

A little known poem by Phillis Wheatley, not included in her collected poems.

A pen drawing from a rare print of Phillis Wheatley.

By W. E. Braxton

TO A GENTLEMAN, ON HIS VOYAGE TO GREAT BRITAIN FOR THE RECOVERY OF HIS HEALTH

By PHILLIS WHEATLEY

While others chant of gay Elysian scenes,
Of balmy zephyrs, and of flowery plains,
My song, more happy, speaks a golden name,
Feels higher motives and a nobler flame
For thee, O, R——, the muse attunes her strings,
And mounts sublime above inferior things.
I sing not now of green embowering woods—
I sing not now the daughters of the floods—
I sing not of the storms o'er ocean driven,
And how they howled along the waste of heaven:
But I to R—— would paint the British shore,
And vast Atlantic, not untried before.
Thy life impaired commands thee to arise,
Leave these bleak regions and inclement skies,
Where chilling winds return the Winter past,
And nature shudders at the furious blast.

O, then, stupendous, earth-enclosing main,
Exert thy wonders to the world again!
If e'er thy power prolonged the fleeting breath,
Turned back the shafts, and mocked the gates of death;
If e'er thine air dispensed a healing power,
Or snatched the victim from the fatal hour,—
His equal care demands thy equal care,
And equal wonders may this patient share
But unavailing—frantic—is the dream
To hope thine aid without the aid of Him
Who gave thee birth, and taught thee where to flow,
And in thy waves his various blessings show.

May R—— return to view his native shore
Replete with vigor not his own before:
Then shall we see with pleasure and surprise,
And own thy work, great Ruler of the skies!

(The fervent wish of the gentle Phillis was not granted. The subject of her invocation died in Bristol, England, soon after his arrival, about the year 1778. Mr. Ricketson has helped us to determine the date of the poem. The above poem was located in Daniel Ricketson's "History of New Bedford," New Bedford, 1858, 8vo, 412 pages, at page 253).

IGNATIUS SANCHO
A mezzo-tint from a painting by Gainsborough

FRANCIS BARBER
From a painting by Sir Joshua Reynolds

A drawing by Charles Cullen

The Runaway Slave at Piligrim's Point

By ELIZABETH BARRETT BROWNING

I.

I stand on the mark, beside the shore,
    Of the first white pilgrim's bended knee;
Where exile changed to ancestor,
    And God was thanked for liberty.
I have run through the night—my skin is as dark—
    I bend my knee down on this mark—
I look on the sky and the sea.

II.

O, pilgrim-souls, I speak to you:
    I see you come out proud and slow
From the land of the spirits, pale as dew,
    And round me and round me ye go.
O, pilgrims, I have gasped and run
    All night long from the whips of one
Who in your names works sin and woe!

III.

And thus I thought that I would come
    And kneel here where ye knelt before,
And feel your souls around me hum
    In undertone to the ocean's roar;
And lift my black face, my black hand,
    Here in your names, to curse this land
Ye blessed in Freedom's heretofore.

IV.

I am black, I am black,
    And yet God made me, they say:
But if He did so—smiling back
    He must have cast his work away
Under the feet of His white creatures
    With a look of scorn, that the dusky features
Might be trodden again to clay.

V.

And yet He has made dark things
    To be glad and merry as light;
There's a little dark bird sits and sings;
    There's a dark stream ripples out of sight;
And the dark frogs chant in the safe morass,
    And the sweetest stars are made to pass
O'er the face of the darkest night.

VI.

But we who are dark, we are dark!
  O God, we have no stars!
About our souls, in care and cark,
  Our blackness shuts like prison-bars!
And crouch our souls so far behind,
  That never a comfort can they find,
By reaching through their prison bars.

VII.

Howbeit God's sunshine and His frost
  They make us hot, they make us cold,
As if we were not black and lost;
  And the beasts and birds in wood and wold,
Do fear us and take us for very men;—
  Could the whipporwill or the cat of the glen
Look into my eyes and be bold?

VIII.

I am black, I am black,
  And once I laughed in girlish glee;
For one of my color stood in the track
  Where the drivers' drove, and looked at me;
And tender and full was the look he gave!
  A Slave looked so at another Slave,—
I look at the sky and the sea.

IX.

And from that hour our spirits grew
  As free as if unsold, unbought;
We were strong enough, since we were two,
  To conquer the world, we thought.
The drivers drove us day by day:
  We did not mind; we went one way,
And no better a liberty sought.

X.

In the open ground between the canes,
  He said "I love you" as he passed
When the shingle-roof rang sharp with the rains,
  I heard how he vowed it fast,
While other trembled, he sat in the hut
  And carved me a bowl of the cocoa-nut
Through the roar of the hurricanes.

XI.

I sang his name instead of a song;
  Over and over I sang his name.
Backward and forward I sung it along,
  With my sweetest notes, it was still the same!
But I sang it low, that the slave-girls near
  Might never guess, from what they could hear,
That all the song was a name.

XII.

I look on the sky and the sea!
  We were two to love, and two to pray,—
Yes, two, O God, who cried on Thee,
  Though nothing didst thou say,
Coldly thou sat'st behind the sun,
  And now I cry, who am but one,—
Thou wilt not speak to-day!

XIII.

We were black, we were black,
  We had no claim to love and bliss—
What marvel, ours was cast to wrack?
  They wrung my cold hands out of his—
They dragged him—why, I crawled to touch
  His blood's mark in the dust—not much,
Ye pilgrim—souls,—though plain as THIS!

XIV

Wrong, followed by a greater wrong!
  Grief seemed too good for such as I;
So the white men brought the shame ere long
  To stifle the sob in my throat thereby.
They would not leave me for my dull
Wet eyes!—it was too merciful
To let me weep pure tears, and die.

XV.

I am black, I am black!
  I wore a child upon my breast,—
An amulet that hung too slack,
  And, in my unrest, could not rest!
Thus we went moaning, child and mother,
  One to another, one to another,
Until all ended for the best.

XVI.

For hark! I will tell you low—low—
  I am black, you see;
And the babe, that lay on my bosom so,
  Was far too white—too white for me,
As white as the ladies who scorned to pray
  Beside me at the church but yesterday,
Though my tears had washed a place for my knee.

XVII.

And my own child—I could not bear
    To look in his face, it was so white;
So I covered him up with a kerchief rare,
    I covered his face in, close and tight!
And he moaned and struggled as well as might be,
    For the white child wanted his liberty,—
Ha, ha! he wanted his master's right.

XVIII

He moaned and beat with his head and feet—
    His little feet that never grew!
He struck them out as it was meet
    Against my heart to break it through.
I might have sung like a mother mild,
    But I dared not sing to the white faced child
The only song I knew.

XIX.

And yet I pulled the kerchief close;
    He could not see the sun, I swear,
More then, alive, than now he does
    From between the roots of the mangles-where?
I know where!—close! a child and mother
    Do wrong to look at one another
When one is black and one is fair.

XX.

Even in that single glance I had
    Of my child's face,—I tell you all,—
I saw a look that made me mad,—
    The master's look, that used to fall
On my soul like his lash,—or worse,—
    Therefore, to save it from my curse,
I twisted it round in my shawl.

XXI.

And he moaned and trembled from foot to head,—
    He shivered from head to foot,—
Till after a time, he lay, instead,
    Too suddenly still and mute;
And I felt, beside, a creeping cold,—
    I dared to lift up just a fold,
As in lifting a leaf of the mango fruit.

XXII.

But my fruit! ha, ha!—there had been
  (I laugh to think on 't at this hour!)
Your fine white angels,—who have been
  God secret nearest to His power,—
And gathered my fruit to make them wine,
  And sucked the soul of that child of mine,
As the humming-bird sucks the soul of the flower.

XXIII.

Ha, ha! for the trick of the angels white!
  They freed the white child's spirit so;
I said not a word but day and night
  I carried the body to and fro;
And it lay on my heart like a stone—as chill;
  The sun may shine out as much as he will,—
I am cold, though it happened a month ago.

XXIV.

From the white man's house and the black man's hut,
  I carried the little body on;
The forest's arms did around us shut,
  And silence through the trees did run!
They asked no questions as I went,—
  They stood too high for astonishment,—
They could see God rise on his throne.

XXV.

My little body kerchief fast,
  I bore it on through the forest—on—
And when I felt it was tired at last,
  I scooped a hole beneath the moon.
Through the forest-tops the angels far,
  With a white fine finger in every star
Did point and mock at what was done.

XXVI.

Yet when it all was done aright,
  Earth twixt me and my baby strewed,—
All changed to black earth,—nothing white—
  A dark child in the dark.—ensued
Some comfort, and my heart grew young;
  I sat down smiling there, and sung
The song I told you of for good.

XXVII.

And there we two were reconciled,
   The white child and black mother, thus;
For, as I sang it,—soft and wild,
   The same song, more melodious,
Rose from the grave whereon I sat!
   It was the dead child singing that,
To join the souls of both of us.

XXVIII.

I look on the sea and the sky!
   Where the Pilgrims' ships first anchored lay,
The great sun rideth gloriously!
   But the Pilgrims' ghosts have slid away
Through the first faint streaks of the morn!
   My face is black, but it glares with a scorn
Which they dare not meet by day.

XXIX.

Ah! in their stead their hunter—sons!
   Ah, ah! they are on me! they form in a ring!
Keep off—I brave you all at once,—
   I throw off your eyes like a noisome thing!
You have killed the black eagle at nest, I think;
   Did you ever stand still in your triumph, and shrink
From the stroke of her wounded wing?

XXX.

(Man, drop that stone you dared to lift!)
   I wish you, who stand there, seven abreast,
Each for his own wife's grace and gift,
   Little corpse as safely at rest,
Hid in the mangles! Yes, but she
   May keep like babies on her knee,
And sing the song she liketh best.

XXXI.

I am not mad,—I am black!
   I see you staring in my face,—
I know you staring, shrinking back,—
   Ye are born of the Washington race!
And this land is the Free America,—
   And this mark on my wrist,—(I prove what I say)
Ropes tied me up here to the flogging place.

XXXII.

You think I shrieked there? not a sound!
   I hung as a gourd hangs in the sun;
I only cursed them all around
   As softly as I might have done
My own child after. From these sands
   Up to the mountains, lift your hands
O slaves, and end what I begun.

XXXIII.

Whips, curses! these must answer those!
For in this Union, ye have set
Two kinds of men in adverse rows,
Each loathing each! and all forget
The seven wounds in Christ's body fair;
While he sees gaping everywhere
Our countless wounds that pay no debt.

XXXIV.

Our wounds are different—your white men
Are, after all not gods indeed,
Nor able to make Christs again
Do good with bleeding.   We who bleed,—
(Stand off!)—we help not in our loss—
We are too heavy for our cross,
And fall and crush you and your seed.

XXXV.

I fall,—I swoon,—I look at the sky!
The clouds are breaking on my brain:
I am floated along, as if I should die
Of Liberty's exquisite pain!
In the name of the white child waiting for me
In the deep black death where our kisses agree.—
White men, I leave you all curse—free,
In my broken heart disdain!

If you know well the beginning
The end will not trouble you much.
—*An African Proverb.*

AN AFRICAN TYPE, *by Baron von Ruckteschell*

THE NATURAL HISTORY OF RACE PREJUDICE

By Ellsworth Faris

N reading the title *Natural History of Race Prejudice,* the reader is asked to regard the occurrence of race prejudice as a natural phenomenon, just as truly as drought, an earthquake, or an epidemic of small pox. Race prejudice is defended by some as desirable, it is deprecated by others as an evil. Men have their opinions and attitudes on this subject but it is not the purpose here to discuss this phase of it. However good or bad it may be, it is assumed that it is possible, and believed to be advantageous to view the matter with detachment and to look to the conditions under which it appears, the cause or causes of its origin, the forms it assumes, the conditions under which it has increased or diminished in intensity, and whether it disappears, and why. This paper is too brief to do more than suggest a treatment of the topic.

The advantage of this mode of procedure is apparent. The history of science seems to show that this method is more fruitful. Knowledge is power; science gives control; to see is to foresee. We can effectively change and control only those events that we can formulate.

Race prejudice is a special form of class prejudice and does not differ in attitude. The only difference is in the object. There may be in a community a prejudice against preachers or soldiers or Republicans. The prejudice against radicals is like the prejudice against Negroes except for its mutability. Religion or politics are voluntary and can be changed, while race is relatively independent of the will.

But class and race prejudice in turn are special forms of a larger category of human experience, namely, prejudice in general. Men speak of prejudice against the Anti-saloon League, too short skirts, the yellow press, cigarettes and small towns.

Prejudice is not easy to define for it is bound up with emotion and contains usually an element of reproach. The dictionary may tell that prejudice is "an opinion or leaning adverse to anything without just grounds or sufficient knowledge," but is is not easy to agree as to what grounds are just or what knowledge is sufficient. And race prejudice, like all prejudices after they endure over a period of time, tends to be supported by arguments. The grounds may not be rational to a critic, but they may seem rational to those who hold the views. It often happens that prejudice is denied by one in whom others confidently assert it.

Nevertheless, for practical purposes, this difficulty is not great. Race prejudice is recognized as a feeling of antipathy or a tendency to withdraw or limit one's contacts toward the members of a certain racial group.

It is important to observe that race prejudice is typically a collective thing. It characterizes a group. It is not private, it is public. Of course, the manifestations are individual, but the point is that race prejudice is of no importance unless the same or similar attitudes and feelings occur in many people at once. Race prejudice then belongs in the field of public opinion or public sentiment.

It is of importance also to point out that race prejudice is attached to the soil. It characterizes a given area and a study of race prejudice can never be adequately made without a map. The significance of this fact arises when we discover that individuals migrating into an area where a certain prejudice exists tend to acquire it although it was absent from their original region. One cannot discuss the subject concretely without a reference to certain areas. The student thinks of the prejudice against Jews in Roumania, against Negroes in Mississippi, against Japanese in California.

In attempting to understand the nature of race prejudice it is important to observe its wide extent. The Japanese have been referred to as the object of prejudice in California, but in Japan the Eta people who number well over a million are the objects of an extreme form of prejudice. An Eta is not supposed to enter the temple for worship. In one recorded instance an Eta insisted on being allowed to worship and said to those who deterred him, "I also am a human being. Why cannot I worship the gods?" The crowd set upon him and he was killed. When his friends complained to the magistrate they were told, "One human being is equal to seven Etas. A man cannot be punished for killing one-seventh of a man. Come back to me when six more of you have been killed." There is prejudice against the Eurasians in China, against the natives, the mulattos and Hindus in South Africa, against the Mexicans in Southern Texas, against the Jews in most parts of the world, and so on around the map.

If now we inquire into the conditions under which the phenomenon appears, we are able to say that there is a quantitative requirement or precondition which seems necessary. If only a few members of an alien group appear they do not usually call out any such attitudes. The first Japanese were received with every evidence of welcome. Thirty years ago a Japanese gentleman married an American girl in Chicago. The wedding was the occasion of widespread interest and one newspaper devoted a whole page of its Sunday edition to pictures and description of the event. The prejudice against them did not arise until they had appeared in far larger numbers. The same remark applies to the Armenian in the West. In Natal in South Africa the British residents invited and imported men from India to work. This was in 1865. They were welcomed and it is agreed that their labor saved the colony from financial disaster. Thirty years later there were more than a hundred thousand, and the prejudice against them was intense. There were Jim Crow laws for the railroads, but they were forbidden on the street cars altogether. Moreover, they were forbidden to walk on the sidewalk and restrictions and social ostracism took an extreme form.

These and similar facts have led to the statement very widely accepted that race prejudice is caused by economic competition. Undoubtedly economic competition does occasion such sentiments, but it appears not to be everywhere the case. There is at present a widespread and very strong feeling in China against two racial groups, the Japanese and the English. Not only has there been an economic boycott, merchants refusing to handle the goods from these nations, but the coolies have refused to work for any Englishman or Japanese, and prominent Chinese have dropped their membership in clubs because of their feelings. This movement is so recent that we can state the facts with confidence. The Japanese hostility was occasioned by the fear of aggression, brought to a dramatic climax by the twenty-one demands, while the hostility to the English grew out of their refusal in the Washington Conference to allow the Chinese to regulate their own tariff provisions. In both cases the feeling was stirred up by the Chinese students who were hardly in any noticeable condition of competition, at least economic. The students petitioned the government, interviewed the merchants, and harangued the coolies. The effect was quite typical but the cause is not apparently the one ordinarily assigned.

Race prejudice has often been asserted by popular writers to be instinctive or hereditary. While this is apparently a complete misstatement it is a very excusable one. The error arises from the normal tendency of unsophisticated people to confuse the customary with the natural. When children grow up in a community they take on the customs and attitudes prevailing, some of which are very old while others are quite recent in origin. But the children can make no distinction between the new and the old and when the attitudes have become second nature they are often thought of as innate or natural. It is said to be "in the blood."

That this is not true can be shown by a comparison in space and time of the same racial stock in respect of this prejudice. The English in South Africa manifest it to an intense degree, as they do also in China against the natives, in sections of Canada against the French, and in parts of India and particularly in Australia. Yet these same English in New Zealand do not have much prejudice against the Maoris who differ from them far more in complexion and civilization than do the Canadian French. Moreover, the prejudice against Jews in England has greatly mitigated. No doubt some exists but it is undeniable that there has been an important modification in the direction of assimilation.

Nor is it possible to assert that wherever two races meet each other there will be prejudice. A list of the areas where it does occur would be too long but we may repeat that in South Africa the English have prejudice against at least four groups, and in Turkey the phenomenon was intense. The Poles and Lithuanians furnish an extreme example, the prejudice between the French and English in Canada has been mentioned, the Negroes in the United States are the objects of it, while in Haiti it is possible to describe a prejudice of the blacks against the whites. The French have their anti-semitism which is perhaps most severe in Roumania. The list if complete would be very long but I mention that in the last few months in Chicago there has developed a racial prejudice between the Polish and the Mexicans, due in part to economic competition and to certain tragic events that accentuated the feeling.

On the other hand race prejudice is relatively absent from Switzerland, the English have lost much of their feeling against the Jews, three races live without race prejudice in Brazil, there is no prejudice against the Indians in Mexico as Indians, two races live without prejudice in New Zealand, several racial groups live together without prejudice in Hawaii, and the phenomenon has never occurred in Greenland in the southern portions of which the common racial type is a mixture of Nordic and Eskimo blood.

If now we inquire more specifically into the conditions of race prejudice it appears that in all cases there is some form of conflict. It may be, and often is, a struggle for money, work, bread, but in many cases it is a struggle for position, status, social prominence, and when it occurs there seems to be a necessity for a definite group consciousness; an esprit de corp arises in one group in contrast to their conception of the other. It is interesting to notice that prejudice is thus double-edged. The prejudice against one group arises with the prejudice for another; prejudice is the other end of one type of loyalty. It is this fact that has made it so easy for those who defend race prejudice and exclusion to present plausible arguments and rationalizations. The extreme form of race prejudice, or perhaps better, one extreme limit of its development re-sults in a condition of stability in which it is some-times difficult to recognize the main features of prejudice. I refer to the accommodation or ac-ceptance of the situation on both sides, in which case the inferior group ceases to struggle against the controlling one. This characterizes much of the relation between the southern masters and their slaves before the war. It is seen in its extreme form in the caste system of India. Now it would be a profitless argument to insist that caste is not prejudice, but for the fact that the acceptance does alter the whole psychology. At the present time when caste in India is beginning to disintegrate prejudice is more easy to find.

Now the caste lines are, or were, extremely rigid. The members of a caste had the same oc-cupation and what we call the social ladder which is used by the social climbers did not and could not exist. A poor man's children could never expect to rise in the world by getting into another group. Moreover, a person could not marry save in his own caste. He could not eat with another not in his own caste, his meals must not be cooked except by one of his own caste, neither could the cooked food be handled by anyone of another group. The interesting thing to the psychologist here is in the form which the defense of such a situation normally takes. Anyone familiar with the literature of edu-cated Indians on this subject will recall how often the condition has been defended as being desirable because of the benefits to civilization and humanity which flow from loyalty to one's own group. Ex-actly the same arguments occur in the writings of Americans in general and southerners in particu-lar on the question of race mixture in the South. The current activity of the Ku Klux Klan abounds in highly idealistic phrases of loyalty and devotion to the precious heritage of the superior group. Race prejudice takes the form of altruistic devotion. The hostility masquerades as love and the wolf of hatred wears the sheep's clothing of affection and solicitude for the beloved group.

This leads us to the question of the motives which govern race prejudice, and the social psy-chologists have discovered an important principle which applies. It is now known that in the case of an ancient custom the motives are certain to vary. This is partly due to the fact that the custom is more difficult to change than its motive. Children carry on the custom without any motive, and if the old motive must be given up a new one spontan-eously arises and men try to phrase their motives so that others will not condemn them. It is hard to imagine the published defense of race exclusion assigned to the motive of hatred or of fear. It is not conscious hypocracy; it is the normal thing in human nature to attempt to make our actions ap-pear as defensible as possible.

There are thus survivals in the plays and games of children, in the customs of weddings, funerals,

and baptisms which go back to rather humble origins but which continue from approved modern motives. Likewise with race prejudice. Sometimes the despised race is represented as inferior but a recent writer in California defended the severity toward the Japanese and concluded with the state-ment, "If the Japanese are superior people so much the worse." One can read rationalizations which take the form of a pseudo-scientific assertion, that while both races may be good, the mixture is bad. There is nothing in this except the ingenuity of an anthor who rather pathetically grasps at a poor reason when he has had to abandon the others.

Race prejudice thus can be shown to be founded not on reason but on sentiments lying deeper and to be relatively impervious to rational arguments. Defenders of the Negro can martial many interest-ing and important facts. In 1870 the Negro in the United States owned 12,000 homes, 20,000 farms, and property to the value of $20,000,000. At the present time they own 700,000 homes, 1,000,000 farms, and are worth $1,800,000,000. They own 22,000,000 acres of land, which is equal to the area of New Hampshire, Vermont, Massachusetts, Rhode Island, and Connecticut. These facts are very interesting and very important, but when they are quoted to a person who is defending race preju-dice in America their effect is sometimes absolutely nothing.

In the concrete social phenomena, particularly those of a collective nature, we may distinguish two parts or elements. One of these is relatively changeable and arises from the need men feel to be logical and the desire they have to appear rea-sonable to their fellows. The other element is rela-tively invariable and is based upon, or the expres-sion of the interests and the emotions which lie deep in the personality. These are the social atti-tudes, and race prejudice is one of them. It is not the result of calm reasoning but arises from an emo-tional condition in a specific social setting. This atti-tude is defended by arguments but is not necessarily altered by counter arguments.
If the reasons assigned for the prejudice are shown to be bad the usual effect will be the abandonment of the reasons and the assertion of new reasons for the same old attitude. Race prejudice, as will be later shown, can be lost and does on occasion disap-pear, but it is perhaps futile to expect the attitude to yield to mere arguments, though of course there is no reason why men who who wish to argue may not do so.

We may attempt to summarize the views here expressed under the following heads:

1. Race prejudice is very widespread. It is al-most universal. Indeed, sociologists would agree that it might appear anywhere on the planet and has actually been manifested by every racial group. Those who are the victims of exclusion in some areas are themselves exclusive in other places. The Chinese may be discriminated against in America,

but the Chinese in China have exhibited the same antagonism against other racial groups. The Japanese are discriminated against but at times they themselves are discriminating, and so with the peoples of India, whether Hindus or Mohammedans, not to mention the various color lines which exist among American Negroes. We shall therefore be most accurate in our formulation of race prejudice if we regard it as a natural phenomenon and normal in the sense in which Durkheim speaks of crime as normal or poverty or suicide, by which he means that under given conditions the statistical facts force the prediction that the phenomenon will continue to occur.

2. Race prejudice is not one culture pattern but many. It takes many forms and exhibits many degrees. There is always involved a collective attitude of exclusiveness, the object of prejudice being kept at a greater distance than the members of one's own race. But this social distance varies and a rough measure or scale could be made, and has indeep been attempted. The members of the out-group are in some places completely excluded from every form of contact as for example in India where the very shadow of an untouchable is a contamination, or again, the out-group may mingle freely in public thoroughfares but may not sit as neighbors in a public assembly. Sometimes the line is drawn at eating together where it forbids or permits public assemblies of a religious nature, and so on through separate scales to complete "social equality" and the approved courtship and marriage between the young people of the two groups. The exact conditions under which the line is drawn in each case might be historically accounted for, but there is little or no logic in it and it can easily be shown to be absurd. As before remarked, however, one may admit the absurdity and retain the attitude.

3. When race prejudice arises it appears to follow a pattern which has been set locally in the mores if such pattern be present. Thus the extreme form of exclusiveness toward the Indians in South Africa can only be explained by the previously acquired attitudes toward the native Negroes. Feeling against the Indians was no higher in Natal than against the Japanese in California, but the form of exclusion is different, and this pattern was followed in each case. A recent court decision in Mississippi excludes Chinese from the public schools. This is understandable if we recall the pattern existing with reference to the Negroes in the south. It may be called a certain consistency in exclusiveness and follows a certain law of habit.

If prejudice arises where there is no pattern or tradition it may take original forms. Thus the children of the slave women in the south who were not acknowledged by their fathers and who lived with their mothers brought about the classification of mulattoes and full-bloods as members of the same excluded group. In the Portuguese colonies where such children were recognized and publicly ac-

knowledged by the father, the mulatto came to be classed with the white group. In Cape Colony the mulatto received certain concessions, as for example, the right to vote which tended to make them into a third caste quite different from the situation in the two other cases.

4. Race prejudice having arisen it may be intensified or mitigated by social experiences. It is aggravated by any conflict between the groups. If conflict ceases entirely, a condition of equilibrium known as accommodation ensues and the feeling is reduced to a minimum. If, however, the conflict or hostility arises in a form where the in-group and out-group unite against a common antagonist or enemy the result is always to mitigate the prejudice and to act in the direction of its removal.

During the World War there was a period when the Negro soldiers and the Negro man-power were regarded as valuable assets to the nation. Men who had never done so before used the words "we" and "us" to include the Negro and white groups taken together. Had the conflict lasted longer, and had it at the same time threatened to go against us, this common feeling would have been more enduring. What happened is a matter of common knowledge. The unexpected armistice released the tension and in some places a very strong reaction took place. Nevertheless, the period is part of the experience of the nation, and the ultimate result in social evolution will be affected by what happened in 1917-18.

5. Race prejudice is increased both in intensity and in duration when to the difference in heredity is added the factor of religious or other social barrier. Anti-semitism seems almost perennial and part of the explanation may be looked for in the multiplicity of barriers to freedom of social intercourse. Each new wave of immigration supplies a group who differ even in dress. The dietary differences are by no means negligible though these tend to disappear, but the religious separation continues to accentuate and emphasize the objects of exclusion when the original motives and occasions have disappeared. Still it is possible to over-state this point. The definition of the we-group and out-group depends upon the arousal of group consciousness and this may take place in disregard of any single type of separation, whether religious, racial, or any other. The massacre at Amritsar united for the time being men in south India with the inhabitants of the Punjab in an intense feeling of brotherhood in spite of many differences and in spite of ancient historical antipathy. It is a common practice of Hindu students in American universities to wear a turban or some distinctive mark so that they will not be classed as Negroes. Yet it sometimes happens that a series of unpleasant experiences will entirely change this attitude and the Hindu will class himself as a colored man, aligning himself with the American Negro. This phenomenon follows

the normal law of group consciousness which perhaps needs no further illustration.

6. Race prejudice cannot only be mitigated, it can disappear. In many cases it has entirely disappeared and in other situations it is obviously decreasing. The Norman Conquest of England was followed by a period of racial hostility and prejudice, but at the present time there is hardly a vestige of the feeling remaining. There was an unmistakable race prejudice against German immigrants in this country and the successive groups of Germans, Irish and French felt the effects of this same phenomenon. At the present time the race prejudice against these three groups is hardly more than vestigial. The hostility which the Germans and Irish encountered is now turned against Italians, Poles, Mexicans and others, but there seems no discoverable difference between the treatment of these last and the way in which the former groups were originally received.

7. If we inquire more particularly into the stages of integration it seems that there can be distinguished certain generalized aspects. There is first of all the gradual taking over of the customs of the dominant group. This is observed first in the costumes, particularly the costumes of the men who go freely among the natives, and of the children and young people who are sensitive to the criticism of those among whom they move. Costume is more conservative in the case of the older women chiefly because of the domestic isolation. Next follows the matter of language. The first generation learns to talk English if possible, but they are sometimes too busy. The second generation has usually two languages, but the third generation often discards the heritage of their fathers for the custom of the country.

The sociologist sees in the public schools of America the real melting pot. The immigrant children are confronted with the new culture in a way that forces them to adopt it. The methods are sometimes brutal, the ridicule of the natives being the most cruel weapon, and because the children are young and defenseless they capitulate rather promptly and are absorbed into the cultural life of their schoolmates. We can generalize all these processes under the head of common experiences which, as before mentioned, are the sources of group consciousness and group loyalty. The bi-racial committees in the south have often been little more than informal conferences by leading members of both races to talk over a situation to see what can be done. These committees help to create a temporary we-group and add ever so little to the stock of traditions which forms the stream of social evolution.

An important means or method for the mitigation of race prejudice lies in the realm of art. To join with an Irish girl in order to help her persuade her father to let her marry a Jewish boy is not given to many Americans. But in the theatre we may do this for two interesting and amusing hours. Art is an experience, a sort of vicarious experience, and yet however vicarious it may be, it is an emotional experience and always modifies our emotional attitudes. The exhibition of primitive African sculpture may have little effect, but it may have some. The reading of a powerful novel in which the human qualities of another race are made appealing acts like a powerful social cement to bind together the hitherto unconnected fragments of a social body.

Of course art can work both ways. The Negroes objected to the "Birth of the Nation" and the "Clansman." No one who strongly desired the disappearance of race prejudice between whites and Negroes would care to see this drama continue in its popularity. Indeed, it may be thought of as a direct reaction to "Uncle Tom's Cabin."

8. Race prejudice being at the same time a collective and an emotional condition it is modified slowly. It is not an individual phenomenon, though every serious individual modification may be theoretically assumed to have some effect on the whole. The important point is that the subjective emotions are only half, the other half being the external conditions and organized regulations. It is only partly true to say that religious emotions or principles can remove it. This would be to neglect the necessity of a change in the external conditions. There is, therefore, a double problem; the one psychological, the other institutional. Any attempt to study it or to change it without recognizing this is apparently doomed to disappointment. This is the sense in which race prejudice is appropriately called a natural phenomenon. It changes slowly but it does change. A too sudden modification, either of attitude or institution, is not only impermanent in character but tends to be followed by a reaction which temporarily leaves the last state worse than the first.

9. But to call race prejudice a natural phenomenon is not to assume that it should be endured or accepted. If we may call race prejudice natural we must also admit suicide, murder, and automobile accidents into this same class. These disturb us and we try to mitigate them, but perhaps we shall never wholly succeed. Nevertheless, the unwelcome effects are undeniable and should be clearly kept in mind.

Race prejudice is narrowing. It may intensify loyalty to one's own group; it certainly produces blindness when members of the out-group are considered. We regard as human those whom we can sympathize with, whose motives we understand, and whose feelings we recognize to be like our own. The barriers men erect in prejudice make it sometimes difficult, sometimes impossible to regard the member of an excluded group as being wholly human. If we fight the Germans we tend to regard them as Huns, as man-like beasts, as cruel savages. If we exclude Negroes we call them inferior or patronize them as being emotionally gifted but intellectually deficient. Reactionaries of today speak of the south Europeans as coming from unassimilable stocks. Sometimes a man who feels this way writes a book to prove it and calls it science. But let us not be deceived in such a culture trait. There is always an emotional element which is difficult to alter and even hard to make explicit. It is a sentiment of race prejudice and it narrows the individual life and always weakens the society where it exists.

The effect of race prejudice on individuals who hold it is to limit their power of discrimination. It blinds a man to differences where these would otherwise be easily seen. Persons are treated according to a stereotype and not as separate and distinct individualities. This is a sort of mental laziness due to the emotional attitude which, being directed toward a class, is manifested toward the varying members of the class as if it did not vary.

The object of this paper has been to show that the desire to change a prejudice is more likely to succeed if we first understand fully the nature of prejudice. Those who are interested in removing a social attitude are more apt to succeed if they first are successful in understanding why people have the attitude who do have it.

ELLSWORTH FARIS,
University of Chicago.

SYBIL WARNS HER SISTER

By ANNE SPENCER

It is dangerous for a woman to defy the gods;
To taunt them with the tongue's thin tip,
Or strut in the weakness of mere humanity,
Or draw a line daring them to cross;
The gods who own the searing lightning,
The drowning waters, the tormenting fears,
The anger of red sins . . .
Oh, but worse still if you mince along timidly—
Dodge this way or that, or kneel, or pray,
Or be kind, or sweat agony drops,
Or lay your quick body over your feeble young,
If you have beauty or plainness, if celibate,
Or vowed—the gods are Juggernaut,
Passing over each of us . . .
*   Or this you may do:*
Lock your heart, then, quietly,
And, lest they peer within,
Light no lamp when dark comes down
Raise no shade for sun,
Breathless must your breath come thru,
If you'd die and dare deny
The gods their god-like fun!

Original Paul Laurence Dunbar Manuscripts

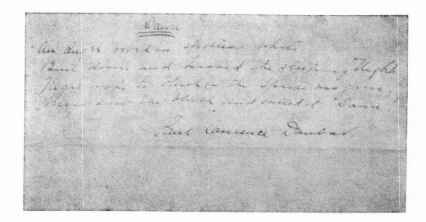

Facsimile

SOME OBSERVATIONS ON THE AMERICAN RACE PROBLEM

By Eugene Kinckle Jones

ECENTLY, I had the pleasure of visiting the cinema version of Harriet Beecher Stowe's *Uncle Tom's Cabin*. So well is the story portrayed that one finds himself living the life of the characters in the slave period of American history. At the end, Eliza and the other members of the Harris family are reunited as the Union soldiers bring freedom to the slaves—Sherman's army passing the plantation of Simon Legree, Eliza's and Uncle Tom's master, at the psychological moment. One sees Old Glory once more flashing triumphantly over the land, and suddenly with the "finis" the theatre lights flash on and I am transported over a period of sixty-two years to find myself once more in America in 1927, a Negro facing many whites—all of whom seem to be saying "What a metamorphosis. How can it be that these same men of sixty years ago now possess so many of those qualities which reflect civilization as we know it!"

The period of the Negro's life as free men in America since the Civil War has been the most progressive period of the Negro's experience anywhere in the world, and it is doubtful that any group of human beings anywhere has made as much advancement under similar circumstances as they have made in so short a time. The last fifteen years of this period have been the most favorable of this sixty-odd year period. The social forces at work during the time just before the entrance of America into the World War and the demand on the Negro during and since the war are recorded as stimuli to this remarkable advancement. But one should not overlook the fact that the Negro -must long have been on the alert for the appearance of his chance and was psychologically prepared to throw himself vigorously into situations from which he would emerge with profit.

In the very beginning of the race's life as free men in the South, it was a group of saintly, self-effacing white missionaries, men and women, of the North who went to the South, established schools for the education of the Negro and breathed the spirit of hope into this benighted group, that has since been leading Negroes out of the wilderness of ignorance and despair.

Many persons today are under the impression that race relations are more strained in America now than at any time during the past fifty years. But my opinion is that this is due to confusion in thinking. The situation should be appraised relatively. It is true that the spirit of tolerance seems

to be strained in certain quarters although no one would question the statement that the attitude of white employers towards their Negro servants and other menial and unskilled employees is much better. The point of strained relations seems to be where Negroes who have gained education and industrial efficiency seek choice positions or better homes in neighborhoods where whites because of their economic status have not before had Negro neighbors. My impression is that these evidences of intolerance are the inevitable results of the so-called inferior group bringing pressure on their obstacles as they themselves acquire higher living and intellectual standards and assume the rights and the attitude of developing men. And in the game of life, just as in athletic contests, the opposition is greatest nearest the goal line. To illustrate this point: Forty-five years ago, in Richmond, Virginia, the public schools maintained by the city for colored children had local white teachers. My father, a native of Virginia, but a graduate of Colgate University, Hamilton, New York, who was then teaching in one of the missionary schools in Richmond, began to advocate the employment of Negro teachers in Negro public schools there. His argument was that if the Negroes were to be separately educated they should have their own teachers. And if the white teachers were to be associated in the schools with the colored children and brought into frequent contact in conferences with the pupils' parents, he saw no reason why this system should not be extended and Negro and white children be educated together in the same schools. He was publicly attacked in the white press and by white clergymen (!) as a Negro advocating miscegenation and amalgamation of the races. Today there are colored teachers in all the public schools there and it is not considered at all out of place for a Negro leader to advocate the use of colored men as principals of the colored schools. Already we see many evidences of the acceptance of the Negro in his new status. Naturally, you would look for this evidence at the top. Negro intellectuals find very little discrimination in the intellectual world. Artists, musicians, literary men of both races mingle freely in the discussion of their major interests. And this is not only true in the North but it is increasingly becoming true in the South. Students in southern white and Negro colleges are having joint group discussions and there is talk of exchange professorships on special sociological problems between certain southern white and colored colleges. Within the

EUGENE KINCKLE JONES
From a drawing by Francis Holbrook

last six months in one of the largest southern cities, an intellectual white man entertained his friends of similar interests in honor of a popular Negro poet. Among the masses, there are evidences also of a growing understanding. Of course, it takes about twenty-five years for the theories expounded in the universities to gain currency among the people at large; but the confusion that has been created by the failure of the theories as to racial inferiority when decided by unbiased scientific measurements has led the outstanding professors in Anthropology, Psychology and Sociology to admit to their students that at least these beliefs have not been substantiated and before many years lay America will admit at least

as much as Lothrop Stoddard does, that any separation of the races must be based *not* upon ideas of inferiority of racial groups but only on the theory of difference, even though this difference has not been and will not be explained.

Slavery left attitudes in whites towards Negroes which the generations since have not entirely eradicated. But gradually Negroes are being recorded as persons capable of becoming self-contained individuals who do not have to depend upon white sufferance and philanthropy for their salvation. This is the most encouraging phase of the whole relationship and it should stimulate philanthropy to **more** determined endeavor in behalf of the Negro group as this is America's ideal, that its citizenry shall be able to adjust themselves to their environment and make of themselves self-possessed, independent, resourceful, productive citizens. No matter what the disposition of the whites as a whole may be to hinder or to help, measurable social improvement in the Negro must be provided for in any permanent solution of the so-called problem.

Some years ago, it was common practice among social and medical scientists to point out the evidence of Negro inferiority in terms of higher death rates and lower physical resistance to diseases. Now with the Negro mortality figures standing about where the white mortality figures were in America twelve or fifteen years ago and gradually getting better, one never hears a reputable physician or statistician presenting such evidence. Similarly, criminologists cited relative prison population figures to indicate the lower moral status of the Negro. When during the prohibition period we see the Negro prison population of North Carolina and South Carolina decreasing and the white prison population greatly increasing to the point where the proportions tend to be equal, critics of the Negro's morals are silenced.

Of course, the atrocity and the violence with which whites in high places have enacted crimes against person, property and the State have never been approached by Negroes of any standing whatsoever in America, and I have personally witnessed many a white audience wilt in a discussion of the subject of Negro crime when a Negro lecturer has facetiously stated: "When will we in America ever make good Americans out of these white people by stopping them from robbing our country's oil lands, and padding the amounts of our public improvements, and doing away with their husbands and wives in order to be safe in clandestine meetings with the third angle of the triangle?"

Personnel managers and large employers of labor no longer speak of Negroes' lack of industrial capacity, efficiency or skill; although they had never employed them. The war time and post-war experience with Negro labor under favorable circumstances has exploded these myths about the Negro's industrial ability. Now it is only a question, employers say, as to whether their white employees will stand for the employment of Negro workers.

While national legislation has provided the atmosphere for the race's development in a democratic form of goverment, the means by which Negroes could acquire most of this unusual progress have been furnished by social, educational and religious agencies—many of them State or municipally supported, but most of them privately maintained. When all of the social agencies in New York touching Negro life—the family welfare group, baby saving movements, community and settlement houses, employment finding and stabilizing agencies, health education interests, churches—combine to wage warfare on the high infant mortality among Negroes in New York City and succeed in

reducing the death rate of Negro babies to a point less than the infant mortality was ten years before and actually less than the white infant mortality in the very district where the Negro rate was more than three times that of the whole city prior to the campaign of course skeptics of the question of the Negro's ability to become acclimated to northern city life are convinced of their error and are silenced. I do not lose sight of those prejudiced individuals who see in this reduction itself a danger to so-called white supremacy and who would rather see Negro babies die than live. But this group is giving away to enlightened intelligence even though in many cases the motive is self-interest as they know that a disease germ knows no color line and a diseased Negro is a menace not only to well Negroes but to healthy white persons also. When we take cognizance of the increase in the Negro population in Detroit from 6,000 in 1916 to 85,000 in 1926 and observe the satisfactory economic and industrial adjustments there with the aid of the Urban League, the Y. M. C. A., the Y. W. C. A., and the churches and other Negro and white social agencies, one can no longer say that competitive industrial life in the northern city is too strenuous for the Negro and that the agricultural south is the only place for him.

Evidences of the effort being put forth to crystallize sentiment in favor of the Negro may be noted in nearly every important social agency, local or national, where the two races come within the scope of the organizations' activities. I think it is pretty generally conceded that regardless of the kindly attitude towards Negroes of a certain simple, harmless type, the Negro as a group needs special aid, as does every handicapped group, to meet the issues of life and to rise in the social scale and thus to merit and receive the approbation of his dominant neighbors.

Practically every community chest organization or local council social agencies in cities where Negroes constitute a goodly proportion of the population has noted the social needs among this element of the citizenry and many of them have inter-racial committees as member agencies, and support definite pieces of social work in behalf of the Negro population. The Boy Scouts of America, the Federal Council of Churches of Christ in America, and the Young Men's Christian Association have national inter-racial committees and the American Social Hygiene Association, the Young Men's Christian Association, the Young Women's Christian Association and the International Big Brother and Big Sister organizations have special work going on in behalf of the Negro population, and in all of these organizations except one, there is Negro representation on their governing boards.

Most criticism by Negroes of activities with the Negro group is based upon uncertainty as to the best method to solve the problem. The Negroes are not satisfied with half a loaf. The whites are not inclined to give a whole loaf. In the shuffle, many cases of injustice may be noted. Many cases of fruitless effort accompanied by excellent intentions may be recorded. But the curve indicating the trend is upward, and a better day is dawning for race relations in America.

The migration of Negroes to the North has been accompanied by a tremendous migration of the southern whites to the North. Northern capital and business interest are being directed in a greater degree annually to the South. The former movement has precipitated an increasing interest in the problems of the Negro on the part of the northern whites and the latter has generated a stronger resolve on the part of southern whites to make an honest effort to help solve the racial difficulties in the interest of the country as a whole as well as in the South. The meeting together of these three points of view—that of the northern white, that of the southern white and that of the Negro—will produce an interesting understanding and will actually result in a better attitude towards the Negro on the part of the whites. America will profit as a consequence and the cause of human understanding and betterment will be promoted.

ARABESQSE
By FRANK HORNE

Down in Georgia
a danglin' nigger
hangin' in a tree
. . . kicks holes in the laughing sunlight—
> *A little red haired*
> *Irish girl . . . grey eyes*
> *and a blue dress—*
> *A little black babe*
> *in a lacy white cap . . .*
> *The soft red lips*
> *of the little red head*
> *kiss*
> *so tenderly*
> *the little black head—*
> *grey eyes smile*
> *into black eyes*
> *and the gay sunlight*
> *laughs joyously*
> *in a burst of gold . . .*
Down in Georgia
a danglin' nigger
hangin' in a tree
. . . kicks holes in the laughing sunlight—

PHANTOM COLOR LINES

By T. Arnold Hill

OW much of the Negro's failure to secure employment is his own fault? Many would answer that most positions are denied because of circumstances chargeable to race. They would tell aptly of instances in which forces beyond the control of the colored applicant or worker kept him out of a job or retarded his promotion. Eligibility would not be questioned since chivalry in war and long citizenship are presumed to establish fitness; and since the Negro's bravery in battle and loyalty to country are acknowledged facts, he is by virtue of such entitled to employment. This irrational conception of values is passing, but it still clings to a class who regards such historical shibboleths as prima facea evidence of acceptability.

Racial prejudice—seldom caste prejudice—is to the casual observer the cause of practically all the dilemmas Negroes encounter in their occupations. A worker, seeing his fellow white workers advancing above him, can assign no cause for it other than disfavor for his race and a corresponding favor for all other races and nationalities.

This is of course a complex question. In it is the recalcitrance of labor unions, the open and subtle antagonism of the snobbish employee, the deliberate revolt of light-headed youth whose bias permits of little reasoning on this or any other subject, the naivete of the employer who honestly believes the Negro incapable of skilled or professional tasks, the dogma of employers who blatantly admit their color prejudices, the traditional hatred of class units who fear the entrance of Negroes into unaccustomed fields, and the public ignorance of the measured steps Negroes have made in recent years. In it, too, is the listlessness of Negro workers, their failure to grasp the subjectiveness of manual labor, the result of which is the absence of a middle group profitably employed, intra-racial antagonism revolting against Negro supervision in plants and the unchecked heresies respecting industrial education against which seldom an effective protest is uttered.

I know Negroes who have worn down their morale in a fruitless effort to secure decent living. I know many who have been discharged when their racial identity became known. Such incidents, and the mockery which makes them incidents, are regrettable. They suggest a topic that might have found place in Stuart Chase's "Tragedy of Waste." But even at this point, where unfairness is plainly revealed, we ask if the Negro should not share a part of the blame for the state of public thought that permits such experiences to continue unabated?

That this has happened so frequently to well-trained Negro youth is of itself reason to ask what is being done to prevent it.

"A bird may be shot upward to the skies by a foreign force; but it rises in the true sense of the word, only when it spreads its own wings and soars by its own living power. So a man may be thrust upward into a conspicuous place by outward accidents, but he rises only in so far as he exerts himself, and expands his best faculties, and ascends by a free effort to a noble region of thought and action." Thus did William Ellery Channing define "elevation" for the working classes. Applying this formula to Negro workers one is moved to overlook failures because the past has not provided opportunity for independent thought and action. Members of this race did not emerge from slavery free moral agents of their own destinies. Freed in the latter half of the nineteenth century they helped America struggle for and secure ascendancy over her European rivals.

But they could not rise when slavery had left them doubtful of their own value, unprepared for industrial labor and illiterate. Negroes were emerging from serfdom when the princely fortunes of the elder captains of wealth were taking form. They had neither personal qualifications of heart or mind and they had no encouragement from others to corner the untouched resources that are the foundation of big estates. The Negro had to be educated. He had to house himself without the aid of masters. He had to work to feed himself and family; there was no time for planning a future.

There is no desire to cavil over the racial shortcomings that may be traced to the effects of slavery. The criticism is not that the race did not make preeminent progress in occupational spheres, but rather that today they give little thought to achieving it.

The proportion of Negroes ten years of age and over gainfully employed, approximately sixty per cent, is larger than that of any other group in the census reports for 1920. The distribution is likewise disproportioned. Of the 4,824,151 Negroes employed, the proportion engaged in the trades, professional service and clerical occupations is far below the average for all classes. The average in domestic and personal service is higher and in transportation the average is not far below. They are numerically strong in agriculture, forming 16.8 per cent of the workers employed in this industry. They are losing ground in domestic and personal service. They have usually been employed when white labor was not available and often discharged when the white shortage subsided. Though they have made undeniable progress in recent years, expanding their diversification until it includes in New York and Chicago practically all important occupations, they are still confined to unskilled and the most onerous tasks, and are often underpaid. The cessation of immigration from abroad, if continued long enough, will undoubtedly be beneficial to them. If the immigration restrictions are modified so as to permit throngs of aliens to rush to our shores, competition between Negroes and immigrants will again be set up just as it was in the sixties and seventies when results disastrous to Negroes ensued. All in all the future is uncertain. It rests upon the Negro's own application to a degree of indispensability that will make replacement unnecessary and expensive.

Some progress is being made in this direction, doubtless the result of exposure to rigid industrial requirements. Critical observations of themselves by groups of workers, called to discuss their problems in industry, are typical of the introspection going on in many parts of the country. The following comments were made in such a conference in Milwaukee:

"An attendant at an oil filling station said his ungovernable temper had caused him to lose several jobs. On his present job he has seen some of the white attendants "balled out" by the superintendent for various reasons but took it calmly. The following day all seemed well. The men did not lose their temper and quit work. He was following their example now and felt if other Negroes did likewise they would not change jobs so much and learn there is really nothing to a lot of this "balling out."

"A moulder having been on one job about two and one-half years said, 'Every day I work side by side with white men, some have been snobbish but are my best friends.' Men who have moulded many years longer than himself have given him a number of fine points which he didn't know. Feels if colored men in various lines take the same interest with other colored men who may be new on the job it will be of much help. Also found since he has become a home owner he gains more respect from the superintendent.

"A sand-blaster said that he has had audience with the foundry superintendent as to why some colored men were not promoted to mechanical jobs. Superintendent felt Negroes couldn't make good on technical work, seemed to be thick headed. Said he noticed white boys were given jobs as apprentices and were better qualified from a technical point of view. He also said the Negro's temper and lack of stability in many instances had caused foremen to refuse them jobs in their department. He stated one colored man had nine fights on a job in one day.

"Mr. J. said he had been a moulder on one job four years. There are a number of jobs, particularly the better paying jobs, which are not given Negroes. Some moulding jobs pay whites more than Negroes on same pattern. He said that most of the preju-

dices which he had experienced came from subforemen because they were prejudiced."

The Negro worker lacks apperception. He is part of an industrial plant but not part of the industrial life of a community. He does not think seriously of his work as he does of his lodge and his church. Unlike the professional man who knows the organizations he should join, the laws and the ethics he must obey, the fee he is to collect, the periodicals he should read, and certain routine he must follow, the manual worker enters upon his duties knowing nothing of and caring less for the besetments he is sure to encounter. He philosphizes on the "Negro problem," but never on the economic side of it except to assign causes for failure. It is not exceptional to find one who can recite verbatim long passages from a ritual of a lodge and who can interpret adequately its purposes and precepts.

Recently I heard presidents of two Negro colleges say that not enough attention is being given to the men and women who toil with their hands. One felt that the whole system of industrial education in the private schools and colleges will have to be reshaped, in order to meet the demands of today. The other believed that the average Negro worker, as distinguished from the professional man, does not know "what its all about." Colored employees are far removed from the problems which concern organized workers. They take little or no pains to learn the laws which govern and protect wage-earners in the various states of the union. They are unfamiliar with the charges of scabbing and the significance of these charges made against them so often by union members. They are unacquainted with the successes of members of their race who have won, by virtue of personal worth, places in the skilled and industrial forces of the country. They still expect advances in positions without corresponding advances in preparation.

The more than sixty national secret and fraternal organizations among Negroes in the United States have an estimated membership of upwards of two million five hundred thousand. Their property holdings are thought to exceed twenty-five million dollars. They have large bank deposits in white institutions, sometimes said to aggregate more than a million dollars in a separate bank. They make extended plans for sickness and death but little provision for economic security. They have great difficulty financing a building of modest dimensions. The added strength to these fraternal organizations and to the race, if they should give attention to business and commerce, would be tremendous. The potentialities for corporal development by virtue of resources, material and human in these fraternal organizations, would long have been seized upon by any group properly conscious of its strength and sufficiently aware of the relationship between economics and the whole problem of the Negro in this country.

There were in 1926, according to the Negro Year Book, 47,000 churches with 5,000,000 communicants and 46,000 Sunday schools with 3,000,000 scholars. Church properties were valued at $98,500,000. They contribute comfortable sums to home and foreign missions, have some splendid denominational publishing houses, make provisions for retired ministers and give large sums to educational and beneficent institutions. The Negro church is the most poignant illustration of organization the race possesses. But their material contributions have been confined almost wholly to the acquiring and building of church properties. There is latent within this group, long accustomed to unified effort, monetary and mental resources that should be released for more substantial racial achievement.

In charging that the Negro lacks apperception I am not forgetting the criticisms of inefficiency which so frequently are lodged against them by those who know only part of the problem. As to how proficient a group of colored workers is when compared with a similar group of workers of another race there is considerable difference of opinion among employers who hire them. What we often mistake for lack of ability or lack of will to do is but an effect, the cause of which has deep psychological foundation. Thus the significance of work in the pattern of life is not appreciated. Inability to remove the obstacles of racial discrimination has dwarfed the faculties the Negro needs for this conception. As a consequence he reasons that a job is but a job and that no matter how industrious he may become, he will remain hopelessly tied to casual occupations.

In the midst of such despondency the National Negro Business League can never thrive to the point its leaders would have it. The trouble is not wholly with the merchants. It is partly within the cerebral reactions of the masses of Negroes to Negro business; for the same disregard for economic relationship and value we have observed in industry and commerce is a vital deterrent to the success of business operated by the race. A Negro Business League must have other purposes than those which are connected with business. If Negro business would succeed it must deal with a state of public mind which has not yet seen the parts of the "problem" in their relationship to the whole. There is room for correlation of effort in this field on the part of the Business League, the lodges, the churches, the schools and the social agencies.

The prominence given today to the cultural achievements by Negroes makes it more necessary than ever that the economic side of Negro life should be strengthened. Most of the researches and practically all books have omitted discussions of this phase of Negro life. We need a more positive material foundation to maintain the host of intellectuals we so proudly boast of today. More than one professional man has moved within the past six months because there was not enough stability and permanence to Negro workers to support them.

That we are denied opportunities for employment is partly due again to our neglect through our failure to popularize the successes attained at work. There is many an employer honestly ignorant of what we have achieved. There are a number who sincerely believe that trouble is fomented whenever white and colored workers are associated together. There are those who still persist that cold weather can not be endured by sons of Ham from the torrid regions of the South. There are perhaps pioneers who have sacrificed along with their intellectual brothers and who have made valuable contributions to race relationship of whom we do not know. Their exploits have not been given publicity and as such they do not provide incentives for others to do likewise nor illustrate the possibilities in a field in which our capacity is so often questoned.

A large share of the Negro's failure to secure employment is his own fault—not so much the fault of the job-seeker, but more the indifference of those whose positions entitle them to lead. We would improve the training which our schools are giving, adding courses that once were thought unnecessary because of the limitations in employment. We would appeal to a fair American sentiment to live up to appropriate ideals of democracy. We would have our white youth increase the understanding it is so rapidly acquiring of Negro life. We would continue to advise organized groups of employees to annex their fellow colored workers. But we would insist upon a more mature understanding and concentration than the Negro has yet given his work problems. In the guidance of this knowledge he must be helped by his leaders who have at their command resources for the infusion of the high spiritual substance against which foreign forces will thrust in vain.

DRAWINGS FOR MULATTOES—Number 1

By Richard Bruce

DRAWING FOR MULATTOES—Number 2

By Richard Bruce

DRAWING FOR MULATTOES—Number 3
By Richard Bruce

DRAWING FOR MULATTOES—Number 4

By Richard Bruce

THE CHANGING STATUS OF
THE MULATTO

By E. B. Reuter

T IS a generally known fact that in the Negro population of the United States the group of bi-racial ancestry has contributed more than its proportionate share of prominent individuals. But the degree to which this is true is perhaps not realized outside the group of professional students. The names that come first to mind when the question of racial talent and leadership is mentioned — Douglass, Washington, Tanner, Williams, Aldridge, Chestnutt, DuBois, Johnson, et al— are not the names of black men. Paul Laurence Dunbar, Kelly Miller, Roland Hayes and Robert R. Moton are perhaps the only men of relatively uncontaminated Negro blood who have achieved a national reputation. In all fields of endeavor, in proportion to their number in the general Negro population, the mulattoes have furnished a disproportionate percentage of the conspicuously successful individuals.

All through the period of Negro residence in America, the outstanding individuals of the race, in the great majority of cases, have been men of mixed blood. In the various slave insurrections they had a prominent part. Within the slave regime they were the ones least accommodated to the status of servitude, the ones who most often came into conflict with the institution, the ones who most frequently led others in revolt against the status. In the realm of intellectual and semi-intellectual pursuits their part was conspicuous. Benjamin Banneker, perhaps the most capable of the early American Negroes, was a free man because of his descent from a white woman. James Durham, the Negro physician, was a mulatto. George Lisle, Andrew Bryan, Samuel Haynes, and other early preachers of note were men of mixed ancestry. In the later days of the slave institution the percentage of mixed bloods among the leaders was high. With one or possibly two exceptions the dozen or twenty colored men most prominent in the anti-slavery agitation were mulattoes. In the post Civil War decades the mixed bloods were conspicuous in the political and other activities opened to the members of the race. In the ministry, in the early literary and artistic strivings, and in the struggle against oppression the mulattoes played a leading role.

The significance of this distribution of superior men has commonly been misunderstood. It seems on first blush to be somehow indicative of an underlying difference in capacity, to imply a marked superiority rooting in the fact of a white ancestry and relationship. This reading of the facts has been all the more acceptable for the reason that it contributes, in a not too subtle way, to the racial self-feeling of the culturally dominant group. The egocentric bias of popular thought has been reinforced by the biological bias of an unarrived psychology. The mixed ancestry of so many Negro leaders has given support to the biological bias at the same time that it has served as evidence to prove the incapacity of members of the Negro group.

In the situation it is not beyond understanding that Negro writers have not emphasized the fact of mulatto leadership, that they have sometimes minimized it, and that in some cases they have attempted to refute the implied or asserted inferiority of the race by denial of the facts themselves. But such tactics are futile. Not only that: they are ill-advised. The facts will be known and in the present case it is to the advantage of the racial group that they be known. In the cultural superiority of the mulatto lies what is, when comprehensively understood, the most complete refutation of the theory of Negro inferiority.

It is, however, only within the past decade that the facts have been comprehensively understood and a tenable hypothesis has gained currency. And even today, and even among students of social and race psychology, the explanation of social phenomena in biological terms is perhaps the rule rather than the exception.

II

IN explanation of these facts it is usual to resort to the doctrine of racial inequality. Since the white man is superior to the Negro, the mulattoes, who are intermediate between the racial extremes, are superior to the one and inferior to the other. It does not appear to be necessary, however, to resort to this order of explanation in order to account for all the facts before us.

Almost from the beginning of Western culture in America, distinctions were made in the servile class on the basis of blood intermixture. This was in part the result of the doctrine of white racial superiority. But there were other facts making for class separation on this basis.

The first mulattoes were of course the result of primary crosses. They were the sons and daughters of white men or women. In consequence there was often a sentimental factor operating to favor the child. The relations between the parents of the mixed-blood children, at least in some cases, were based on mutual affection. White men were sometimes inordinately fond of their colored babies. This matter of relationship and personal affection was a thing of first-rate importance in those cases where the mulattoes were children of the slave owner or of some member of his family. Being the owner as well as the father or uncle of the mulatto child he was in a position to give it special consideration. The cases where the masters were the slave owners of their own relatives and favored them above other slaves are numerous. Such children were often freed, sometimes they were educated, and generally they were directed into the more stimulating and less deadening sorts of occupation.

Another important factor in the differentiation came in very early. Some of the mulattoes were the children of white mothers and Negro fathers. When the question of the legal status of the Negroes came to be defined in law, a distinction was made on the basis of parentage. It became a rule at law that the status of children should follow that of the mother with the result that some percentage of the mulatto children were free persons. This group perhaps did not include a very considerable proportion of the total mulatto population but it contributed to the increase of the group of free Negroes and to the percentage of mulattoes in the group. The frequent emancipation by slave holders of their mixed-blood relatives also added to the mulatto character of the free Negro population.

Within the slave order itself the mulattoes were commonly favored. The assumption of the greater native ability of the persons of mixed blood led to their being trained for skilled and semi-skilled occupations. They were most frequently selected for positions of responsibility and for positions involving personal and confidential relations. They were everywhere in demand for house servants. They were more generally than the average of the population, city residents. Whatever the reason, and the reasons were different in different cases, the mulattoes were commonly assigned to the more stimulating types of work, were given more education and freedom, and had the advantage of more contact and association with cultured people.

The distinctions thus made in the Negro population afforded the mulattoes on the average more freedom and opportunity and this registered very early in the greater cultural advance of these persons. They furnished most of the individuals of any prominence and achievement. They came to occupy a somewhat special status; they stood somewhat apart from the field hands and common laborers. This class division was of course nowhere complete. There were always black men in the special positions and there were always mulattoes among the field and labor gangs. Some of the leaders were black men. But the distinction was sufficiently marked to be recognized by the Negroes and the mulattoes as well as by the whites. And the explanation, subsequent for the most part to the fact, came to be the same for each of the groups.

III

THE external situation was reflected in the social and psychological attitudes; the sentiments and beliefs came to be in harmony with the external social order. Men developed the type of mind and the set of habits necessary to a tolerable life. The white group, superior in status and culture, developed the psychological characteristics that go with power and responsibility. The Negroes, repressed and backward, accommodated themselves to the inevitable and developed the reciprocal type of mind.

In the situation, the mulatto was in cultural advance as well as in appearance an intermediate type of man. His white relationship, his somewhat superior status, and his greater degree of accomplishment raised him somewhat above the general level of the Negro population. But the same group of facts placed him below as well as outside the white group. The whites treated them as somewhat superior to the Negroes. They thought them superior and expressed the belief in their treatment. At the same time they believed them to be inferior to the whites and treated them as inferiors. The Negroes, reflecting the white attitude in this as they did in most other matters, looked upon the mulattoes as being of a higher caste and as being natively superior men. In much the same way the mulattoes came typically to conceive of themselves. They were a numerically minor group and the conceptions that they came to hold of themselves and of their natural place in the social order was determined in major part by the beliefs and attitudes of the major groups. The Negroes looked up to them, they looked down upon the Negroes; the whites looked down upon them, they looked up to the whites. A body of popular doctrine thus developed out of the cultural situation. The separation and relative status was a fact imposed from without. It favored the mixed bloods at the expense of the unmixed Negroes. The resulting sentiments and beliefs presently came to operate as an independent force making for the perpetuation and increase of the separation that, in the first instance, gave a basis for the body of belief.

As the differentiation advanced, the mulatto sense of superiority increased. The internal bonds, which distinguish a genuine class organization from a group held together by external forces, formed and strengthened. The mulattoes developed a common body of sentiment and belief that fostered their closer association. They held themselves more and more aloof from the backward Negroes and avoided association with them. In some cases very definite and highly exclusive mulatto societies were formed. Color or its absence came more or less to be a badge of the élite. This separation, seldom complete and often potential rather than realized, continued well into the present period.

It was inevitable that the Negro and mulatto individuals of education and refinement should desire association with persons of like culture. They had little in common with the illiterate laboring groups. They lived in a somewhat different universe. Their whole cultural orientation was toward the white rather than toward the Negro group. Ethically they were frequently more white than Negro. In tastes and ideals, interests and ambitions, standards and education, they were drawn to the dominant culture group. Opportunity for tolerable life and individual success was, or at least seemed to be, greater there.

But, regardless of education and refinement, they were excluded from participation in the white society. An assumption of inferiority and uncleanness attached to them and the traditional definitions classed them with the Negroes. They resented the classification. They had little in common with the rank and file of the Negroes with whom association was often offensive and always depressing. In the situation they were typically discontented, unhappy, rebellious persons. There was a long period during which the educated mulatto was a pathetic figure. His wishes could not be satisfied within the existing social order.

In some cases there was a possibility of individual escape. Where the physical marks were not conspicuous, they simply passed as white men. The number who have thus changed their racial classification with a change of residence is often grossly exaggerated, but that the number was considerable there is no doubt. This became increasingly frequent as continued intermixture and European immigration tended to blur the lines of race distinction, as the technique for concealing tell-tale racial marks increased, and as the anonymity of urban life increased. But large or small in amount, it is an evidence of the mulattoes, protest against an anomalous social status. But it was no solution except in individual and exceptional cases.

Others accepted, at least outwardly, the inevitable, identified themselves with the Negro groups, and assumed its leadership. For this they were prepared by the facts of superior education, a longer and more varied experience, a certain prestige, and a sense of superiority and self-confidence which the black group lacked because they lacked experience. The mulatto aristocracy was a generation or so ahead of the bulk of the race. They came to compose the bulk of the growing business and professional classes. This mulatto leadership the Negro group more or less willingly accepted. They could not do otherwise in the absence of education, status, experience, and self-confidence.

IV

NOT all the Negro leaders were mulattoes. They were more numerous and generally more prominent, capable, and influential. But there were also many influential black men. This was particularly true in certain lines of work, as church leadership, where the absence of education was not a serious handicap. Since the church touched the common Negro at so many points, the minister was always a man of local importance. The mulattoes never reached the dominating position in church affairs that they did in the professional and intellectual pursuits.

There was also, at all times, a more or less unanalyzed opposition on the part of the Negroes to the mulatto leadership and representation. There was a vague irritation arising from the mulattoes' assumption of superiority, an inarticulate desire among the masses for a black leadership. Even among his followers and admirers, Washington was often referred to in disappointed tones as a "little yellow man." The prominence in racial affairs of certain men has certainly been due in part to the fact that they were obviously and conspicuously not mixed bloods.

As the general Negro population gained in education and advanced in economic status more of the latent talent of the race had opportunity to get expression. As educational opportunity was extended through the public schools and in some degree equalized the talented children of the masses had some chance to emerge. And the success of every black child contributed to the growing self-confidence of the group. As time goes on the sheer weight of numbers will also be felt. The Negro group is four or five times as large as the mixed-blood group. Assuming the practical equality of native ability in the two groups, the Negroes will produce four or five times as many outstanding men when the opportunities of the groups have been equalized.

With the general economic and cultural advance of the group there is a greatly increased need for educated men. The number of physicians and lawyers and other professional men is far below the group needs. This has provided and will continue to provide an opportunity for the ambitious black boy. In every group leadership comes chiefly from the favored classes. It is only in exceptional times, when the need for superior men exceeds the capacity of the aristocracy to produce them, that talented individuals born in the lower orders are able to emerge. In the present and recent past the mulatto class, from which Negro leadership has traditionally come, is not able to supply the number of leaders needed.

The growing solidarity of the race operates to the same end. Regardless of the evaluative attitude that one takes toward the growth of racial self consciousness, it makes a place for an additional number of popular leaders and provides a background of racial self-respect that assures their appearance. And it makes certain that, other things approximately equal, the individuals not conspicuously unlike the masses in physical appearance will have some initial advantage. Because of or in spite of conspicuously Negroid features, superior individuals will have an increased opportunity to rise.

There is at the present time another force of some importance operating to equalize the opportunities of the Negroes and mulattoes. This is the growing disposition to judge the work of Negroes by the same standards as are elsewhere applied.

There have always been many sentimental and non-critical individuals ready to applaud any artistic effort of a Negro no matter how crude. They have done the cause of Negro advancement much harm as have also the white faddists who are always ready to patronize any Negro who gains momentary notoriety.

But there is an increasing group of more or less influential men who have become skeptical of the doctrine of race superiority and of the popular idea that native talent and ability are localized in certain favored economic and social classes. They are disposed to offer encouragement to unknown Negroes as well as to others of literary and artistic promise. Back of this interest, in some cases, is a belief that because of a peculiar racial temperament, Negroes are able to make a unique contribution to American culture. Others anticipate a distinctive culture contribution because the body of social experience of the Negroes is distinctive and peculiar. Still others look upon talent as a matter of individual variation as likely to appear in one place as another. They are concerned to discover and recognize it regardless of race or social class.

This relatively new interest has the effect of stimulating the Negroes' artistic efforts. They are assured of an appreciative and sympathetic audience for any meritorious work. So far as the productions of individuals are evaluated in objective terms, the Negro and the mulatto stand on exactly the same level, and a difference in the amount of talent emerging from the two groups is a measure either of the artificial differences in education, tradition, and economic status still existing, or of a difference in the number of favorably varient men that the two groups produce.

V

ALL such changes operate to a reduction in the advantage that the mixed bloods have traditionally enjoyed. In certain fields the Negro gets recognition and award proportional to accomplishment.

The present tendency of liberal-minded white people to discount the accidents of birth and economic status and to recognize individuals on the basis of personality and inherent worth removes in part one of the greatest handicaps of the Negro. He is not prejudged. There is no longer an assumption that his capacity varies inversely as his skin color. This new attitude of the liberal group stimulates and reinforces the growing self-respect of the black man. He can be a Negro, he can even be proud of the fact, without of necessity being a fool. The fact of Negro blood does not of necessity carry with it the presumption of incapacity. It may put certain more or less inconvenient obstacles in the way of the individual's advance. But the obstacles are external: they are in

the social organization rather than in the psychology of the individual. External handicaps may be overcome. But there was no advance possible so long as the individual Negro accepted the general belief in the innate incapacity of the black man.

This change in the Negro's attitude toward himself removes one important advantage historically enjoyed by the mixed bloods. There is no longer the same assumption of mulatto superiority. The Negroes are rapidly developing a confidence in their own ability to manage their own affairs and to produce their own talented men.

As a result of the changing situation there is an increasing number of relatively black Negroes among the successful and prominent men.

In the future we may anticipate a farther decline in the preponderance of mixed bloods in the economic, political, and intellectual leadership. With the equalization of opportunity the Negroes, assuming equality in the distribution of native ability, will produce an increasing proportion of the prominent men.

But the advantage that the mixed bloods have enjoyed, and in a measure still enjoy, will continue.

It is not reasonable to anticipate that the difference will disappear in one generation. The mixed bloods have a long start and their tradition of superiority will persist. The doctrine of racial inequality is perhaps more firmly fixed in popular thought at the present time than it has ever been. It is not likely to be dislodged in any reasonable period of time. So long as it persists the mulattoes will enjoy an intangible but very real advantage that will get expression in their relative degree of success. It will require a long period for the Negroes to overcome the handicap of the later start and the popular assumption of lower capacity.

At the present time the mixed bloods occupy a somewhat superior status. As a result superior individuals are attracted to the group and tend to reinforce and perpetuate the status. Individuals born and reared in the group have an initial advantage in the struggle for success.

Again, the mixed bloods have the advantage of better education and more secure economic position. This gives a prestige at the same time that it assures better education, better homes, and greater economic security for the succeeding generations. This operates and will continue to operate to the advantage of the mulatto group.

But these differences are, on the whole, on the decline. With the spread of education, the growth of race consciousness, and the attitude of the liberal white people, the Negroes of talent will more and more come to the front. Ultimately, if the races are in reality equal in capacity, the Negroes will produce as many prominent men, in proportion to their number, as any other element in the population. The fact that the mulattoes have in the past produced more prominent men should be understood as a simple and obvious consequence of the historic circumstances that have favored them.

SUFFRAGE

By WILLIAM PICKENS

HERE ultimate power resides in voters, the importance of the right to vote cannot be overestimated. In its last analysis political suffrage means brute force, as one discovers in a state of war, or in the hands of a policeman. The importance of the right to vote is minimized by men only when they seek to deprive others of the right: it is never minimized when they seek or defend it for themselves.

The right of the individual to cast a vote equal to the vote of any other individual subject to the power of the same government—this right has climbed wearily in American history. And the suffrage articles of many of our state constitutions indicate that there is yet a long climb ahead. The right to vote has been supported by two different theories: the theory of "natural rights" and the theory of the good of the state. The natural rights theory looks backward; the good-of-the-state theory looks forward. The good of the state, which I interpret to mean the highest average good of everybody in the state, will prove to be the victorious idea. "Natural rights" is a beautiful sentiment, but one right is not more natural than any other in the state, where all right depends upon might. The good of the state is a progressive idea, based in reason and experience, and that may be advanced even by experimentation. Today the individual or group which seeks to acquire or defend its right to vote, must justify the claim in the good of the whole people, and not in poetic theories about primitive individualism and original compacts.

On the other hand, the idea of the good of the state is limited in its usefulness by the prevailing idea as to who or what constitutes the state. If the emperor be the state, the good of the state is a very small good. If the imperial family and the nobility be the state, the majority of inhabitants are left out; for the whole population cannot join the nobility, unless like the Romans they make all the rest of the world their subjects and slaves. And if, as in Mississippi, the state means only the white inhabitants, the pursuit of the good of the state will, at its best, aim to include less than fifty per cent of the people. Certain limited classes are excluded more or less temporarily from participation in government,—such as children and other dependents and wards. Children up to a certain age would be excluded by nature if not by law. Their exclusion is only temporary. They are the future state. Idiots and criminals are excluded; that is, the *known* and *registered* idiots and the *convicted* and *incarcerated* criminals. But idiots may become sane, and law-breakers may

become law-abiding, so that even these classes suffer only a conditional and possibly temporary exclusion.

These types of exclusion are, therefore, more reasonable, or rather less unreasonabe, than racial exclusion. Exclusion on account of race is a permanent disability, as irrational as it is inalterable. It is not a challenge to ambition but a fixed barrier. Apologists for racial disability have tried to justify it by references to children, paupers, criminals,—and they have used to cite the case of unenfranchised women, until the women destroyed the point of that citation by enfranchising themselves. But none of these cases parallels racial exclusion. Even economic-class exclusion is not a parallel. Excluded day-laborers might become capitalists and employers. The nearest parallel to the exclusion of a racial blood is the exclusion of some lower caste where law and tradition prevent the sons of such peasantry from rising above the status of their fathers. But even peasanthood may be overcome by social evolution or political revolution. The barrier against race is without a rival the most reasonless of all barriers.

Other apologists for racial exclusion remind us that even the favored race did not at first enjoy universally the right of suffrage; that the right was originally based in the possession of real estate, and advanced only gradually to a normal manhood basis. Inhabitants had to own so much real estate, so many acres, to vote. But the growth of industrial cities, where even the richest may not own acres of land, caused a change from this specific basis to an *ad valorem* basis, so that the voter no longer had to own so many acres but only real estate valued at so much, or on which he received a minimum rent or payed a minimum tax. Again, as industrial centers grew populous, it became evident that many good men in cities could not own even a foot of land, that there was not land enough to go round; and so a minimum valuation of personal property and belongings was admitted to qualify the voter. Later still it occurred to some that a man might not own any taxable property, real or personal; and yet be a human being and a decent member of society; therefore capitation taxes, poll taxes, were offered as compromises. A fellow with no property could pay a tax on his head. But even this head-tax was a surviving mark of the tyranny of property, as the appendix in the human body is a survival of some lower animal function. The battle front therefore advanced further toward manhood suffrage by reducing and minimizing taxes and offering alternatives and substitutes, such as service in the army, literacy, general intelligence, and even that indefinable thing called "good moral character." Thus the tyranny of property, with its heraldry of taxes, died a slow and stubborn death, and in some communities it is not yet dead.

This homage to the title-holder of property and to the so-called tax payer is ridiculous in the light of modern economic knowedge. It assumed that the whole burden of taxation and support of government rested on those who held the property and took the tax receipts. How slowly men's minds came to understand that the greatest payment of tax is the indirect payment: that the heaviest tax is paid by those who work and consume honestly. The level of wages and of the cost of necessaries is influenced by the tax burden of government. When a man buys a pair of shoes, he pays a share of the tax of the factory that made them and of every middleman that handled them; for the tax is a part of the expenses of the business and is figured into every pair of shoes. The tax is paid by every honest consumer of a hen from the hennery, of an apple from the orchard, and of a peanut from the farm. The poor man who pays the rent on a shack, pays the taxes on that shack,—not the man who collects the rent and gets the tax receipt. Those of us who own houses for rent, know how we arrive at fixing the rental figure against the tenant: first, we value the house at more than we could sell it for, and decide that we must earn the usurious rate of ten percent on that valuation; to this we add fifty dollars a year for repairs, and do not make any repairs; then we add the taxes, insurance, water rent, and all other imaginable costs for the year. If we let the place by the week, we next divide this sum by 48, instead of by 52, allowing 4 weeks for improbable vacancies, and by dividing the debt 48 times, we find what the debtor must pay us 52 times in order to discharge it; and finally, when this quotient turns out to be $7 a week, we charge him $10, just to be on the safe side and to simplify bookkeeping. And yet in spite of this chain of evidence, some people do not yet comprehend the truth that not those who get the tax receipts but those who work and honestly consume, especially those who work, pay the taxes, support the government, and are entitled to a vote.

The humbler members even of the dominant races have had to overcome this false notion of the exclusive relationship of property to production and of tax receipts to the ultimate burden of government. And yet the exclusion of the unpropertied and the non-tax-paying is no parallel to the exclusion of a race or blood. A fee simple deed can be acquired by the individual; membership in a favored race cannot be acquired by the individual. If poverty be a bar to citizenship, it can be overcome; but those who have in their veins the blood of any race, will always have it, and their children will have it to a thousand generations. The exclusion of a sex is more nearly like the exclusion of a race. But even sex is permanent only during the life of the individual; the children of a voteless woman might be males and become voters. Besides, mothers, wives, sisters, daughters, who share the social and private economic life of the voters, can have more influence on their male electors than could the members of any separate race. By every comparison it is clear that race is the most unreasonable basis for citizenship, law or justice.

The citizenship of the Negro is the real test of American democracy. The front of liberty has advanced somewhat against the power and privilege of property but is being held back at the barricade of the color line. The first barrier was slavery. That was demolished in civil war. The way was next blocked by prejudice against ex-slaves, which continues almost unabated against their free-born descendants. Sumner, Chase and Frederick Douglass believed that an emancipated people, unenfranchised, might fall into a condition worse than slavery: for in the slave somebody has a private investment and a personal interest, but an anomalously "free" people without rights or power would be like unclaimed cattle,—wild buffaloes to be hunted by whoever had the inclination. To enfranchise ex-slaves was, of course a serious matter: an evil, but the lesser evil. Some say that so soon after emancipation was not "the best time" to enfranchise the Negro, and that he should have been educated and trained first. This argument makes two wrong assumptions: first, that real prejudice would be more willing that Negroes should get education than that they should get votes, and second, that the amendments made it necessary for unfit Negro individuals to be admitted to suffrage. The constitution forbids discrimination against the Negro on account of race or previous condition of servitude, but still permits discrimination on account of individual unfitness. Prejudice is not more willing that educated than that uneducated Negroes should vote, and the Negro needs the vote to get education. The last fifty years bear no evidence that the unaided sentiment of Mississippi or South Carolina would have enfranchised the Negro in the next two hundred years. There has been but one time when those amendments could have been ratified, and that was before the ex-slave-holding south regained complete local control. Logically, the *only time* when a thing can be done, is always the "best" time to do it; and the *worst time* in all eternity to do a thing is when it cannot be done. The conscience of the people, quickened by the sacrifices of the war, offered the opportunity of an epoch to broaden the base and strengthen the bulwark of popular suffrage. "An oligarchy of skin" is not more reasonable than one of titles or dollars. And we agree with Charles Sumner, the immortal democrat, that: "It is impossible to suppose that Congress will sanction governments . . . not founded on the consent of the governed."

Some say that the Negro should have come to the voting status by slow and gradual stages, as did the white man. That is a fallacious argument: it would be sound if the Negroes had been left alone in some separate territory, not to be governed or disturbed by others who voted. When a people is suddenly placed in an advanced environment, they must meet that environment by the educational, and not by the evolutional, process. In the school of an exacting environment, centuries must be overpassed in a decade, milleniums in a generation; otherwise, instead of teaching it to our children in schools, we should leave them to discover, as their ancestors discovered, the organization of the solar system and the surgery of the vermiform appendix. If Japan, instead of adopting dynamite and airplanes from the white man, had elected to evolve them slowly, as did the whites, that would have been nice—for everybody except Japan. Sumner and Douglass were immediately and abundantly justified by the double-decade of trickery and violence which followed the re-enfranchisement of the ex-slaveholders, from 1870 to 1890. Some of the tricks were: stealing and stuffing ballot boxes; false arrest the day before election and false counting the day after; voting "repeaters" or duplicating votes by thin tissue ballots; and sometimes by advertising the polling place as at one address and suddenly changing it to another. The violence, ranging from ordinary thuggery to murder, continues slightly abated to the present moment, but most of the unlawful tricks have been enacted into trick laws. The courts were apathetic to the brutality and dishonesty and have generally upheld the trick laws. These laws represent an effort to save the sickening conscience of the south, but they usually go only so far as to clothe dishonesty in legal immunity and specious respectability. Men said, as it were: "We are sick of robbing the Negro of his vote illegally, therefore we will revise the constitution and do it legally."

Constitutional conventions and legislatures endeavored to regain political respectability by juggling property requirements, indefinite "educational tests," residence and registration pitfalls, "good character" loopholes for the favored, and the threat of perjury against the disfavored. And in spite of the fact that all the registrars and other officers were white, some of these Negro-catching devices proved to be boomerangs to white applicants. Therefore South Carolina, the mother of nullification, secession and oppression, in a desperate example to save the superior white majority of the south from being surpassed by an inferior black minority, invented and enacted into law in 1895 the most brazen of all tricks,—the so-called "Grandfather Clause." The general architecture of "grandfather" legislation was this: first, the constitutional convention would lay down detailed and treacherous registration requirements for everybody in the state, with no mention of race or color,—and so far to square with the 15th amendment. But then a later clause or section would be added to the effect that those who were eligible or whose ancestors were eligible to vote in 1867 or 1868, could still register without these requirements. The essence of time in this lit-

tle device exempted the whole white population from the consequences of its shortcomings and left the black population at the mercy of the all-powerful registrars,—who knew their business. For nearly two decades this travesty was enforced in Southern states until declared unconstitutional under an organized attack of the Negro in 1914.

Men thought to salvage political honor and to salve their remarkable religious consciences by legalizing dishonesty. Many new constitutions were made, and their suffrage articles, with their labyrinthine catch-clauses, reveal their origin and purpose. States with no trick to try, no trap to set, and no fundamental national law to evade, sometimes write the suffrage articles of their constitutions in a single page, half a page, or a paragraph or so. But when we come to a state like Alabama and its constitution of 1901, the suffrage article consists of seven closely printed pages with twenty sections,—every section being a double-jawed trap with the trigger under the thumb of the registrar. The humble citizen may even be required to "understand" the constitution, something which, after more than a hundred years of serious study, the Supreme Court has not yet accomplished. But the courts, including the Supreme Court, have connived at and abetted these tricks and trick laws. Usually they require the disfranchised and aggrieved Negro to prove what everybody, including the court, already knows: namely, that he was denied the right to vote on account of his race or color. What is well known may be the hardest thing to prove. But when uneducated officials in Alabama refuse to register a Negro graduate of Yale, Harvard or Tuskegee, pretending to disqualify him on his lack of intelligence and not on his race, the presumption ought to lie in favor of that Negro—in a court of justice.

The worst trick, next to the "grandfather clause" itself, is the "white primary," which is a survival of the era of force and violence, a relic of the time when anti-Negro mobs generally bluffed, bullied and beat black men from the polls. A white primary conducted by the party which will also control the regular election, disfranchises the Negro as effectually as if he were on the moon. For example, a white Democratic primary election in Mississippi requires that the voter shall be not only a Democrat but also white. In most southern states the Democratic primary election determines absolutely and invariably the result of the regular election,—and in such regular election the Negro can cast only a perfunctory and unnecessary vote to ratify the nominations already made by whites. The Negro is thus a dis-service by enacting this bold trick into law and making it liable to more direct judicial attack. This was the meaning of "The Nixon Case," won by the colored people of El Paso in 1925. If "white primaries" are constitutional for Democrats, they are also lawful for Republicans, Socialists and all others; so that colored people, or any other minority race or class, could be disfranchised by any dominant political party.

If a race primary is reasonable, a sex primary is more reasonable, and women may be kept out of office and power by the primary-exclusion method. Women should remmber that the anti-slavery struggle gave the first real impetus to woman-suffrage. And so long as women could not vote, they were continually comparing their situations to that of the enslaved or disfranchised Negro: but since women have become enfranchised, their leaders have changed into regular politicians, like the men, forgetting the former comradeship of their cause, dodging moral issues and dealing in political expediences. But it was the World's Anti-Slavery Convention in London in 1840 which inspired its American women delegates to organize the first women's rights convention in New York in 1848. Frederick Douglass, the great Negro anti-slavery leader, was a loyal and life-long friend of woman-suffrage. As late as 1870 a Vermont constitutional convention turned down woman suffrage by the disastrous vote of 233 to 1,—but less than fifty years later women were enfranchised by ratified act of Congress. Will white women now prove that they are indeed the "equal of men" in political chicanery, or will they remember that colored women are still disfranchised by trick laws and maladministration?

Men like a good excuse even for a bad action. Therefore some say: "The Blacks of the south should take their own right to vote. The law is on their side. They are the majority in some localities. White men would die for their rights." All this declamation is the merest bunk. The Negro may be a majority in some locality, but he is a minority in the south as a whole, and a still smaller minority in the nation. State lines are artificial and invisible; so far as the Negro minority is concerned, South Carolina and Mississippi are one community with Virginia and Texas. If Mississippi were a separate and independent nation, free from all outside interference, its colored people could not be held in their present plight for 30 days. Not only the rest of the south, but the United States army is back of every petty official in Mississippi, if his act be technically sanctioned by local law, however otherwise unjust. A black majority in an Alabama county is a mere local phenomenon, to be weighed against the greater white majority of the United States. White people of Massachusetts and Minnesota, by their very existence as parts of the republic, and especially by their silence and apathy, are the potential and the actual oppressors of the Negroes of the Mississippi deltas.

The whole people have a political and moral, even a physical relation to the status and rights of the smallest minority or the humblest citizen. The right of equal suffrage among a free citizenship is the one fundamental right which should not be abandoned to local prejudice and control. If the voter is the ultimate source of governmental power, the right to vote is primary among rights. If it is successfully denied, other rights become illusions. The solution of the suffrage problem involves the permanent solution of other problems: In every 100 persons in Georgia there are 54 whites and 46 blacks. If the Negro there could vote his 46 percent, he would get better schools by electing some of the school administrators; he would get more justice by defeating the unjust judges; he would have less oppressive laws by electing many of the legislators; he would be seldomer lynched and burned, for in the succeeding election he would defeat the unfaithful or cowardly sheriff. But against the fundamental wrong of racial disfranchisement, philanthropists and humanitarians might spend their money to the end of time trying to help the Negro to these desirable ends. The most economical help is to help one into a position of self-help. Impartial suffrage legislation and administration may not bring the millenium much nearer to the nation as a whole, but it would bring the Negro minority much nearer the millenium.

CONSECRATION

By Lois Augusta Cuglar

My sweet, red blood to snuff the Yellow hate,
My proud, White flesh a Black girl's pangs to ease,
My muscles wrenched a Red-skin's wrongs to crush,
My entire body diced to clean the slate,
Sheer mock-heroics? They'll have love of me:
The long-enduring, mystical Chinese,
The colored girls whose goodness makes me blush,
The kind-faced squaws who peddle basketry.
They'll have it. Great God, surely it is right?
He taught it . . . Thy son pleasing in Thy sight—
No dawdling, half-way measures satisfy—
I must earn sure approval in Thine eye.
Failing, I plunge (may nothing me exempt)
In cauldron—seething, scalding self-contempt.

UNDERGRADUATE VERSE
FISK UNIVERSITY

YOUTH OF TWENTY CONTEMPLATES SUICIDE

By T. Thomas Fortune Fletcher

Life is a book
I have read
Twenty pages
The book
Is not beautiful
It bores me.
I do not wish
To read
The rest.
Life is a book
I have read
Twenty pages.

POEM

By Richard Jefferson

You went away.
A sharp, green star
Shot through my heart.
I want you back.
The green-gold flame
Burns sharp as steel
You do not come
Pin pointed sparks of pain
Prick out
The soft flesh
Around my heart
And leave a hard
And ashen skin
Unfeeling, cold and passion-spent.
I do not want you any more.

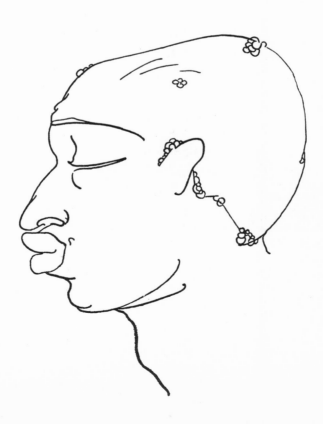

The child that does not cry,
  Dies on its mother's back.

        —*An African Proverb.*

A DRAWING, *by Charles Cullen*

OUR LITTLE RENAISSANCE

By ALAIN LOCKE

OW that the time has come for some sort of critical appraisal, what of our much-heralded Negro Renaissance? Pathetically pale, thinks Mr. Mencken, like a candle in the sunlight. It has kindled no great art: we would do well to page a black Luther and call up the Reformation. Fairly successful, considering the fog and soot of the American atmosphere, and still full of promise—so "it seems" to Mr. Heywood Broun. I wonder what Mr. Pater would say. He might be even more sceptical, though with the scepticism of suspended judgment, I should think; but one mistake he would never make—that of confusing the spirit with the vehicle, of confounding the artistic quality which Negro life is contributing with the Negro artist. Negro artists are just the by-products of the Negro Renaissance; its main accomplishment will be to infuse a new essence into the general stream of culture. The Negro Renaissance must be an integral phase of contemporary American art and literature; more and more we must divorce it in our minds from propaganda and politics. Otherwise, why call it a renaissance? We are back-sliding, I think, into the old swamp of the Negro problem to be discussing, as we have been of late, how many Negro artists are first-rate or second-rate, and how many feet of the book-shelf of leather-bound classics their works to date should occupy. According to that Hoyle, the Grand Renaissance should have stopped at the Alps and ought to have effected the unification of Italy instead of the revival of Humanism.

To claim the material that Negro life and idiom have contributed to American art through the medium of the white artist may seem at first unfair and ungracious; may even be open to the imputation of trying to bolster up with reenforcements a "wavering thin line of talent." But what is the issue—sociology or art—a quality of spirit or complexions? The artists in question themselves are gracious enough, both in making their acknowledgements to the folk spirit, and in asserting the indivisible unity of the subject-matter. Only recently, confirming her adoption of Negro material as her special field, Mrs. Peterkin has said: "I shall never write of white people; to me their lives are not so colorful. If the South is going to write, what is it they are going to write about—the Negro, of course." Still more recently, the distinguished author of *Porgy* applauds shifting the stress from the Negro writer to the "Negro race as a subject for art" and approves of "lifting the material to the plane of pure art" and of making it available to the American artist, white or Negro, "as native subject-matter." And if there is any meaning to the term universal which we so blithely and tritely use in connection with art, it must be this. There is no other alternative on the plane of art. Indeed, if conditions in the South were more conducive to the development of Negro culture without transplanting, the self-expression of the "New Negro" would spring up just as one branch of the new literature of the South, and as one additional phase of its cultural reawakening. The common bond of soil and that natural provincialism would be a sounder basis for development than the somewhat expatriated position of the younger school of Negro writers. And if I were asked to name one factor for the anemic and rhetorical quality of so much Negro expression up to the present, I would cite not the unproved capacities of our authors but the pathetic exile of the Negro writer from his best material, the fact that he cannot yet get cultural breathing space on his own soil. That is at least one reason for the disabilities of the Negro writer in handling his own materials with vivid and intimate mastery.

More and more the younger writers and artists are treking back to their root-sources, however. Overt propaganda now is as exceptional as it used to be typical. The acceptance of race is steadily becoming less rhetorical, and more instinctively taken for granted. There was a time when the only way out of sentimental partisanship was through a stridently self-conscious realism. That attitude stripped the spiritual bloom from the work of the Negro writer; gave him a studied and self-conscious detachment. It was only yesterday that we had to preach objectivity to the race artist to cure the pathetic fallacies of bathos and didactic approach. We are just beginning perhaps to shake off the artifices of that relatively early stage; so to speak the Umbrian stiffness is still upon us and the Florentine ease and urbanity looms just ahead. It is a fiction that the black man has until recently been naive: in American life he has been painfully self-conscious for generations—and is only now beginning to recapture the naivete he once originally had. The situation is well put in a stanza of Mae Cowdery's poem—"Goal,"

> I must shatter the wall
> Of darkness that rises
> From gleaming day
> And seeks to hide the sun.
> I will turn this wall of
> Darkness (that is night)
> Into a thing of beauty.

I will take from the hearts
Of black men—
Prayers their lips
Are 'fraid to utter,
And turn their coarseness
Into a beauty of the jungle
Whence they came.

So, in the development of the materials of Negro life, each group of artists has a provincialism to outgrow; in the one case narrowness of vision, in the other, limiting fetters of style. If then it is really a renaissance—and I firmly believe it is, we are still in the hill-town stage, and the mellowness of maturity has not yet come upon us. It is not to escape criticism that we hold it thus; but for the sake of a fair comparison. The Negro Renaissance is not ten years old; its earliest harbingers cannot be traced back of the beginning of the century; its representative products to date are not only the work of the last three or four years, but the work of men still in their twenties so far as the producing artists are concerned. Need we then be censured for turning our adjective into an affectionate diminutive and for choosing, at least for the present, to call it hopefully "our little renaissance"?

MY HEART HAS KNOWN ITS WINTER

By ARNA BONTEMPS

A little while spring will claim its own,
In all the land around for mile on mile
Tender grass will hide the rugged stone.
My still heart will sing a little while.

And men will never think this wilderness
Was barren once when grass is over all,
Hearing laughter they may never guess
My heart has known its winter and carried gall.

PREMONITION

By ARCADEO RODANICHE

The moon looks like a bleached face
against the sun
that moves on
along the edge of night
which ruins the abysmal lands of yesterdays;
and as it hovers
over the mist of times unborn,—
staring at tomorrows—
it pales with dread
at the sight of the chaos it beholds
undergoing gestation
in the womb of time yet to come.

RACIAL SELF-EXPRESSION

By E. Franklin Frazier

I.

CONCURRENT with the growing group consciousness among the colored people there has come into prominence two rather widely divergent opinions as to the principles which should govern the development of the group in America. The opinion represented by one group is that colored people should undertake to conform in every respect to the culture about them, while another group holds that they should develop their own unique culture. Although these two viewpoints can not be said to take this apparently mutually contradictory form in the minds of all leaders, they indicate to a large extent two emerging philosophies of racial development which are receiving emphasis by their respective protagonists. Moreover, it should be added that these two theories have been present since the Negro began to assert himself as a free man in this country, but have received new accentuation by the so-called renaissance of Negro artists and thinkers. The debate in the NATION between Langston Hughes and George Schuyler was a skirmish in the clash between these two viewpoints. While the younger Negro artists are generally regarded as exponents of the opinion favoring a unique culture among the colored people, there is apparent disagreement among them. Countee Cullen's insistence that he wants to be a universal poet rather than a Negro poet is indicative of this lack of unanimity.

The issue between these two theoretical standpoints should not be confused with the more practical but less critical programs of certain Negro leaders and Southern whites, based upon the assumption that innate but not unequal racial endowments make it necessary that each race develop its own separate culture, with the corollary often expressed but always implied that intermarriage would cause a confusion or neutralization of their respective racial endowments. This new appreciation of the racial gifts of the Negro is naïve and seems to be a sublimation of the old admonition to the Negro that he should strive to be the "best possible Negro and not a poor imitation of the white man."

While it is improbable that either of these theoretic viewpoints will issue into immediate practical consequences, it is well to examine the assumptions upon which they are based. It is likely that both philosophies are rationalizations of tendencies which are observable in the different developments which are taking place in the experience of the col-ored group in America. In this essay, the writer hopes to contribute to the clarification of the issues involved and to evaluate the claims of the respective schools of opinion. As a first step in this analysis, the writer should say something about the relation between race and culture.

II.

ONE of the first results of the general acceptance of the evolutionary hypothesis was the attempt to explain racial differences in terms of the evolutionary process. For example, an attempt was made to show that contemporary "savages" possessed keener sensory powers than civilized man and therefore stood in the evolutionary scale closer to the lower animals than modern man. The comparatively smaller average of brain volume of certain races was taken as conclusive evidence of the retarded evolution of these races. Likewise the assumed mental traits of primitive man were supposed to bear testimony to his inferior evolutionary status. According to Spencer, primitive man lacked emotional control and the power of intellectual concentration. He was explosive and showed a marked deficiency in the capacity for abstract thought. Moreover, according to the classical anthropologists, social evolution followed a unilinear course; and that among the peoples of simple culture today, we had a view of the past evolution of modern man. But of greater importance to our subject was the assumption that primitive man's simple culture was a reflection of his incomplete or arrested physical and mental evolution.

These á priori assumptions based upon superficial observations and favorable data have been totally discredited by the critical field studies of modern anthropologists. Even the recent claim of Bean to having discovered significant anatomical differences in the Negro's brain has been discredited by Mall's subsequent findings. There is a tendency to discard even the term 'primitive' and substitute 'preliterate' in referring to peoples possessing simple cultures both because of the connotations of the older term and because the essential difference between primitive and modern man seems to be the absence of a written tradition among the former. The sensory powers of primitive peoples as well as their capacity for emotional control and abstract thought do not appear to differ essentially from those of civilized man. The recent attempt on the part of Levy-Bruhl, a French sociologist, to establish chiefly on the basis of accounts of travellers and missionaries a different order of mentality for preliterate peoples, has met a similar fate at the hands of field workers, who have shown that preliterate peoples are as logical as modern man in the sphere of secular activities of life. There is a rather general agreement among ethnologists and sociologists that cultural advance is due to the contact of peoples rather than the flowering of the genius of a particular racial stock.

There are, however, some sociologists who, while recognizing the inadequacy of the other criteria of racial differences, hold to the theory of differences in temperamental endowment in races. According to this theory, races select different elements of a culture when brought into contact with it. The writer will postpone comment on this assumption until he considers more specifically the issue which is the occasion for this essay.

III.

THE foregoing all too brief summary of the conclusions regarding the relation between race and culture would lead us to believe that there is scarcely any warrant for the proposal that the Negro develop a unique culture in harmony with his racial characteristics. This opinion receives further support even from those authorities who hold to differences in the intellectual capacity of different races. These authorities hold that the intellectual powers of the Negroes and whites show the same range but that there is a greater frequency of those of superior intelligence among the whites. If the Negro were not differentiated from the whites by color, individuals under our competitive social organization would find their places according to their merit and the question of uniqueness of culture would never have been raised. The issue between the philosophies we are examining seems to resolve itself into the old issue of every nationalistic group. At first the group attempts to lose itself in the majority group, disdaining its own characteristics. When this is not possible there is a new valuation placed upon these very same characteristics and they are glorified in the eyes of the group. The same tendencies are observable in the case of the Negro group. There is, however, a conflict between the two tendencies noted above. On the one hand there is an attempt to efface Negroid characteristics and among the extremists of this group to dispense with the appellation, Negro; and on the other hand a glorification of things black. If the New Negro is turning within his group for new values and inspiration for group life, he is following the course of other nationalistic groups.

But to turn within the group experience for materials for artistic creation and group tradition is entirely different from seeking in the biological inheritance of the race for new values, attitudes and a different order of mentality. In the philosophy of those who stand for a unique culture among the Negroes there is generally the latter assumption. Moreover, while the group experience of the Ne-

groes in America may be a fruitful source for the materials of art and to some extent a source of group tradition, it offers a very restricted source for building up a thorough-going group life in America. By the entrance of the Negro into America, he was practically stripped of his culture. His whole group experience in America has been directed towards taking over cultural forms about him. In spite of the isolation in which he has lived, the Negro has succeeded in doing this to a remarkable degree. From the beginning he has not been able to draw upon a group tradition outside of America. When he has been charged with imitation of white models, he has been forced to plead guilty because there were no others. If the Negro had undertaken to shut himself off from the white culture about him and had sought light from within his experience, he would have remained on the level of barbarism. Even at the present time, if the Negro seeks relief from his conflict with the white majority by a flight from the reality of the culture about him, his development will be arrested and he will be shunted from the main highway of American life. In this respect the Negro's position is different from any other nationalistic group in America. While they can maintain their group life by drawing upon the national tradition from the Old World, and participate only to a small degree in the American tradition, the Negro has no source to draw on outside of America and only an inadequately assimilated American tradition from his past in this country.

It is quite possible that those who advocate a unique culture among Negroes would agree on the whole with the position taken above but would insist that the main point at issue is the difference in temperamental endowment. Therefore, as promised above, we shall turn to the consideration of this question. It has been pointed out by some that the facility with which the evangelical denominations spread among Negroes as well as the spirituals, and the seeming lack of strong economic motives, are indications of the peculiar racial temperament of the Negro. In the latter respect he is often contrasted with the Jew. But even here we can not say dogmatically that racial temperament has been the decisive factor in the emphasis placed by the Negroes on certain elements of American culture. There are historical and social factors which are adequate reasons to account for the fact that the majority of Negroes are Baptists and Methodists as well as the predilection of the Jew for economic activities. In Africa the Negro has always been a trader and his markets are an outstanding feature of African cultures. Even in America we find a remarkable development of business enterprises and this type of activities has become for many of the younger Negroes the surest means for the group to acquire status.

Mr. James Weldon Johnson has indicated, it appears to the writer, in "God's Trombones" the unique contribution of the Negro artists. In this unique work of art he has used the literary language of America to give artistic expression to the racial experience of the Negro in America. Whatever of racial temperament there is in these poems has been made articulate through cultural forms which were acquired by the artist in America. This does not deny that it is possible that the Negro artist working on the materials of the Negro's experience in America will create greater works than white artists. But we can not overlook the fact that at present white writers have surpassed Negro writers on the whole in the use of this material. While it may be true that at times the Negro has attempted to appropriate elements of American culture which have justified the rebuke that he was a "poor imitation of the white man" it was due to the fact that his group experience in America had not prepared him for such a rôle, but not because anything in his biological inheritance made the appropriation of such cultural traits incongruous. As the Negro group becomes more differentiated we see developing the same social types that are found in the white majority. There is a growing group of black Babbitts who are indistinguishable in their mental attitudes from the white Babbitts. The racial temperament of the Negro will assert itself in the cultural traits which he takes over; but such an indeterminable factor can not become the norm for determining the lines along which the Negro should build his culture. But it may be asked if it is desirable for the Negro to acquire uncritically all the traits of American culture. The remainder of this essay will be directed to an attempt to give a brief answer to this question.

The very fact that the issue between these two philosophies of racial development has been raised indicates a sophistication that could never have developed in cultural isolation. Negro leaders have enjoyed a cosmopolitan experience that enables them to view objectively their racial experience, as well as American culture and cultural traits in general. This appears to be increasingly one of the chief functions of the Negro intellectual. His strategic position makes him a critic of values for his group. But it still remains an open question how far the Negro group can escape the adoption of the cultural forms of America. One example will suffice to show that even in the sphere of economic life some selection may be possible the Negro must fit into the competitive industrial life about him either as a laborer or capitalist; but if the co-operative system of production and distribution offers superior spiritual values, then as far as practical he should develop in his economic life a co-operative economic technique. This he should do rather than slavishly take over both the form and spirit of modern industrialism. If such a course finds support in the racial experience of the Negro in America or in his temperamental endowment, the task will be easier and will be a distinct contribution to the general fund of American culture. Likewise, if because of racial temperament there is

a greater disposition on the part of Negroes to enjoy life than among the whites and this is recognized as a superior value, without sacrificing the efficiency of the group this trait should not be smothered by forcing the Negro's life into generally accepted molds.

Something should be said about another aspect of this question; namely, the building up of a group tradition. It seems to the writer that any such effort should be encouraged only so far as it is compatible with a fuller participation in American culture. In this matter the experience of immigrant groups has a lesson for the Negro. Those immigrant groups which have maintained the greatest group efficiency have suffered the least amount of social mal-adjustment. The efficiency of their group organization has been the best means for fitting their members for participation in American life. One of the primary needs of the Negro in America where he is not treated as an individual is the development of group efficiency. The work of the Association for the Study of Negro Life and History under Dr. Carter G. Woodson is very rapidly creating a group tradition which is necessary for group morale. This is a socializing process through which the individual members of a group acquire status. This is a healthy sign among Negroes and need not be incompatible with their struggle for fuller participation in American culture so long as it does not increase their isolation.

IV.

THIS discussion has undertaken to evaluate the over-simplified assumption expressed and implied by those who are advocating a unique cultural development for the Negro, that our modern culture is the expression of certain special intellectual and temperamental traits and that the Negro should build a culture in harmony with his racial endowment. It was pointed out that the racial experience of the Negro was unique because of historical and social factors rather than of biological inheritance. Even those traits which are so universally ascribable to temperamental rather than intellectual differences were shown to have a possible explanation in social factors. While for the artist this unique experience was recognized as a fertile source, it was not deemed adequate for the building up of a thorough-going racial tradition which would afford maximum individual development. On the other hand, the utility of a group tradition built even upon African material for group efficiency was given due recognition. But finally it was shown that any nationalistic program that made the Negro seek compensations in a barren racial tradition and thereby escape competition with the white man which was an inevitable accompaniment of full participation in American culture, would lead to intellectual, spiritual and material impoverishment such as one finds among the Southern mountain whites.

OUR GREATEST GIFT TO AMERICA

By George S. Schuyler

N divers occasions some eloquent Ethiop arises to tell this enlightened nation about the marvelous contributions of his people to our incomparable civilization. With glib tongue or trenchant pen, he starts from the arrival of the nineteen unfortunate dinges at Jamestown in 1619, or perhaps with the coming of the celebrated Columbus to these sacred shores with his Negro mate in 1492, and traces the multiple gifts of the black brethren to the present day. He will tell us of the vast amount of cotton picked by the Negro, of the hundreds of roads and levees the black laborers have constructed, of the miles of floors Negro women have scrubbed and the acres of clothes they have washed, of the numerous wars in which, for some unknown reason, the Sambo participated, of the dances and cookery he invented, or of the spirituals and work songs composed by the sons of Ham and given to a none too grateful nation. The more erudite of these self-appointed spokesmen of the race will even go back to the Garden of Eden, the walls of Babylon, the pyramids of Egypt and the palaces of Ethiopia by way of introduction, and during their prefatory remarks they will not fail, often, to claim for the Negro race every person of importance that has ever resided on the face of the earth. Ending with a forceful and fervent plea for justice, equality, righteousness, humanitarianism, and other such things conspicuous in the world by their absence, they close amid a storm of applause from their sable auditors—and watch the collection plate.

This sort of thing has been going on regularly for the last century. No Negro meeting is a success without one or more such encouraging addresses, and no Negro publication that fails to carry one such article in almost every issue is considered worthy of purchase. So general has the practice become that even white audiences and magazines are no longer immune. It has become not unusual in the past few years for the Tired Society Women's Club of Keokuk, Iowa, or the Delicatessen Proprietors' Chamber of Commerce or the Hot Dog Vendors' Social Club to have literary afternoons devoted exclusively to the subject of the lowly smoke. On such occasions there will be some such notable Aframerican speakers as Prof. Hambone of Moronia Institute or Dr. Lampblack of the Federal Society for the Exploitation of Lynching, who will eloquently hold forth for the better part of an hour on the blackamoor's gifts to the Great Republic and why, therefore, he should not be kept down. Following him there will usually be a soulful rendition by the Charcoal Singers of their selected repertoire of genuine spirituals, and then, mayhap one of the younger Negro poets will recite one of his inspiring verses anent a ragged black prostitute gnawing out her soul in the dismal shadows of Hog Maw Alley.

It was not so many years ago that Negro writers used to chew their fingernails and tear as much of their hair as they could get hold of, because the adamantine editors of white magazines and journals invariably returned unread their impassioned manuscripts in which they sought to tell how valuable the Aframerican had always been to his country and what a dirty shame it was to incinerate a spade without benefit of jury. Not so today, my friends. The swarms of Negro hacks and their more learned associates have at last come into their own. They have ridden into popular demand on the waves of jazz music, the Charleston, Mammy Songs and the ubiquitous, if intricate, Black Bottom. Pick up almost any of the better class periodicals of national note nowadays and you are almost sure to find a lengthy paper by some sable literatus on the Negro's gifts to America, on his amazing progress in becoming just like other Americans in habit and thought, or on the horrible injustice of jim crow cars. The cracker editors are paying generously for the stuff (which is more than the Negro editors did in the old days), and as a result, the black scribblers, along with the race orators, are now wallowing in the luxury of four-room apartments, expensive radios, Chickering pianos, Bond Street habiliments, canvasback duck, pre-war Scotch and high yellow mistresses.

All of which is very well and good. It is only natural that the peckerwoods, having become bored to death with their uninteresting lives, should turn to the crows for inspiration and entertainment. It is probably part of their widespread rationalization of the urge they possess to mix with the virile blacks. One marvels, however, that the principal contribution of the zigaboos to the nation has been entirely overlooked by our dusky literati and peripatetic platform prancers. None of them, apparently, has ever thought of it. While they have been ransacking their brains and the shelves of the public libraries for new Negro gifts of which to inform their eager listeners at so much per word or per engagement, they have ignored the principal gift sprawling everywhere about them. They had but to lift their eyes from the pages of their musty tomes and glance around. But they didn't.

"And what," I can hear these propagandists feverishly inquiring with poised fountain pens and notebooks, "is this unchronicled contribution to the worth of our nation?" Well, I am not unwilling to divulge this "secret" that has been all too apparent to the observing. And though the brownskin intelligentsia are now able to pay for the information—and probably willing to do so—I modestly ask nothing, save perhaps a quart of decent rye or possibly one of the numerous medals shoveled out each year to deserving coons. Hence, like all of the others, I now arise, fleck a speck off my dinner jacket, adjust my horn-rimmed nose glasses, and, striking an attitude, declaim the magic word: Flattery!

Yes folks, the greatest gift we have made to America is flattery. Flattery, if you please, of the buckra majority; inflation of the racial ego of the dominant group by our mere proximity, by our actions and by our aspirations. "How Come?" I am belligerently and skeptically quizzed, and very indulgently I elucidate. Imitation, some one has said, is the sincerest flattery. It is quite human to be pleased and feel very important when we are aped and imitated. Consider how we Negroes shove out our chests when an article appears in an enterprising darkey newspaper from the pen of some prominent African chief saying that his dingy colleagues on the Dark Continent look to their American brethren, with their amazing progress, for inspiration? How sweet is flattery, the mother of pride. And pride, we have been told, is absolutely essential to progress and achievement. If all of this be true of the dark American, mow much truer must it be of the pink American? By constant exposure to his energetic propagandists in press, on platform and in pulpit, the colored brother has forged ahead—to borrow an expression from the Uplift—until he can now eat with Rogers silver off Haviland china, sprawl on overstuffed couches and read spicy literature under the glow of ornate floor lamps, while the strains of "Beer Bucket Blues" are wafted over the radio. This is generally known as progress. Now if the downtrodden Negro, under the influence of his flattering propagandists, has been able to attain such heights of material well being, is it any wonder that the noble rednecks have leaped so much farther up the scale of living when surrounded by millions of black flatterers, both mute and vocal? Most certainly not.

Look, for example, at Isadore Shankersoff. By hook or by crook (probably the latter) he grabbed off enough coin of his native land to pay his passage to America. In Russia he was a nobody—hoofed by everybody—the mudsill of society. Quite naturally his inferiority complex was Brobdingnagian. Arriving under the shadow of the Statue of Liberty, he is still Isadore Shankersoff, the prey of sharpers and cheap grafters, but now he has moved considerably higher in the social scale. Though remaining mentally adolescent, he is no longer at the bottom: he is a white man! Over night he has become a member of the superior race. Ellis Island marked his metamorphosis. For the first time in his life he is better than somebody. Without the presence of the blackamoor in these wonderfully United States, he would still know himself for the thick-pated underling that he is, but how can he go on believing that when America is screaming to him on every hand that he is a white man, and as such entitled to certain rights and privileges forbidden to Negro scientists, artists, clergymen, journalists and merchants. One can understand why Isadore walks with firmer tread.

Or glance at Cyrus Leviticus Dumbbell. He is of Anglo-Saxon stock that is so old that it has very largely gone to seed. In the fastnesses of the Blue Ridge Mountains his racial strain has been safely preserved from pollution by black and red men, for over two hundred years. Thus he is a stalwart fellow untouched by thrift or education. Cy finally tires of the bushes and descends to one of the nearby towns. There he finds employment in a mill on a twelve-hour shift. The company paternalistically furnishes him everything he needs and thoughtfully deducts the cost regularly from his slender pay envelope, leaving him about two dollars for corn liquor and moving pictures. Cy has never had cause to think himself of any particular importance in the scheme of things, but his fellow workers tell him differently. He is a white man, they say, and therefore divinely appointed to "keep the nigger down." He must, they insist, protect white womanhood and preserve white supremacy. This country, he learns, is a white man's country, and although he owns none of it, the information strikes him not unpleasantly. Shortly he scrapes together ten dollars, buys Klan regalia, and is soon engaged in attending midnight meetings, burning crosses, repeating ritual from the Kloran, flogging erring white womanhood for the greater purity of Anglo-Saxondom, and keeping vigilantly on the lookout for uppish and offensive zigaboos to lynch. Like the ancient Greeks and Romans, he now believes himself superior to everybody different from him. Nor does the presence of jim crow institutions on every hand contribute anything toward lessening that belief. Whatever his troubles may be, he has learned from his colleagues and the politicians, to blame it all on the dark folks, who are, he is now positive, without exception his inferiors.

Think, also, of demure little Dorothy Dunce. For twelve years she attended the palatial public school. Now, at eighteen, having graduated, she is about to apply her Latin, Greek, English Literature, Ancient History, Geometry and Botany to her everyday work as packer in a spaghetti factory. When she was very young, before she entered the kindergarten, her indulgent parents used to scare her by issuing a solemn warning that a big, black nigger would kidnap her if she wasn't a good little girl. Now that she has had American popular education turned loose upon her, she naturally believes differently: i. e., that every big, burly, black nigger she meets on a dark street is ready to relieve her by force of what remains of her virtue.

A value is placed upon her that she would not have in Roumania, Scotland, Denmark or Montenegro. She is now a member of that exalted aggregation known as pure, white womanhood. She is also confident of her general superiority because education has taught her that Negroes are inferior, immoral, diseased, lazy, unprogressive, ugly, odoriferous, and should be firmly kept in their place at the bottom of the social and industrial scale. Quite naturally she swells with race pride, for no matter how low she falls, she will always be a white woman.

But enough of such examples. It is fairly well established, I think, that our presence in the Great Republic has been of incalculable psychological value to the masses of white citizens. Descendents of convicts, serfs and half-wits, with the rest have been buoyed up and greatly exalted by being constantly assured of their superiority to all other races and their equality with each other. On the stages of a thousand music halls, they have had their vanity tickled by blackface performers parading the idiocies of mythical black roustabouts and rustics. Between belly-cracking guffaws they have secretly congratulated themselves on the fact that they are not like these buffoons. Their books and magazines have told them, or insinuated, that morality, beauty, refinement and culture are restricted to Caucasians. On every hand they have seen smokes endeavoring to change from black to white, and from kinky hair to straight, by means of deleterious chemicals, and constantly they hear the Negroes urging each other to do this and that "like white folks." Nor do the crackers fail to observe, either, that pink epidermis is as highly treasured among blacks as in Nordic America, and that the most devastating charge that one Negro can make against another is that "he acts just like a nigger." Anything excellent they hear labeled by the race

conscious Negroes as "like white folks," nor is it unusual for them, while loitering in the Negro ghetto, to hear black women compared to Fords, mulatto women to Cadillacs and white women to Packards. With so much flattery it is no wonder that the Caucasians have a very high opinion of themselves and attempt to live up to the lofty niche in which the Negroes have placed them. We should not marvel that every white elevator operator, school teacher and bricklayer identifies himself with Shakespeare, Julius Caesar, Napoleon, Newton, Edison, Wagner, Tennyson and Rembrandt as creators of this great civilization. As a result we have our American society, where everybody who sports a pink color believes himself to be the equal of all other whites by virtue of his lack of skin pigmentation, and his classic Caucasian features.

It is not surprising, then, that democracy has worked better in this country than elsewhere. This belief in the equality of all white folks—making skin color the gauge of worth and the measure of citizenship rights—has caused the lowest to strive to become among the highest. Because of this great ferment, America has become the Utopia of the material world; the land of hope and opportunity. Without the transplanted African in their midst to bolster up the illusion, American would have unquestionably been a much different place; but instead the shine has served as a mudsill upon which all white people alike can stand and reach toward the stars. I submit that here is the gift par excellence of the Negro to America. To spur ten times our number on to great heights of achievement; to spare the nation the enervating presence of a destructive social caste system, such as exists elsewhere, by substituting a color caste system that roused the hope and pride of teeming millions of ofays—this indeed is a gift of which we can well be proud.

EFFIGY

By LEWIS ALEXANDER

FORM

You stood in the yard
Like a lilac bush
With your head tossed high
As if to push
Your hair in a blossom
About your head
You wore the grace
Of a fragile reed.

FASHION

Your gown crackled loud
Like the swish of leaves
Being flitted about
By a lyric breeze
Your step was like a dainty fawn
Breathing the nectared air at dawn,
Oft have I seen the rose in you
But it never bloomed such a brilliant hue.

THE NEGRO ACTOR'S DEFICIT

By Theophilus Lewis

HE actor makes the theatre. He creates the theatre by distinguishing himself from a crowd of worshippers or revellers by his special talent for mimicry or simulation. His ability to give clever and convincing imitations of familiar persons and situations and well known objects of nature excites widespread curiosity. By improving his talent he crystalizes transient curiosity into continued interest and makes the theatre a permanent institution of public amusement.

The theatre has now become an independent institution. Formerly it was an appendage of the church. Its performances were a part of religious ritual, religious propaganda or religious orgy. Now its performances attract a definite social interest on their own merits—an interest, separate and distinct from all other interests, which no other institution can satisfy. People no longer go to see the actor simulate the story of the Passion. They go to see him jig a lively step or enact a contemporary and perhaps humorous version of the story of Potiphar's wife. The actor, who began as a subordinate of the priest, has achieved his autonomy and decides for himself whether he shall devote his talent to making people good or to making them happy.

He usually decides to make them happy. As the servant of the church the actor devoted his skill to making his audience reverent. As the master of the theatre he specializes in making his audience merry. He eliminates the elements of ceremonial and worship and restricts the theatre solely to amusement. But the relationship between the church and the theatre has not been completely severed. Neither the church, dominated by the priest, nor the theatre, controlled by the actor, offers its patrons any material boon. Each is strictly a spiritual institution. The church endures because it satisfies men's deepest emotional cravings; the theatre, in its immature state, thrives because it caresses their lighter emotions.

I have not, of course, attempted to trace the literal steps by which the acolyte becomes the actor and the mystery tableau or the revel evolves into the theatre. I am seeking, merely, to isolate the origin and the nature of the theatre as a means of leading up to the final responsibility and test of the actor. The theatre, when it has once been established as an autonomous institution, can be imported from one country to another. America, for example, borrowed its theatre along with other fundamentals of culture from Europe. We Aframericans borrowed our theatre from our white compatriots. But transferring the theatre from one continent or culture to another continent or culture does not change its essential nature any more than importing English sparrows from abroad made them Baltimore orioles.

The theatre is a spiritual institution in America and Australia as well as in Greece and England. It obtained its original license from the church and it has a similar spiritual function to perform. The actor began as a subordinate of an institution designed to exalt men. When the theatre became independent he found himself head of an institution devoted merely to entertaining them. This, in a sense, is cultural degradation. If the actor permits the stage to remain at this level he is a social factor of negligible significance, except, perhaps, to the police. If, on the other hand, the actor advances the theatre to a point where it exalts as well as entertains, where it both colors and reflects social conduct, he becomes a cultural agent coordinate with the priest and one of the most precious members of society.

I can now consider what Negro actors have done with their theatre, or, if you prefer, what they have accomplished in the theatre. The test will be empirical. I will not compare the accomplishments of Negro actors with an ideal or a theory. I will compare their accomplishments with what actors of other peoples have accomplished, making due allowance for whatever extenuating circumstances exist in favor of Negro actors if they have failed to make the grade.

The theatre, excepting the church and sports, is the most democratic of spiritual institutions. Since sports are hardly influenced by art at all while the church employs art merely as a handmaiden the theatre is really the most democratic of all artistic institutions. It evolved out of a crowd and its entertainment has always been adapted to mass rather than to individual enjoyment. More than any other esthetic institution it reflects the spiritual life of a whole people. This is not to say the theatre appeals to every individual of a group. It means that the theatre, if it is in a healthy state, will attract representative individuals from every class of society from the lowest to the highest. If it draws its patrons from any one class, either the lowest or the highest, to the exclusion of other levels of society, it will become either spiritually anaemic or spiritually crapulous, hence unable to keep pace with the cultural progress of the group.

It seems like a waste of words to describe the audience of the Negro theatre for the reader is doubtless familiar with it already. It is well known that the Negro theatre appeals only to the lowest elements of the race. Not the lowest class economically, but the lowest intellectually and morally —the ignorant and depraved. The poorer respectable classes either avoid it or attend its performances with shamefaced apologies. The middle and upper classes hold it in contempt and the more intelligent actors themselves are disgusted with it. There is no better way to describe the attitude of respectable Negroes toward their theatre than to point to their indifference to its frequent indecency. Unlike the white public, which is often alarmed by the moral tone of its theatre, the colored respectable classes seldom protest against the tendency of their stage toward turpitude. As they never attend its performances its indecency does not offend them and they do not care whether it continues or not.

The cause of the indifference of the better classes is obvious and the cause of the interest of the lewd element is equally so. The general tone of the Negro stage has never risen above the level of the burlesque show. Its performances consist of a continuous display of imbecile and obscene humor. An actor with a deformed mouth will sing a song and vibrate his lips. An elongated comedian with legs like broomsticks will sing a song and proceed to make letter Z's and figure 4's with his limbs. When an actor has no physical deformity to capitalize he will make up for the deficiency by arraying himself in a suit of trick clothes. A derby three inches in diameter will perch perilously atop his poll, a ten-inch safety pin will hold his coat together, thirty-inch shoes will encase his feet and a red flannel patch will adorn the seat of his black breeches. Add to this a patter which depends on the mispronunciation of words for its humor and some by-play of ribald sex jokes and you have the entire gamut of amusement offered by the Negro stage. What it was thirty years ago it is today. Amusement of this sort, once the novelty has worn off, can divert only the dull and depraved. The progressive classes are revolted by it.

Fully eight out of ten colored actors will admit the deplorable condition of the Negro stage, only they will demur responsibility for it and place the blame on the public. They argue that if respectable colored people would patronize the theatre they (the actors) could raise the standard of amusement, but since only members of the lower element fill the auditorium they must play down to the level of their audience. This sounds plausible enough but it is nevertheless highly specious. The public has no business in the theatre except to be entertained and occasionally exalted. The rest is up to the dramatist, whose part we will not consider for the present, and the actor.

The actor is an artist, or he ought to be, and he must assume the same responsibility to the public every other artist assumes. A man goes to the theatre to see his spiritual likeness just as he goes to a portrait artist to have his physical likeness depicted. There is a little bit of Henry V in every Englishman, a mite of Cyrano de Bergerac in every Frenchman and a bit of Toussant l'Ouverture or Booker Washington in every Aframerican. The Englishman, the Frenchman and the Aframerican each wants to see the stage reflect his inner heroism, nobility and wit. No one wants to see the actor depict him as a gorilla no more than he wants to see a portrait artist paint his picture with the snout of a boar or the ears of an ass. It is not his business to tell the painter what brushes or pigments to use. Neither is it his concern what methods the actor employs. He has fulfilled both his duty and his right when he expresses approval or disapproval of the finished work.

The artist, whether he is actor, painter or poet, is a spiritual pioneer. Gainborough did not ask the citizens of London how he should paint the Blue Boy, Keats did not canvas the town on how to write the Ode to a Nightingale nor did the Parisians specify how Coquelin should portray the role of Cyrano. Each of those artists divined the spiritual needs of the time and proceeded to satisfy those needs. He did not say people have never seen a picture, poem or acting like I have in mind so I must not produce it till they let me know they are ready to appreciate it. Still that is precisely what the Negro actor says in substance when he complains that the absence of the better classes from the theatre prevents him from raising the standard of entertainment.

If the Negro actor was the artist he should be, he would not complain of being dominated by his audience. Instead he would master his audience and make it like a progressively higher form of amusement. It goes without saying that no actor, whatever his genius, can make a *How Come?* audience like the Master Builder. On the other hand it is hard to conceive how an actor can be so bad as to make any audience dislike Cyrano de Bergerac. It can be logically objected that heroic plays like the latter are few and far between. It can be just as logically replied that melodramas are easy to obtain and that they would uplift the present audience of the Negro theatre and at the same time attract patrons from higher levels of the race. The fact that Negro actors have not brought their stage to this transition period from a lower to a higher form of amusement simply means they lack imagination and energy. It is easier to wear the same old trick clothes and spiel off the same old patter than it is to learn the lines of a play, so our actors follow the line of no resistance and keep doing the same old stuff. It is not true that they are compelled to play down to their audience. They are playing up to the limit of their own ability. The only thing that distinguishes the flashily dressed hoodlum in the box seat from the actor on the stage is that the former eats more and drinks less.

Like most shoddy characters the Negro actor, as a rule, is wholly lacking in race pride. This is not surprising, for pride of race is akin to pride in self, and incompetence and lack of patriotism commonly go together. The genuine artist is always a patriot at bottom. He may incessantly bawl his countrymen out to the dogs but in his heart he cherishes an intense affection for them. Some first rate artists like Paderewski even do not disdain to assume political office.

The artist imbued with a sense of race pride and responsibility, like Ethel Waters or the late Bob Cole and Florence Mills, is a rare bird in the ranks of Negro performers. Instead of doing their best to make the Negro theatre a house of loveliness for the diversion of Negro audiences most colored actors are forever trying their hardest to get out of it altogether, using it only as a stepping stone to popularity with white producers. Broadway or Big Time vaudeville is the goal of every colored performer. Not all of them reach their goal, of course, but it is always present in their dreams; and they do not feel that they have made a success until they have heard the applause of Caucasian palms.

The Negro stage is so much a thing apart from the interests of the race at large that it is hardly probable that any colored apologists for it will be found outside the ranks of professional actors. There may be some, however, and they may argue that the colored actor cannot have made such a dismal failure of his theatre, for white people frequently attend its performances and enjoy them. These white visitors, it may be pointed out, are often members of the cultured classes and quite familiar with the best their own stage affords. The answer is plain. These white visitors have not seen the same actors doing the same thing year after year for two decades. Hence they mistake what is novel to them for originality on the part of the actor just as they are likely to mistake his obscenity for sophistication. Even so, they do not compare the Negro stage with their own, for they think of the latter in terms of drama while they think of the Negro stage in terms of vaudeville.

Drama and vaudeville. The comparison epitomizes the Negro actor's deficit. We think of the French theatre in terms of its Talmas, Coquelins, Bernhardts and Guitrys. We think of the English theatre in terms of its Burbages, Irvings, Garricks, Siddonses, Bracegirdles and Ellen Terrys. We think of the American theatre in terms of its Forests, Hacketts, Fiskes and Barrymores. We think of the Negro theatre in terms of Johnny Hudgins, Billy Mills, Hamtree Harrington and Miller and Lyles. But what about our Cloughs, Pryors, Desmonds and Bishops? Simply this. If the whole kit and caboodle of them were worth the grave dust of Joseph Jefferson they wouldn't have to hang around Broadway stage doors crying for dramatic handouts at $35 a week top.

The cultural value of the actor, I said in the beginning of this article, must be judged by his ability to raise the theatre above the plane of amusement and make it an instrument for the expression of the higher spiritual life of his people. The theatre should be a dynamic institution that both reflects and colors the general pattern of life of which it is a part. The Negro actor has not only failed to make the stage a vital part of our cultural life; he has degraded it below the notice of the better classes of the race. Our stage does not influence our culture even to the extent of providing matinee idols for romantic schoolgirls. Instead it panders exclusively lasciviousness of the feeble minded and depraved elements of the race. Worse. The majority of our actors are ignorant of both the nature and the history of the theatre and have only the vaguest suspicion why the respectable classes ignore their existence. The few performers intelligent enough to sense what is wrong with our theatre lack sufficient energy to make even a gesture of reform. In his account with his race the balance of the Negro actor remains heavily in the red.

TWO POEMS

By EDWARD S. SILVERA

THE UNKNOWN SOLDIER

"Behold our son, our valiant dead,"
They say to one another—
And all the while
None ever thinks
That he might be my brother:
But I am glad he holds his peace,
I'm glad he can't come back;
I'd hate to see Love crucified
If he, by chance, were black.

OLD MAID

The fires of a thousand loves
Burned bright within her
Night and day,
The years like bellows
Fanned the flames
Which ate her heart and soul away.

DUNCANSON

(An American Artist Whose Color Was Forgot)

W. P. Dabney

STRANGE to say, the world, or rather our world, knows little of R. S. Duncanson, a native of Cincinnati, Ohio, who years before the Civil War had established a reputation as an artist of high rank. The ignorance arises from the fact that in this country, his associates were artists and his color was rarely mentioned.

Though self-taught, his pictures early attracted attention. The Art records of England mention and describe some of the paintings he exhibited when making a tour of Europe. His associates even in his home town were men of international reputation, among them Farny, Lindsay, S. Jerome, Uhl, and Henry Mosler, who afterwards located in New York. Among his paintings, now in Cincinnati, are a full size portrait of William Cary which hangs at the Ohio Military Institute, and a life size picture at Ohio Mechanics' Institute of Nicholas Longworth, I. There are several other pictures in existence, among which are magnificent landscapes.

One of the finest, *The Western Hunters' Encampment,* was purchased by me from a connoisseur of the fine arts who had treasured it for years. It hangs on the wall of my library and there, mellowed by the light that falls upon it from above, its marvelous lineal precision, its magnificent coloring accentuated by age, reveal a touch that ever characterizes the work of the masters.

The following brief extract is taken from the *Enquirer* of December 21, 1924:—

"In 1857, Cincinnati was a large art center, the most prominent west of the Alleghenies. Already the city was known for the fame of Hiram Powers, a sculptor, and a score of painters headed by James H. Beard, Thomas Buchanan Read and Robert S. Duncanson, the phenomenal colored man, whose father was a Scotchman of Canada, and whose mother was a mulatto.

"Seventy-five years ago, according to Charles Cist's 'Cincinnati in 1851,' Cincinnati had numerous

artists who had already become, or were about to become, distinguished for work. One of these was the colored man, Robert S. Duncanson, who was then already prominent for such historical pieces as 'Shylock and Jessica,' 'Ruins of Carthage,' 'Trial of Shakespeare,' 'Battle Ground of the River Raisin' and 'Western Hunters' Encampment.'

"In 1865, November 24, there appeared in the Cincinnati Daily Gazette the following item from Moncure D. Conway of Cincinnati, who wrote from London, England, telling of the advance of Robert S. Duncanson:

"In walking through the gallery of miniatures, at the South Kensington Museum the other day I met Duncanson, whom some of your readers will remember as one who, a few years ago, was trying to make himself an artist in Cincinnati, and who had already produced a worthy piece of imaginative art in a picture of Tennyson's 'Lotus Eaters.'

"Duncanson subsequently left Ohio and repaired to Canada, where his color did not prevent his association with other artists and his entrance into good society. He gained much of his culture and encouragement in Canada, retouched his 'Lotus Eaters,' produced one or two still better paintings and set out for England. In Glasgow and other Scotch cities he exhibited these paintings with success."

"He has been invited to come to London by various aristocratic personages. Among others, by the Duchess of Sutherland and the Duchess of Essex, who will be his patrons. He also received a letter from the poet laureate, Tennyson, inviting him to visit him at his home, in the Isle of Wight, where he will go and take with him the 'Lotus Eaters.' Think of a Negro sitting at the table with Mr. and Mrs. Alfred Tennyson, Lord and Lady of the ·Manor, and Mirror of Aristocracy—and so forth! (Signed) "Aubrey" Moncure D. Conway.

"In 1866 there appeared in 'The Art Journal,' of London, England, the following tribute to American Art. It was headed, 'The Land of the Lotus Eaters. Painted by R. S. Duncanson.'

" 'America has long maintained supremacy in landscape art, perhaps indeed its landscape artists surpass those of England. Certainly we have no painter who can equal the works of Church; and modern British School. Duncanson has established high fame in the United States and in Canada. He is a native of the States and received his art education there, but it has been "finished" by a course of study in Italy, by earnest thoughts at the feet of the great masters and by a continual contemplation of nature under Southern skies.

"We therefore may add this picture to the many works of rare value supplied to us by the landscape artists of America.

"Many wonderful tributes have been paid to this man, so worthy, yet so little known among us. A genius of 'purest ray serene,' 'Dunc,' as his contemporaries called him, was temperamental to the extreme. He worshipped his art, idolized the children of his brain and brush. While painting, he would often sing, laugh or even weep, for his soul was in Paradise.

"The time came when the fervor of his emotions, shook asunder the ties of sanity, and then, 'God gathered him to his Fathers.' "

YOUTH

By FRANK HORNE

I am a knotted nebula—
a whirling flame
Shrieking afiire the endless darkness . . .
I am the eternal center of gravity
and about me swing the crazy moons—
I am the thunder of rising suns,
———the blaze of the zenith—
. . . the tremble of women's bodies
in the arms of lovers . . .
I sit on top of the Pole
Drunk with starry splendor
Shouting hozzanas at the Pleiades
. . . booting footballs at the moon—
I shall outlast the sun
and the moon
and the stars. . . .

A Drawing by Aaron Douglas

The Prospects Of Black Bourgeoisie

By Abram L. Harris

HE slave regime furnished the basis for the racial distinctions which it projected and crystallized into a social psychology which in turn became the sentimental bulwark of the slave power and its legacy upon dissolution. In order to hold the system intact, the exploitation of black labor was justified on ground that the Negro was inherently unfitted for independent participation in western culture. Even to the poor white worker whose status was only theoretically superior to that of the slave, the Negro was accursed of God, and "to labor was to work like a nigger." On the other hand, the social superiority of the master class exerted a subtle influence on the Negro slave. Conscious of his own social and economic debasement and contemptuous of the poor white man's economic infirmity, he desired to be like the old masters. The complexity of these attitudes made it impossible for the lower white and black classes to divest themselves of mutual animosity.

When freedom came, the Negro, who, in culture and refinement, more nearly approximated the white man, comprised a sort of natural aristocracy which furnished the race with leaders. Under the slave regime these leaders had been the house servants and artisans. Their proximity to the dominant class of whites and, sometimes, blood relationship predisposed them to an affectation of aristocratic graces, traditions, and manners. But their social philosophy was of northern origin.

This early Negro leadership was mainly political in its purpose and outlook. While the more astute Negro politicians may have perceived some of the economic factors in the race problem, only ephemeral contact was established with the labor movement of the 60's and 70's when competition provoked certain white unions to take the initiative in organizing Negro workers. Of course, many of the unions, like the typographical that was malicious in its discriminations against Negro printers, intensified the Negro worker's skepticism of white labor, particularly when organized. But the chief element that perpetuated discord and profited by it was the Negro politicians who were Negro labor's spokesmen during this period. These politicians were aligned with the Republican Party. When the white workers projected an independent labor party, the Negro Republicans naturally exclaimed that their party was the fountain of all social reform. The masses of Negro laborers believed in the political faith of their leaders; and their social experience could not

lead to any appreciation of labor legislation such as was proposed by their white contemporaries. Not that the Negro worker disapproved class legislation. The fact was that he did not approve class legislation when it was designed to ameliorate specific racial handicaps.

On the economic side, the chief undertaking directly after emancipation was the incorporation of the Freedmen's Savings Bank by the Federal Government. This too was tainted with Republican politics. It was not conceived by Negroes as a step in the race's economic elevation. It was organized for Negroes by their political guardians. Although the Bank was a hot-bed of corruption and exploitation, it served to bring the Negro closer to the *habits of thought* that prevailed in the capitalistic economy. Along with this indoctrination in the cultus of savings and private enterprise went habituation to the ideology of the middle-classes.

In later years the racial philosophy which expounded industrial efficiency to the Negro masses became the embodiment of economic individualism and business enterprise, but eschewed political alliances—even with the political power that symbolized these virtues. More paradoxical than this was the fact that business enterprise as a philosophy of racial advancement was made synonymous with the industrial education of the Negro, since they both claimed to be the means of Negro economic emancipation.

II

As social ostracism increased, and the Negro's industrial education—such as it was—counted for little in the competitive economy, the philosophy of business enterprise succeeded in establishing its conceptual independence of the old dualism in economic thinking of Negro leaders. It became *the* means of promoting Negro independence of existing economic arrangements; and now, in our contemporary culture, it bids fair to pre-empt the field of racial betterment philosophies. The practical validity of Negro business enterprise is claimed to be attested by the surpluses of wealth individual Negroes have accumulated. The adherents to the doctrine do not advocate increasing the number of really middle-class Negroes through an increase of independent Negro farmers, even though sound business enterprise must rest as much upon such a class as upon industrial and fiscal fact. In the surrounding white population, business enterprise rests upon a fairly even distribution of functional classes, cultivation of natural resources and ownership of complex industrial arrangements. In the Negro population functional classes are most unevenly distributed; and, of course, the Negro has little industrial control and possesses a small share of the nation's natural resources. The Negro middle-class is comprised of small shop keepers, a small group of independent farmers, and persons engaged in rendering professional and personal service. Here of late a decided growth in industrial wage-earners has increased the number of skilled craftsmen in the Negro population while decreasing its agricultural proletariat. At the bottom of the social ladder are to be found the unskilled laborers, domestic servants, and agricultural wage-earners who constitute by far the largest functional groups. The professions are already overcrowded. The desire to escape the lot of the domestic and the poverty of the unskilled laborer accounts for the disproportionate share of Negroes that has been attracted to the healing, teaching, and exhorting professions. Relief from this top-heaviness among Negro functional classes is promised by those who undertake business enterprise as the plan of racial salvation. What are the Negro's prospects of realizing these ideals in American life? Upon the answer to this question hinges the probability of the Negro's continued social performance in accordance with bourgeois logic as well as the prospects of a strictly racial business enterprise, the material base without which, his middle-class bias must become a useless psychological vestige of social heritage.

III

Let us examine the postulates of business enterprise as a racial philosophy. Its adherents maintain that since the Negro problem is purely economic, the solution is the creation of competitive business enterprises within the Negro group so as to afford employment to Negroes. It is further contended that a state of racial economic sufficiency will be attained only when the Negro consumes less and produces more.

The growing prevalence of the above type of reasoning undoubtedly marks a renaissance of Negro economic learning; but one whose philosophic validity was lost upon the advent of modern capitalism. Before the rise of the *bourgeoisie,* the doctrine that guided the economic policy of nations was mercantilism. It held that a nation's stock of gold was the best measure of national wealth and power; and that the way to increase national wealth and power was by producing goods that could be exported for money returns and by consuming less of other nation's goods. As modern industrial society gradually developed, the economists saw that interdependence and not self-sufficiency was the basis of economic and social progress. Today, even in that sphere of economic life known as international trade, this hoary fallacy of economic self-sufficiency has lost much of its pristine virtue. The doctrine of *comparative costs* which is but an extension of the principle of *division of labor* is of greater importance in international trade than is this notion of the self-

contained community. Obviously in a complex culture based upon specialization and interdependence of classes and individuals there can be little approximation to individual, racial or national self-sufficiency.

The absence of statistics on the comparative industrial efficiency of racial groups makes it impossible to ascertain the productivity of different races. Such data are not necessary for a refutation of the insinuation that the Negro is a parasitical class in industrial society. What on earth has the Negro been doing these last three hundreds in America if he has not been producing? To what has his manpower been devoted if not to the increase of wealth and services? It is a fact, however, that the Negro has rarely owned or controlled the instruments and machines of production, i.e., social capital. Nor have the great entrepreneurs been recruited from the Negro race. The Negro as a freeman arrived very tardily on the scene of capitalistic enterprise and adventure. The greater portion of the Negro population has been wage-earners and chiefly unskilled laborers. This can by no twist of economic logic be construed into meaning that the Negro has been more of a consumer than a producer. And it is futile to point out that after all, consumption is merely a demand for production and *vice versa:* for; what these advocates of racial business mean by increased productivity is that the Negro should procure some of the wealth producing factors of the community—which is very different from admonishing him to become more productive. How great are the Negro's possibilities in achieving this goal? If some individuals among the Negroes are to suceed as business undertakers, must their success be a purely racial phenomenon; or can it result from general conditions of the competitive economy? Social attitudes being what they are, will not the racial identity of Negro enterprise restrict its utility to the Negro group? When pushed to its logical extremity, must not this doctrine of Negro business enterprise reckon with the feasibility of erecting within the already existing national economy, a purely racial one?

Thus far the Negro's largest economic institutions have been banks, insurance, and real estate corporations and secret fraternities. In short his most important economic institutions have been financial. Now, the financial superstructure of modern capitalism has been built up in order to hold together the underlying and somewhat diversified but interstitial parts of industry, commerce, and agriculture. Industry proper is devoted to the production of goods. Investment banks supply fixed capital, and commercial banks and paper houses supply working capital for transferring the commodities produced. While financial institutions perform a useful function in production and exchange operations of industrial society, their existence is contingent, not only upon savings, but a market for the capital which savings place at their disposal. The existence of Negro finance organizations may be assured by the savings of the masses. But what about the demand for these savings, i.e., the market for capital-disposal? If the funds of Negro finance institutions flow to the general money market, these institutions must ultimately lose their racial significance in the melée of competition—which may not be a bad thing;—but more of this later. If the available funds do not flow to the general market, they must be confined to investments within the race. Where is the Negro or group of Negroes who owns or controls interest in factories, mines, or public utilities that have need of fixed or liquid capital? Negro business men do operate funeral and embalming, and hair straightening concerns of not ordinary capitalization. These are not sufficiently numerous or potent to give solidity and flexibility to any large financial superstructure. The advances that Negro finance organizations make must take the form of short time consumption loans or, when made for a larger period, take the form of a mortgage on real property. At all events their assets are of a non-shiftable type. But this does not check the Negro's ambition for multiplying banks and finance corporations.

One argument for the creation of Negro banks is that they enable the Negro to keep his earnings within the race. The chief lamentation of Negro business enterprise is that Negroes carry large deposits with white banks. One Negro banker upon visiting New York saw that a great many Negroes were depositing their savings with the United States Postal Savings Department. This was very distasteful to him. He seemed to have felt that a Negro bank should be organized as depository for these funds. Perhaps it never dawned on this banker that the United States Government was at that time employing in New York City, alone, more Negroes than all of the Negro finance institutions combined. Little do these banking promoters realize that they and their institutions rest upon the savings of Negro masses who are employed, not by Negro but by white capitalists.

Another argument for the creation of Negro banks is that they give Negro business men greater credit accommodations. White banks, for example, refuse to extend the same credit terms on a mortgage in real property in a Negro as in a white community. It seems that the policy is not always racial. Very often it is economic. A white business man who seeks a loan on property which he owns in a Negro neighborhood is likely to receive much better terms from a white bank than a Negro owning the same piece of property. The white borrower's direct or indirect credit standing in the business community, apart from the security offered, plays an important part in the transaction. Moreover, it is not unlikely that this hypothetical white borrower of superior credit standing could obtain better accommodations from a Negro creditor than could the average Negro borrower. Aside from the comparative borrowing strength of the Negro and

white business man, what is the character of the security offered, i.e., the real property in the Negro community? Is it good business practice to extend the same credit on it as on property of the same appraised value in a white community? The opinion seems to be that it is not. In certain Negro communities some property is in exceptional physical condition, but the surrounding property has suffered such rapid physical depreciation that the whole section is undesirable for residential purposes. The value of first class Negro property must for this reason fall below what its normal price would otherwise be. Moreover, once property is let to Negro tenants, its vendibility is restricted and its market value reflects the limitation in demand. One may easily deplore these conditions but not deny that business actuated by the *profit motif* in a competitive society is forced to discriminate against mortgages on property in Negro communities. And the prime position that the real estate mortgage occupies in Negro financial operations gives Negro banking a rather non-flexible and investment character.

To the extent that Negro finance institutions assist black wage-earners to acquire property, they are beneficial, though limited in function. Their serviceability could as a matter of fact be heightened by organization upon a co-operative basis which would permit Negro savers to share in the surpluses. But these organizations are conceived in the spirit of business individualism. They are not organized for racial service but for private profit. The surpluses must therefore go to the entrepreneurs. And in Negro business enterprise an inordinately high proportion of the gross profit is diverted by the entrepreneur from reinvestment in the business enterprise and appropriated to his personal consumption which is usually more conspicuously wasteful than that of wealthier and more efficient capitalists in the world of great economic achievement. As a general tendency undue absorption of profits will inevitably weaken the whole fabric of Negro business. It has already led to what a Negro business man called over-expansion which is not over-expansion in any real economic sense of over-investment. It is rather under-investment; the quest for greater and greater profits in face of the limitations placed upon Negro finance institutions by their absence of industrial foundation and inadequate market for capital, leads the Negro entrepreneurs into promotions of dubious worth. Investments are made in amusement corporations and other perpetual motion machines that are perpetual only to the extent that they secure perpetual instalments of investment. But why can't Negro finance institutions secure a firm footing in economic life by purchasing the shares of industrial corporations or by organizing new ones?

Before the Negro was emancipated, the great American fortunes were in the making. When he became a freeman, the foundation of the continental railway systems and the later development of mines, factories and fields had been laid. A score of years after his emancipation, huge combinations capitalized in hundreds of millions arose stifling competition and establishing monopoly in industry. Today some of these vertical and horizontal combinations are capitalized at more than a billion dollars (***). They have not only established a sort of hegemony in industry but have set up interlocking directorates and communities of interest in the financial domain. Does anyone acquainted with this economic evolution believe that the Negro, as such, at this late date can by some financial wizardry acquire much of the nation's sources of raw material, or, obtain control of any of the productive factors?

Of course the shares of large industrial and public utilities are purchasable on the market. Suppose the Negroes in the United States could be prevailed upon to pool their wealth and place it in the hands of Negro enterprises so as to gain control of some of the numerous corporations by mopping-up their securities. Any one of a thousand investment bankers could bankrupt the whole Negro race between tickings of the stock-exchange tickers. No doubt some sagacious and thrifty Negro individuals, or corporations, may purchase securities of existing, or new corporations or portions of the issues of foreign and domestic governments. Such operations must of necessity be limited. When conducted on a wide scale, the Negro business is forced to take chances in the general competitive market where small and inexperienced economic endeavor is disadvantaged. Capitalize some racial enterprise at a billion dollars. If it would live it must ultimately compete with white business. This, for the reasons already alluded to, would be its undoing.

The financial prowess of the Jewish capitalists is often cited for Negro emulation. But the existence of a large population of poor Jews who—no more than Negroes, the occasional object of Jewish capitalists' charity—have escaped the wage-earning class merely because of the existence of Jewish financiers, is usually ignored. A more important fact of Jewry is ignored: the financial history of the Jew

(***) Vide Taussig, Principles of Economics, I, 59. Also Moody, The Truth About Trusts.

which dates back to the Middle Ages when the Church's edict against usury gave the Jews monopoly of money lending.

The logical conclusions from these observations may be summarized.

(1) Negro financial institutions can neither hope to exert any considerable control over national industry requiring fixed capital nor over purely commercial transactions necessitating working capital.

(2) Social attitudes being what they are, the racial identity of Negro economic institutions will, perforce of these attitudes, confine their services to the Negro race.

(3) The restriction of the dealings of Negro finance institutions to the race will shunt them from the general investment market, thus further proscribing their utility.

(4) These institutions may incidentally assist some Negroes to acquire a stake in the economic order and furnish employment to a limited number of educated Negroes, but the masses of Negroes must continue to look to white capitalism for employment.

(5) They are a sort of illogically necessary appurtenance in an economic world where the large capital accumulations necessary for production must depend on Negro as well as on white savers, but where it is felt desirable for social reasons to maintain white and black institutions even at the cost of tragic waste.

(6) The philosophy of wealth and economic enterprise grips the imagination of the Negro even in the lower stratum.

(7) The tenacity with which this belief in racial economic independence is held results from a fructification of the bourgeois ideals that social pressure has forced Negroes to emulate, irrespective of social class.

(8) And while there is need for theoretical formulation of Negro economic experience, there are few, if any, trained Negro economists. But even if theoreticians existed in the Negro population, their profoundest formulations, however rational, when contrary to popular assumptions would be futile speculation to a racial group that is looking for solutions and is impatient of theory.

TO A YOUNG POET

By GEORGE CHESTER MORSE

Lincoln University

Just as molten thoughts o'erflow
From an unknown fiery source
To form themselves in poetry;
Such is the wavering self in woe
Seeking life's straight or winding course
To infinity.

A PAGE OF UNDERGRADUATE VERSE

TO A MOCKING BIRD
By HERMAN E. FIELDS
Shaw University

I have listened, oft have listened
To a voice I love to hear;
Soft its echo oft resounded,
Falling faintly on my ear.

And I asked me as I listened
To that voice, so clear and sweet,
As I wandered in the wildwood,
As I heard the notes repeat.

Could this voice of wondrous beauty,
Trilling anthems so divine,
Be a seraph, nymph, or angel,
Thus to cheer this soul of mine.

Was it spirit, the harp of Nature,
Chanting praises to the skies,
Or the loving voice, transcendent,
Of a bird in Paradise?

And when evening falls upon me,
Still its little form I see,
Flitting in the pale blue heaven
Or about the leafy tree.

Even then the echoes haunt me;
Even yet I hear the cry,
Ringing still though but a memory
That will live and never die.

CONGENITAL
By KATHERINE JACKSON
Tougaloo College

A pig will be a pig
It matters not his name—
Whenever he is fed,
He always acts the same.

IDYLL
By GLADYS M. JAMESON
Howard University

Tall, straight birches
Starkly etched against the sky—
Virgin slim they stand, mutely questing,—
Silver fingers pointed upwards.
Lissom willows bend
Their silver leaves cast dappled shade
Upon the dimpled bosom
Of the placid, dreaming stream.

If nothing touches the palm leaves
They do not rustle.

　　　　—An African Proverb.

A DRAWING FOR

COPPER SUN, *by Charles Cullen*
Courtesy of Harper and Bros.

VERISIMILTUDE

By JOHN P. DAVIS

I am a rather young man, with no especial knack for writing, who has a story to tell. I want to tell it as I feel it—without restraint—but I can't do that. Critics are already waxing sarcastic about this way of doing things. They think it is too emotional, too melodramatic. I am going to attempt to tell the story I have in me without any fuss or sensation. To achieve "grandeur of generality," to attain the "universal" rather than the "specific"—these are the things I am trying to do. I want you to say when you have finished reading: "That reminds me of . . . ," or "There are thousands like that character; I may never have known one, but there are thousands, thousands. There must be."

Now you can help me, if you will forget everything else in the world except this story. Whether it actually happened or not is of little consequence. The important thing is that it might have happened, that, in mathematical or scientific terms, given such causes working on such characters, the results about which I am going to tell you would have happened. If at any time you feel that there is something in the story that couldn't happen on your own main street then stop reading. I don't want to create monsters, but real, living characters.

Now this is the story of a man. A man is the hero of most stories. Man is the hero of life. This man was a Negro. Negroes are common enough. There are fifteen million, more or less, in the United States alone. This Negro man was in love. Love is the theme of ninety percent of all fiction. I doubt that it is the theme of ninety per cent of life. But no matter, it is common enough in these days.

The next fact in the plot may seem to point the way to something grotesque, something that veers away off from the center of normal human existence like a comet. The Negro man loved a white woman. Are you disappointed already? Well, I am sorry. But I was a census-taker in Virginia. And you woud be surprised at the number of cases of intermarriage I found. That is why they passed an anti-intermarriage law there. There are such laws in nearly all southern states. There must be a reason back of these statutes. Legislatures don't pass laws for nothing. So it wouldn't be strange if I wrote a story about a Negro man who loved a white woman and married her. But I have no intention of marrying my characters. In fact my plot exists because they did not marry. I say only that he loved her. Whether she loved him, I leave you to judge when you have read the story.

This Negro man was tall, young, and brown. There is nothing to quarrel with here. I haven't said he was handsome. Surely, young, tall, brown Negro bundle-wrappers in down-town New York department stores are common enough not to shock you out of belief. And just as ordinary and matter-of-fact are slim, little, rather-nice-looking white salesgirls.

You see these two characters now, don't you? You see them working side by side ten hours a day. One is selling yard after yard of vari-colored cambric to fat house-wives who are harder to please than you would expect Mrs. J. Pierpont Morgan to be. You see these termagants snarl at the shopgirl and then go to buy cambric at a cheaper price in one of the cut-rate stores. Of course, it is the most natural thing in the world that the shopgirl should get angry and stick her tongue out at them when they have turned their backs.

Take a look at the other character. He is at the end of the counter wrapping up package after package which the girl hands him. He hears the housewives quarrelsome babble. He sees the girl make faces at them. He sympathizes and smiles at her as if to say: "I understand how it is with you." The girl has caught the smile and thrown it back. She wants to talk about that last old biddy who put on the airs of her mistress. And she doesn't see why she shouldn't talk to this bundle-wrapper. He smiled; he would understand. She goes over while there is a lull in the sale of cambric and chats with him about "that old fool who expected to get something for nothing and blamed me because Gimbels charged a cent less per yard for cambric than we did. Why the heck didn't she go there in the first place?" He laughs at the way she got back at the woman. She laughs. The tension is broken. They understand. Isn't all this about as natural and plausible as may be? Put yourself in place of either of the characters. Would you have acted differently?

Common suffering leads to mutual interest. That's why men forced to fight against tyranny form friendships for one another. It is just as plausible, then, that this girl and this man, united by laughter, should form a combine against stupid customers. Talk with a man and you find out that he isn't so different after all. "You can't know a man and hate him," said Woodrow Wilson. The girl, Mame, (we might as well call her that as anything else) probably never heard that statement, but she was human nature just the same. She talked with this bundle-wrapper. Let's call him "Paul." Mame found that Paul went to movies, read the Daily Graphic, and was on the whole a normal human being. She forgot to notice any difference in him. And in the little respites from selling cambric she liked to talk to him about this, that, or the other thing. What they actually said doesn't matter. This will serve as a specimen of what they might have said.

Mame: "I'll sure be glad when six o'clock comes."

Paul: "So will I."

Now right here I had better tell you that I am not trying to reproduce Paul's southern accent or Mame's American cockney dialect. How they said things doesn't matter. It is sufficient to give you the impression of what they thought. Your imagination will have to do the rest.

Paul: "Have you heard anything about the new rule for closing on Saturdays beginning in June?"

Mame: "I haven't heard anything definite, but I certainly hope they do."

But enough of this. The things they talked about, then, were just every-day matters-of-fact about work, life, and movies. Paul never tried to go any farther. Mame never said more than: "See you tomorrow," when she pulled the black cloth over the cambric counter and arranged her cloche hat on her sleek round head.

In real life things don't continue as they began ever. You come to know a person as an acquaintance. Then you are thrown into more intimate contact with him. After that it isn't long before you like him better or like him less. That was the case with Abelard and Heloise. It was true of Paul and Mame.

It won't take much imagination to suppose that Mame lived on 119th street and Paul on 131st. White people live on 119th; black people inhabit 131st. It shouldn't strain your fancy either to imagine that they both usually rode home from work on top of a Seventh Avenue bus. Suppose that coming out from work one evening, some two or three months after their first laugh together, Mame should be waiting for a bus at the same time and the same corner as Paul. This might not have happened. Paul might have lived in Brooklyn and Mame have been accustomed to going home on the subway. But it isn't being sensational to throw characters together to aid the action of the plot. So they did meet each other one night about a quarter after six o'clock waiting for a bus. Paul tipped his hat; Mame smiled. Bus Number Two came along crowded. They went up to the top. There was one seat vacant. They sat down together. They talked of everything you think they would talk about. There were no distractions to interrupt their conversation. They talked as they passed throngs of tired everyday toilers pouring out of stores and warehouses at 42nd street. They talked as they passed alongside Central Park. They talked as the bus trundled into upper Seventh Avenue. Mame got off at 119th street. She smiled and said good-bye. There are flaws in this little episode, I admit. A little too much coincidence. A bit too little motivation. But if you are not too fastidious a reader, I think you will let it pass. For at least it is within the realms of plausibility.

Let us say that Paul and Mame did not meet again for a week, two weeks, a month. But don't let us say they never met again. They did. Perhaps Paul covertly planned it. Perhaps Mame did. That doesn't matter. They met. That is sufficient. And they met several times. In fact, it became a habit for them to ride up on the bus together. Am I losing reality? I think not. You see after all the thing I am suggesting is a mere mechanical detail. Although I handle it clumsily, the intrinsic design of the life I am trying to depict cannot be destroyed.

"So far so good," you say, "but whither go we?" or, if you incline to slang, "What has their riding home from work together got to do with the wholesale price of onions?" The answer is simple. It was on such occasions that Mame found in Paul something she liked. What was the "something," you ask? Say Mame discovered that Paul was going to night school in preparation for a clerical examination for a position in the municipal department of New York. Not much to admire from your point of view. But suppose all Mame's life had been one of crowded tenements. Say she lived with a cross old aunt, wanted an escape, wanted to get away from hum-drum life, to be something better, to marry a decent man—(God knows every woman wants that.) Every woman admires a man who is doing things. And Paul from Mame's point of view was doing things. She said to herself: "This colored fellow is different from anybody else I've ever known. He is a man. I like him. I wish Albert (let Albert be what we Americans would call Mame's "steady feller") I wish Albert would go to night school."

And Paul probably thought: "This white girl is a lot less stuck-up than some colored girls I know. She's darn decent to talk with me like this. I wonder if she would go to the movies some night with me."

Here we are hundreds of sentences and thousands of words from the beginning and never a sign of complications. Well, they will be with us in a moment. First I must get Paul and Mame in love. I could spare myself a great deal of tedious detail by just saying they came to love one another. But you would not believe me. All readers come from Missouri. Anyway I am going to compromise with principle and say that Paul came to love Mame first because of novelty and then because he was forced to admire a woman who broke convention to love him. And Mame fell in love with Paul because to her he represented a somewhat better man than any other she had ever known. The process of falling in love is an evasive thing at best. You somehow know you are in love, but when and how and, above all, why defy analysis. It is an elusive something. Say, then, that these two characters fell in love. If you want a dash of sentiment say they saw dawn in each others eyes. There are lovers that do. If you are practical say Mame saw possibilities of a three room apartment and no more drudgery. Repeat for emphasis: they fell in love. What about Albert. Well, let Albert be a wastrel, a drunkard, a loafer. You will find a great many like him. Doubtless, you know a few.

I promised you complications. Life demands them as well as you. Complications? Here they are. Paul takes Mame to see Lya de Putti in "Variety" at the Rialto. A colored fellow whom he knows sees them. Next morning all Harlem is gossiping about Paul who has turned "pink-chaser"—(apologies to Mr. Carl Van

Vechten). When Harlem talks about you it means that you feel curious eyes staring at you. The spirit of scandal stalks your path. People you know avert their eyes as you pass. Stand on the street corner and you stand alone. That is the effect of the colored Mrs. Grundy on a man. The white Mrs. Grundy may look different, but "the lady and Judy O'Grady are sisters under the skins." On 119th street houses have just as many eyes as on 131st. So when Mame let Paul take her home once or twice, people talked. Albert heard about it and "raised Hell." The aunt heard about it and threatened to kick Mame out if she didn't stop "going around with a nigger." Mame looked guilty.

Does this suit you? You have the sunshine and now you see the clouds. Are you worried? You should be. I am not one to lead you up to tragedy and then turn aside to talk about flowers. Well, you know and I know that life wouldn't let this end happily. There has got to be death, there has got to be sorrow. And since it must be, let it come soon.

But I am not quite ready for the show-down. Like a woman who powders her nose before every great moment of her life, I must hesitate, demur—in a word—build up suspense. We need emotional intensification here. For that purpose let Paul be happy enough with Mame to forget the snubs of his own people. Let Mame pacify her aunt temporarily by threatening to leave and thus deplete the family revenue eleven dollars a week. The eleven dollars represents Mame's contribution for room and board. Leave a cancerous wound in the souls of both characters, if you must; but let them live yet awhile. For, like Alamanzor, they have "not leisure yet to die."

Don't be provoked with me. Don't accuse me of "playing in wench-like words with something serious." Peace! brother. Peace! sister. All will be clear in only a little while. Soon you will know. Soon you will sit back in your chair and see Mame and Paul as duly garnished sacrifices. And whether you like them or not, you will know them as they are.

Paul and Mame were happy. They went to Staten Island on picnics. They went to movies. Paul gave Mame candy. Mame gave Paul a tie for his birthday. And love—the ideal of humanity—lived in their hearts. Or if this is too poetic, just say they enjoyed being with one another. I have not explained their love fully enough, maybe—but can you explain it better? If you can, please fill in the facts for yourself.

When two persons become intimate with one another they lose their sense of proportion. They respect neither time, custom, nor place. This fact got Paul and Mame into trouble. They didn't know when it was time to stop talking and pay attention to their work. You see, it was one thing to exchange a few commonplaces while at work; but, it was quite another to delay customers or to smile at each other while the world was waiting for a yard of cambric. Business men know such delays irritate their customers. That is why they hire floor-managers to snoop on their salesgirls. You see what I am driving at, don't you? I am getting Paul and Mame into more trouble. Soon I'll have them discharged. But, not before I give a sidelight on the episode.

Shopgirls have had love affairs before. They have kept customers waiting before; and have got away with it under the very eyes of floor managers. It isn't enough, therefore, for me to offer this as the only excuse for getting Mame and Paul discharged. But I can suggest others. A young Negro man talking to a young white woman for more than five minutes is always subject to suspicion. And when this is repeated again and again, scandal gets busy. You know this as well as I do. There is still another reason. Perhaps, you remember Albert. I shouldn't have had any justification for naming him if I did not intend to weave him into the plot. It would have been faulty technique. So Albert comes in here. He enters through the department store door and makes his way to the cambric counter. Now he is on the scene. He is half-drunk and a little loud. It is ten-thirty in the morning and Albert has come to tell Paul that he had better "damn sight" leave his woman alone—all white women, in fact. That's just what Albert did. He "bawled Paul out" right before a crowd of people. And Mame couldn't keep her temper. She turned red in the face. She dug her nails in her hands and wanted to fly at Albert. Paul held her back. He put his arm around her. The crowd grew larger. A policeman took Albert away. That is all there is for Albert to do in this story. The floor-manager whispered something to Paul and about two hours later both Paul and Mame had their salaries in little manila envelopes. You can't blame the floor-manager very much. It was for the good of the business. Anyway as he told Paul, he had noticed for some time that they were not paying attention to business. He didn't get angry. He was simply hard, cold and matter-of-fact. That was all.

Here we are facing the climax of this personally conducted tour of a short story. Mame and Paul are out of a job. They have to live. Mame is crying. Life seems unfair, bitter, unkind. Don't weep because Mame did. Stand on the sidelines and see the show. What are Hecuba's tears to you, or Mame's? I only record that she wept because, under the circumstances, I think she would have done so. Paul gritted his teeth. They would get a job soon, he told her. And it wouldn't be long before he would be able to take the clerical examination. Then they could get married and go to Atlantic City for a honeymoon. All that is needed here is a little time and a little sanity. But life would cease to be a tragedy, if time would wait for us. The harsh reality, the bitterness of life comes because everything in the world is run by clocks and whistles. Time to get up. Time to retire. Time to live. And time to die. To use a slang expression—Mame and Paul "didn't get the break."

If you have ever hunted for a job in New York, you know what it is like to do so. Your feet hurt after the first two or three days. You get tired of being told that there are no vacancies. Sometimes you go back to the same place on five or six occasions before you can find the employment manager in his office, and then he only shakes his head. Sometimes you think you've got a job; then you are asked where you worked last, how long, why you quit, if you have any references. Your heart sinks and you go out of the door of the inner office, through the outer office, down the elevator and out into the street. And all the time you are saying to yourself: "Oh God, dear God, am I your creature?" A man can stand a great deal more of this sort of thing than a woman. Mame gave up; Paul lasted. There were other reasons for Mame's surrender but this had its share in the result.

Mame, I have said, contributed eleven dollars a week to her aunt. A week or so after she was fired her contributions ceased. Mame hadn't saved up much. Soon that was gone. You understand how that might happen, I know. Money doesn't come from the skies. And the girl's name was Mame and not Cinderella. Mame's aunt was angry with Mame in the first place for "taking up with a nigger." She was angrier when Mame lost her job. "I-told-you-so's" dinned in Mame's ears and buzzed in her head. It was too much for the aunt to stand when Mame couldn't pay her the eleven dollars. Mame had to do one thing or the other: "either get out or give up that nigger." Those were the aunt's own words. Do you think that the aunt is too hard a character? Read any metropolitan daily. The world is getting hard and cold. All the world wants is money. Money was all Mame's aunt wanted. So she turned Mame out. But she wasn't altogether cold. She didn't really mean to turn her out. She wanted only to each Mame a lesson. After all blood is thicker than water. She didn't believe Mame would really go. She wanted her to stop being a fool and come down to earth. There were plenty of decent young white men she could marry. It was infatuation or something that got Mame this way. If she had her way, she'd either put Mame in the insane asyum or that "nigger" in jail. Whoever heard of such "carryings-on?" She was tired of having people talk about her. She wasn't going to be related to a "nigger" even by marriage.

Don't blame Mame's aunt any more than you did the floor-manager or Albert. All—all of them are just cogs in the wheels of the world. If you must fume and fret, say simply that all the world's a pasture and each one in the world, a jackass.

This is what human beings such as Mame's aunt and Albert and the floor-manager might have done to such a girl as Mame. What would Mame have done? Probably, gone to Paul. She did. But he could not take care of her. He had no money. He was being threatened himself with being put out of his rooming house because he didn't pay his rent. It was a poor time to try to bring a young, unmarried white woman into a respectable Harlem rooming house. Go . . . go where? Somewhere, you say? But where? There are streets. But streets in New York are either covered with soft, cold snow, or melted by the rays of a hot blazing sun. Try living in New York without money. Try living anywhere without money. Friends, you suggest? I wish I could. But where are friends when your aunt turns you out of doors and you have done what Mame had done? Then, who with pride would go a begging? Only one thing remains: it whispers in your ear every time there seems no way out—suicide.

Suicide isn't normal. Only abnormal people think of it. Joy may drop from you like a dead bird from a leafless tree, but, somehow, life is still sweet. But too much defeat, too much bitterness make people abnormal. Consider a woman who has drudged all her life; put her in Mame's place. You will find that she is like the string on a violin: draw her too tightly and she snaps. Something snapped in Mame. She kissed Paul goodnight in the park, spent her last dollar and a half to get a room in a settlement house—and turned on the gas. Don't blame Paul. He didn't know she was going to commit suicide. He thought he would see her the next day. Don't say Mame isn't true to life. If you believe she is not, live her life over. Spend two months looking for a job; wandering willy-nilly. Then put her back into the picture as a human being. I think you will succeed.

What about Paul. There isn't much to tell. He stood it. He stood Mame's death. But how he stood it I leave you to imagine. You will agree that he grew bitter. You will not agree that he would commit suicide. That is the sort of melodramatic thing I want to avoid. I am sorry Mame had to commit suicide. But I don't see how she could help it. Do you?

Suppose that after Mame's death Paul got a job as a longshoreman on the New York docks. Not as clerk in the municipal department, mind you. He had given up night school when he lost his job. Then Mame had died and he hadn't gone back. He was bitter, he grew cynical . . . No money, no job, Mame, were the causes. He might have got over it some time, but that time didn't come. Is this anti-climactic? Not quite. Remember Paul is really the chief character.

When you have gone through what Paul went through, you won't be happy and optimistic. You are apt to look on the world and people in it as just so much damned rot. You are apt to walk around with a chip on your shoulder. And a chip on your shoulder doesn't help you any if you are a longshoreman. They are hard working, hard swearing, sweating Negroes, Irish and what-nots—these longshore gangs. And the dock is no place for Hamlet. Even Falstaff would have a hard time getting along. You've got to laugh loudly, work hard, and mix with the gang. Paul did none of these things. He felt just a little above them. He was always moody, introspective, hard to get along with. Even Negroes despised him. You can imagine the opinion that the Irish held.

Under the circumstances can't you imagine Paul becoming a flaming pillar of rage when an Irish longshore boss yelled at him: "Hey, nigger, stop dreaming and go to work. Yes I mean you, you son of a . . . ." But the Irish fellow didn't finish his oath.

Paul hit him over the head with a chisel. Chisels are common on the docks. They are used to open boxes. Paul opened the fellows head with one. He didn't kill him. The Irish foreman lived to testify against Paul. He was quite well when the District Attorney painted a gaudy word picture of how Paul lost his last job. He saw twelve ordinary men, readers of the Daily Graphic, cigar salesmen, shopkeepers, butchers, insurance agents—all, somehow, a little influenced by the way Paul glared at people in the courtroom and by the District Attorney's subtle suggestion that Paul had been the cause of a white woman's suicide. Of course, they thought more about the affair than actually happened. Can't you see that District Attorney? He's running on the State ticket next year. He's got to make a record. Some cases he can't prosecute to win. Politics won't let him. Here is one in which he can have a free hand. Here he can make a name for himself. Look at the jury. They don't know much about sociology, but they know where to get the best beer in New York City. Look at the judge. He's a scholarly man, but he's sick of the crime wave. Something's got to be done. And Paul to him is obviously a criminal. Look at the young man who calls himself a lawyer. He is defending Paul and he means well. But his best is not good enough. Maybe next year or year after he'll be a good lawyer. Paul won't smile, he won't plead. He is obstinate. I think you will find little fault with the verdict. Guilty. The law is the law. He was lucky to get only seven years.

I have outlined this story and set it in New York. If you like you may write it to please your taste and set it any place under the sun. The results would not vary a great deal. If you must have a happy ending, pardon Paul, or, bring him back from prison and regenerate him. But I doubt if you will succeed. It is hard to get a pardon. It is harder to reform a man who looks on life pessimistically for seven years. At least grant that what I have outlined is true or might be true. As someone has written (a Jewish poet, I think):

> The sum and substance of the tale is this
> The rest is but the mise en scéne
> And if I have painted it amiss
> I am a prattler and a charlatan.

Oh yes, you will want a moral. I had forgot. Take it from Shakespeare:—
> "Golden lads and girls all must
> Like chimney sweepers come to dust."

UNDERGRADUATE VERSE
FISK UNIVERSITY

NIGHT
By T. Thomas Fortune Fletcher

Night in the South
Is a black mother
Mourning for murdered sons
And ravished daughters.

LIFE
By Richard Jefferson

Life is a woman's tongue
That babbles on and on
Till quick, impatient death
Weary of hearing it
Constantly rave
Conceals it

WHITE GOD

God is white,
Why should I pray?
If I called Him,
He'd turn away.

POEM
By Richard Jefferson

I longed to write a poem of life,
One that was fierce and bitter, wild.
But wrote of stars when once I saw
A white man strangle his black child.

Mrs. Bailey Pays The Rent

By IRA DE A. REID

Won't you come home Bill Bailey?
Won't you come home,"
She mourns the whole day long.
"I'll do the cooking, I'll pay the rent,
I know I've done you wrong.
Remember that rainy evening
I drove you out,
With nothing but a fine tooth comb?
Aint that a shame,
I know I'm to blame,
Bill Bailey, won't you please come home?"
—Old popular song.

FOR many years it has been the custom of certain portions of the Negro group living in Southern cities to give some form of party when money was needed to supplement the family income. The purpose for giving such a party was never stated, but who cared whether the increment was used to pay the next installment on the "Stineway" piano, or the weekly rent? On the one hand, these parties were the life of many families of a low economic status who sought to confine their troubles with a little joy. On the other hand, they were a wild form of commercialized recreation in its primary stages. Humor was the counterpart of their irony.

No social standing was necessary to promote these affairs. Neither was one forced to have a long list of friends. All that the prospective host required to "throw" such an affair would be a good piano player and a few girls. Of course you paid an admission fee—usually ten cents—which was for the benefit of some Ladies Auxiliary —though it may have been an auxiliary to that particular house. The music invited you, and the female of the species urged that you remain. The neighborhood girls came unescorted, but seldom left alone. Dancing was the diversion and there is no reason to doubt that these affairs were properly named "SHIN-DIGS."

There was "Beaver Slide," that supposedly rough section of the Negro district, situated in the hollow between two typically Georgian Hills. Here lived a more naive group of Negroes whose sociables were certain to make the passers by take notice. The motto for their affairs seemed to be "Whosoever will let him come, and may the survived survive." Twenty to thirty couples packed into two small rooms, "slow-dragging" to the plaintive blues of the piano player, whose music had a boss accompaniment furnished by his feet. The piano was opened top and front that the strains may be more distinct, and that the artist may have the joy of seeing as well as hearing his deft touches (often played by "ear") reflected in the mechanics of the instrument. They were a free-"joy-unconfined" group. Their conventions were their own. If they wished to guffaw they did—if they wished to fight they did. But they chiefly danced— not with the aloofness of a modern giglio but with fervor. What a picture they presented! Women in ginghams or cheap finery, men in peg top trousers, silk shirts, "loud" arm bands, and the ever present tan shoes with the "bull dog" toe. Feet stamped merrily—songs sung cheerily—No blues writer can ever record accurately the tones and words of those songs—they are to be heard and not written—bodies sweating, struggling in their effort to get the most of the dance; a drink of "lightning" to accelerate the enthusiasm—floors creaking and sagging—everybody happy.

During the dance as well as the intermission, you bought your refreshments. This was a vital part of the evening's enjoyment. But what food you could get for a little money! Each place had its specialties—"Hoppinjohn," (rice and black-eyed peas) or Mulatto rice (rice and tomatoes). Okra gumbo, Sweet potato pone—sometimes Chicken—Chitterlings—Hog maws—or other strictly southern dishes. You ate your fill. Dancing was resumed and continued until all were ready to leave—or it had suddenly ended in a brawl causing the "Black Maria" to take some to the station house and the police sending the remaining folk to their respective homes.

And there were those among us who had a reverential respect for such affairs. At that time there was no great popularity attached to a study of the Negro in his social environment. These were just plain folks having a good time. On the other hand, they were capable of description, and to those of us who knew, they were known as "struggles," "break-downs," "razor-drills," "flop-wallies" and "chitterling parties." These they were in fact as well as fancy. It was a struggle to dance in those crowded little rooms, while one never knew if the cheaply constructed flooring would collapse in the midst of its sagging and creaking. What assurance did one have that the glistening steel of a razor or "switch blade" would not flash before the evening's play was done? And very often chitterlings were served—yet by the time forty sweating bodies had danced in a small parlor with one window—a summer's evening—and continued to dance—well the party still deserved that name. But Mrs. Bailey paid her rent.

NEWS ITEM: "Growing out of economic stress, this form of nocturnal diversion has taken root in Harlem—that section known as the world's largest Negro centre. Its correct and more dignified name is "Parlor Social," but in the language of the street, it is caustically referred to as a "house rent party."

With the mass movement of Southern Negroes to Northern Cities, came their little custom. Harlem was astounded. Socially minded individuals claimed that the H.C.L. with the relative insufficiency of wages was entirely responsible for this ignominious situation; that the exorbitant rents paid by the Negro wage earners had given rise to the obnoxious "house rent party." The truth seemed to be that the old-party of the South had attired itself à la Harlem. Within a few years the custom developed into a business venture whereby a tenant sought to pay a rent four, five and six times as great as was paid in the South. It developed by-products both legal and otherwise, hence it became extremely popular.

There has been an evolution in the eclat of the rent party since it has become "Harlemized." The people have seen a new light, and are no longer wont to have it go unnamed. They called it a "Parlor Social." That term, however, along with "Rent Party" is for the spoken word. "Social Whist Party" looks much better in print and has become the prevailing terminology. Nor is its name restricted to these. Others include "Social Party," "Too Terrible Party," "Too Bad Party," "Matinee Party," "Parlor Social," "Whist Party," and "Social Entertainment." And, along with the change in nomenclature has come a change in technique. No longer does the entrepreneur depend upon the music to welcome his stranger guests; nor does he simply invite friends of the neighborhood. The rent party ticket now turns the trick.

There straggles along the cross-town streets of North Harlem a familiar figure. A middle aged white man, bent from his labor as the Wayside Printer, is pushing a little cart which has all of the equipment necessary for setting up the rent party ticket. The familiar tinkle of his bell in the late afternoon brings the representative of some family to his side. While you wait, he sets up your invitation with the bally-ho heading desired, and at a very reasonable price. The grammar and the English may be far from correct, but they meet all business requirements since they bring results. What work the Wayside Printer does not get goes to the nearest print shop; some of which specialize in these announcements.

A true specimen of the popular mind is expressed in these tickets. The heading may be an expression from a popular song, a slang phrase, a theatrical quip or "poetry." A miscellaneous selection gives us the following: "Come and Get it Fixed"; "Leaving Me Papa, It's Hard To Do Because Mama Done Put That Thing On You"; "If You Can't Hold Your Man, Don't Cry After He's Gone, Just Find Another"; "Clap Your Hands Here Comes Charlie and He's Bringing Your Dinah Too"; "Old Uncle Joe, the Jelly Roll King is Back in Town and is Shaking That Thing"; "Here I am Again. Who? Daddy Jelly Roll and His Jazz Hounds"; "It's Too Bad Jim, But if You Want To Find a Sweet Georgia Brown, Come to the House of Mystery"; "You Don't Get Nothing for Being an Angel Child, So you Might as Well Get Real Busy and Real Wild".

And at various parties we find special features, among them being "Music by the Late Kidd Morgan"; "Music by Kid Professor, the Father of the Piano"; "Music by Blind Johnny"; "Music by Kid Lippy"; "Skinny At the Traps"; "Music Galore"; "Charge De Affairs Bessie and Estelle"; "Here You'll Hear that Sweet Story That's Never Been Told;" "Refreshments to Suit"; "Refreshments by 'The Cheater'." All of these present to the average rent party habitueé a very definite picture of what is to be expected, as the card is given to him on the street corner, or at the subway station.

The parties outdo their publicity. There is always more than has been announced on the public invitation. Though no mention was made of an admission fee, one usually pays from twenty-five to fifty cents for this privilege. The refreshments are not always refreshing, but are much the same as those served in parts of the South, with gin and day-old Scotch extra. The Father of the Piano lives up to his reputation as he accompanies a noisy trap drummer, or a select trio composed of fife, guitar, and saxophone.

Apart from the admission fee and the sale of food, and drinks, the general tenor of the party is about the same as one would find in a group of "intellectual liberals" having a good time. Let us look at one. We arrived a little early—about nine-thirty o'clock. The ten persons present, were dancing to the strains of the Cotton Club Orchestra via radio. The drayman was just bringing two dozen chairs from a nearby undertaker's establishment, who rents them for such affairs. The hostess introduced herself, asked our names, and politely informed us that the "admittance fee" was thirty-five cents, which we paid. We were introduced to all, the hostess not remembering a single name. Ere the formality was over, the musicians, a piano player, saxophonist, and drummer, had arrived and immediately the party took on life. We learned that the saxophone player had been in big time vaudeville; that he could make his instrument "cry"; that he had quit the stage to play for the parties because he wanted to stay in New York.

There were more men than women, so a poker game was started in the next room, with the woman who did not care to dance, dealing. The music quickened the dancers. They sang "Muddy Water, round my feet—ta-ta-ta-ta-ta-ta-ta". One girl remarked— "Now this party's getting right." The hostess informed us of the menu for the evening —Pig feet and Chili—Sandwiches à la carte, and of course if you were thirsty, there was some "good stuff" available. Immediately, there was a rush to the kitchen, where the man of the house served your order.

For the first time we noticed a man who made himself conspicuous by his watchdog attitude toward all of us. He was the "Home Defense Officer," a private detective who was there to forestall any outside interference, as well as prevent any losses on the inside on account of the activity of the "Clean-up Men." There were two clean-up men there that night and the H.D.O. had to be particularly careful lest they walk away with two or three fur coats or some of the household furnishings. Sometimes these men would be getting the "lay" of the apartment for a subsequent visit.

There was nothing slow about this party. Perfect strangers at nine o'clock were boon companions at eleven. The bedroom had become the card room—a game of "skin" was in progress on the floor while dice were rolled on the bed. There was something "shady" about the dice game, for one of the players was always having his dice caught. The musicians were still exhorting to the fifteen or twenty couples that danced. Bedlam reigned. It stopped for a few minutes while one young man hit another for getting fresh with his girl while dancing. The H.D.O. soon ended the fracas.

About two o'clock, a woman from the apartment on the floor below rang the bell and vociferously demanded that this noise stop or that she would call an officer. The hostess laughed in her face and slammed the door. Some tenants are impossible! This was sufficient however, to call the party to a halt. The spirit—or "spirits" had been dying by degrees. Everybody was tired—some had "dates"—others were sleepy— while a few wanted to make a cabaret before "curfew hour." Mrs. Bailey calmly surveyed a disarranged apartment, and counted her proceeds.

And so the rent party goes on. In fact, it has been going from bad to worse. Harlem copyists of Greenwich Village give them now—for the lark of it. Not always is it a safe and sane affair. Too many evils have crept in, professional gamblers, confidence men, crooks looking for an accomplice for the night, threats of fights with revolvers and razors drawn—any or all of these things may appear in one party. You are seldom certain of your patrons. However, one entrepreneur is always certain of her guests. She invites only members of the Street Cleaning Department and their friends. She extends the invitation *Viva Voce* from the front window of her apartment. The occupant in the apartment below her once complained to the court of the noise in the course of her parties. The court advised that if the noise were too great she should move. She remained.

At the same time, there may be tragedies. The New York Age carried an editorial sometime ago on a "Rent Party Tragedy." At this affair one woman killed another woman about a third member of the species. The editorial states in part:

> "One of these rent parties a few weeks ago was the scene of a tragic crime in which one jealous woman cut the throat of another, because the two were rivals for the affections of a third woman. The whole situation was on a par with the recent Broadway play, imported from Paris, although the underworld tragedy took place in this locality,—In the mean-

time, the combination of bad gin, jealous women, a carving knife, and a rent party is dangerous to the health of all concerned."

Nowadays, no one knows whether or not one is attending a bonafide rent party. The party today may be fostered by the Tenants Protective Association, or the Imperial Scale of Itinerant Musicians, or the Society for the Relief of Ostracized Bootleggers. Yes, all of these foster parties, though the name is one of fancy. Musicians and Bootleggers have to live as well as the average tenant, and if they can combine their efforts on a business proposition, the status of both may be improved.

It has become in some quarters, a highly commercial affair. With the increased overhead expenses—printing of tickets, hiring the Home Defense Officer, renting chairs, hiring the musicians—one has to make the venture pay.

But the rent parties have not been so frequent of late. Harlem's new dance halls with their lavish entertainment, double orchestra, and "sixteen hours of continuous dancing", with easy chairs and refreshments available are ruining the business. They who continue in this venture of pleasure and business are working on a very close margin both socially and economically, when one adds the complexity illustrated by the following incident:

A nine year old boy gazed up from the street to his home on the "top floor, front, East side" of a tenement on West 134th Street about eleven thirty on a Friday night. He waited until the music stopped and cried, "Ma! Ma! I'm sleepy. Can I come in now?" To which a male voice, the owner of which had thrust his head out of the window, replied,—"Your ma says to go to the Midnight Show, and she'll come after you. Here's four bits. She says the party's just got going good."

SONNET TO A NEGRO IN HARLEM
By HELENE JOHNSON

You are disdainful and magnificent—
Your perfect body and your pompous gait,
Your dark eyes flashing sullenly with hate,
Small wonder that you are incompetent
To imitate those whom you so despise—
Your shoulders towering high above the throng,
Your head thrown back in rich, barbaric song,
Palm trees and mangoes stretched before your eyes.
Let others toil and sweat for labor's sake
And wring from grasping hands their meed of gold.
Why urge ahead your supercilious feet?
Scorn will efface each footprint that you make.
I love your laughter arrogant and bold.
You are too splendid for this city street!

TOKENS

By Gwendolyn B. Bennett

IGH on the bluff of Saint Cloud stands the Merlin Hospital, immaculate sentinel of Seraigne . . . Seraigne with its crazy houses and aimless streets, scrambling at the foot of Saint Cloud's immense immutability. Row on row the bricks of the hospital take dispassionate account of lives lost or found. It is always as though the gay, little town of Seraigne were thumbing its nose at Saint Cloud with its famous Merlin Hospital where life is held in a test-tube, a thing to be caught or lost by a drop or two of this or a pellet of that. And past the rustic stupidity of Seraigne's gaiety lies the wanton unconcern of the Seine. The Seine . . . mute river of sorrows . . . grim concealer of forgotten secrets . . . endlessly flowing . . . touching the edges of life . . . moving purposefully along with a grey disdain for the empty, foolish gaiety of Seraigne or the benign dignity of Merlin Hospital, high on the warm cliffs of Saint Cloud.

A trim nurse had drawn Jenks Barnett's chair out onto one of the balconies that over-looked the Seine. Listlessly, aimlessly he turned his thoughts to first one aspect and then another of the Seine, Merlin Hospital, the cliffs of Saint Cloud, Seraigne . . . over and again . . . the Seine, Merlin Hospital, the cliffs . . . of . . . Saint . . . Cloud . . . silly, little Seraigne. It was a better way—that Seine business. Just swallow up life and sorrow and sadness . . . don't bother about the poor fools who are neither dead nor alive . . . just hanging on to the merest threads of existence . . . coughing out one's heart and yet somehow still keeping heart. Purposeless thoughts these as one just as purposelessly fingers the blanket that covers one's emaciated, almost lifeless legs. But the Seine goes on, and Seraigne continues to be happy, and the pain in one's chest grows no easier.

It so happened that at this particular time there were a number of colored patients at the Merlin Hospital. Most of them were musicians who had remained in Paris after the World War. Two of them had come to London and thence to Paris with Will Marion Cook in the Negro entertainer's heyday. Jenks was one of these. He had been a singer in those days. His voice was now spoken of in the hushed tones one uses when speaking of the dead. He had cherished great plans for himself in those days and no one dared hope otherwise, so rare was his voice in range and quality. That was all changed now. . . .

Merlin Hospital had won nation-wide fame as a haven for patients suffering from tuberculosis. An able staff of doctors and nurses administered daily hope of recovery to broken bodies or perhaps kindly, although inadequate, solace to those whose cases were hopeless. Jenks Barnett had been there five weeks. His case was one of the hopeless ones. The tale of his being there did not take long in the telling. Shortly after the success of Cook's orchestra with its inimitable "singing trombonist" Tollie had come—Tollie Saunders with her golden voice and lush laughter. From the very first she and Jenks had hit it off well together. It was not long before he was inextricably enmeshed in the wonder of her voice and the warm sweetness of her body. Dinner at Les Acacias . . . for Tollie . . . a hat for her lovely head . . . that dress in Chanal's window . . . she wanted one of those large opal rings . . . long nights of madness under the charm of her flute-sweet voice. His work began to suffer. Soon he was dismissed from the orchestra. Singing *soirees* didn't pay too well. And then one day before the pinch of poverty came Tollie had left him, taking with her all the pretty things he had given her . . . leaving no farewell . . . her chance had come to sing in an American production and she had gone. No word of their plan to startle the singing world with their combined talents; no hint of regret that she was leaving . . . just gone. Three nights on a gorgeous drunk and he had awakened to find himself in a dingy, damp Parisian jail with a terrific pain in his back . . . eighteen days in which he moved from one prison-house to another . . . sunshine and air again when his friends had finally found him and arranged for his release . . . sunshine lasts but a short time in Paris . . . endless days of splashing through the Paris rain in search of a job . . . always that pain between his shoulder-blades . . . then night upon night of blowing a trombone in a stuffy little *Boite de Nuit* during which time he forgot the pain in his back . . . and drink . . . incessant drink . . . one more drink with the fellows . . . and after the job cards and more drink. One came to Merlin after one had been to the American Hospital. One came to Merlin after one had been to every other hospital round about Paris. It does not take long to become accustomed to the turning knife in one's chest. It is good for a hopeless case to watch the uncurbed forgetfulness of the Seine.

Spring had sent ahead its perfume this day. It was as though the early March air were powdered with the pollen of many unborn flowers. A haze settled itself in the air and on the breast of the river. Jenks forgot for a moment the relentless ache in his bosom and breathed deeply in sheer satisfaction. In the very midst of this gesture of aliveness the tool of death, lodged in his lung, gave a wrench. A hacking cough rose in his throat and then seemed to become stuck there. His great, gaunt frame was shaken in a paroxysm of pain. The fit of stifled coughing over, his head fell back upon the pillow. A nurse hurried to his side. "Guess you'd better go in now. I told you not to move around."

With quick, efficient hands she tucked the cover more closely about his legs, lowered the back of the invalid chair in which he was sitting, and pushed him carefully back into the hospital. As his chair was rolled through the ward it was as though he were running the gamut of scorn. Jenks was not a favorite at the hospital by any stretch of the imagination. Few of the patients there had escaped the lash of his tongue. Sour at life and the raw deal it had dealt him, he now turned his attention to venting his spume on those about him. Nurses, doctors, orderlies, fellow-patients, persistent friends . . . all shared alike the blasphemy of his words. Even Bill Jackson, the one friend who continued to brave the sting of his vile tongue, was not spared. Bill had known him and loved him before Tollie came. It was in this memory that he wrapped himself when Jenks was most unbearable. He accused Bill of stealing his money when he asked him to bring him something from the city. . . . There had been many who had tried to make Jenks' last days easier but one by one they had begun to stay away until now there was only Bill left. Little wonder the other patients in the hospital heaped invective upon him as he passed.

So thin he was as he lay beneath the covers of the bed that his knees and chest made scarcely perceptible mounds in the smooth whiteness of the bed. The brown of his face had taken on the color of dried mud. Great seams folded themselves in his cheeks. There he lay, the rotting hulk of what he had once been. He had sent for Bill . . . these waiting moments were so long!

"Hi there, Jenks" . . . it was Bill's cheery voice . . . "thought you'd be outside."

"Can't go out no more. Nearly kicked off the other day."

"Thas all right . . . you'll come around all right."

"For God sakes cut it out. I know I'm done for. You know it, too, damn it all."

"Come on now, fella, be your age. You can't last long if you get yourself all worked up. Take it easy."

"Oh I get so damned sick of the whole business I wish I would hurry up and die. But whose business is that but mine . . . got somethin' to tell you."

"Shoot."

"See I'm dyin' . . . get me. They keep stickin' that needle in me but I know damn well I'm dyin'. Now what I want you to do is this . . . I wrote a letter to Tollie when I first came here . . . it's in her picture in my suit-case . . . you know that silver frame. Well when I die I want you to give it to

her, if it's a thousand years from now . . . just a token of the time when we were in love. Don't forget it. Then you remember that French kid that used to be on the ward downstairs . . . she always liked that radium clock of mine. She's been transferred to the Gerboux Sanitarium . . . almost well now. I think they said she would be out in a year. Good kid . . . used to climb up here every afternoon . . . stairs sort of wore her out, too. Give her my clock and tell her I hope she lives to be well and strong 'cause I never'll make it. God, she was an angel if ever there was one . . . she used to sit there on that chair where you're sittin' now and just look at me and say how she wished she could die in my place cause I was such a big man . . . and could sing so. . . . I believe she'd like to have something to remember me by. And, Bill, you take . . . that . . . mmmghgummmm . . . mmm. . . ."

That strangling cough rose in his throat. His eyes, always cruel, seemed to look out softly at Bill. A nurse hurried swiftly into the room and injected a hypodermic needle into his arm. A tremor went through his body. His eye-lids half closed . . . he slept.

The days dragged out in one week after another. Jenks lingered on like the days. Outside the Seine flowed endlessly on unhindered and free. It was all so futile and strange . . . waiting this way.

June had laid her warm mouth upon the face of the earth. With soft languor the sun slid tenderly over the cliffs of Saint Cloud . . . even tenderly over the grey bricks of Merlin Hospital. Jenks had raged so about not being allowed to lie on the balcony that at last the hospital authorities had relented . . . there was such a short time left for him anyway . . . he might as well have what he wanted . . . this was the first day that had been warm enough. As he lay there he looked out across the cliffs, past the little town of Seraigne, out past the Seine . . . on . . . on . . . immune to life . . . conversant with death . . . on to the great simplicities. He got to thinking of when he was a boy . . . the songs he used to sing . . . he almost thought he'd try to sing now . . . what did it matter if he got another coughing spell . . . but then the nurses would all be in a flurry. Nice to be out here once more looking at the Seine and the world where people lived and breathed.

Bill sighed as he placed the little clock on the mantle-piece. Funny world, this! The French girl had died in late May. He had better not tell Jenks . . . it might upset him. No-o-ope better just keep the clock here. Funny how the first kind thing Jenks had done for anybody since Tollie left him should be done for a person who was dead.

High on the bluff of Saint Cloud stands the Merlin Hospital, immaculate sentinel of Seraigne . . . with its crazy houses and aimless streets, scrambling at the foot of Saint Cloud's immense immutability. Row on row the bricks of the hospital take dispassionate account of lives lost or found.

A PAGE OF UNDERGRADUATE VERSE

SIGNS OF SPRING
By HERBERT PICKETT
Tougaloo College

One day, the last of winter,
It was warm as any spring—
I sat in my room, on Sunday,
And heard the bluebirds sing.

The buds had begun swelling,
And the peach trees were in bloom;
I could not but feel happy,
And forget the winter's gloom.

It was during silent hour
When I saw a cloud appear,
But the drops were soft and gentle—
A sign that spring was near.

It was after silent hour,
After the shower of rain,
That the last sign came—white trousers—
When we went to see the train!

THE SOUDAN
By CLARENCE F. BUYSON
Cleveland College of Western Reserve University

The brooding, sullen forest nights are filled
With varied sights and smells. The purple dusk
Of shaded jungle paths, where Njega killed
Of oily, bubbling slime; the Lemur's cry,
A wild crescendo, then a baffling shriek
And dined, is thick with sounds: the reeking musk
Of sluggish snakes beside a stagnant creek
That dies away; a snail's sepulchral sigh
Of endless woe; a leopard's coughing roar
Above the tangled skein; the monotone
Of pounding surf against a hostile shore;
The stench from dripping mangrove roots; the groan,
Below the drifting mists, of fetid mud
Where new life stirs in old life's stagnant blood.

NOTE:—Njega, in the Benga dialect, means leopard. It is pronounced Njega or
Nega, i.e. N—yeaga. A giant snail in the French Soudan gives that peculiar remorseful
sigh, which is heard only at night.
Note B:—That Njega is pronounced with two syllables.

DISILLUSION
By LILLIAN BROWN
Tougaloo College

In a far-away wood there lived two monkeys . . .
They went to town on two old grey donkeys . . .
But when they saw what we call "men,"
They decided to go home again.

THE RETURN

By Arna Bontemps

I

Once more, listening to the wind and rain,
Once more, you and I, and above the hurting sound
Of these comes back the throbbing of remembered rain,
Treasured rain falling on dark ground.
Once more, huddling birds upon the leaves
And summer trembling on a withered vine.
And once more, returning out of pain,
The friendly ghost that was your love and mine.

II

The throb of rain is the throb of muffled drums;
Darkness brings the jungle to our room.
Darkness hangs our room with pendulums
Of vine and in the gathering gloom
Our walls recede into a denseness of
Surrounding trees.   This is a night of love
Retained from those lost nights our fathers slept
In huts; this is a night that cannot die.
Let us keep the dance of rain our fathers kept
And tread our dreams beneath the jungle sky.

III

The downpour ceases.
Let us go back, you and I, and dance
Once more upon the glimmering leaves
And as the throbbing of drums increases
Shake the grass and the dripping boughs of trees.
A dry wind stirs the palm; the old tree grieves.
Time has charged the years and they have returned.
Then let us dance by metal waters burned
With gold of moon, let us dance
With naked feet beneath the young spice trees.
What was that light, that radiance
On your face?—something I saw when first
You passed beneath the jungle tapestries?
A moment we pause to quench our thirst
Kneeling at the water's edge, the gleam
Upon your face is plain; you have wanted this.
Oh let us go back and search the tangled dream
And as the muffled drum-beats throb and miss
Remember again how early darkness comes
To dreams and silence to the drums.

IV

Let us go back into the dusk again,
Slow and sad-like following the track
Of blown leaves and cool white rain
Into the old grey dreams; let us go back.
Our walls close about us, we lie and listen
To the noise of the street, the storm and the driven birds.
A question shapes your lips, your eyes glisten
Retaining tears, but there are no more words.

I—

By Brenda Ray Moryck

HEN I was a very little girl, a strange and unaccountable idea persisted with me that I wanted to belong to the aristocrats of the earth. Psychologists would explain this complex by referring to the African kings and queens who loom so frequently on the horizon nowadays as the direct forbears of every Negro who achieves, and of many who aspire to achieve, but my mother offers a more physical and intimate reason. She spent the lovely Spring months preceding my birth in a serene and exclusive country seat on a tiny farm adjoining a magnificent estate, where the beautiful titled English woman for whom I was subsequently named, and who was graciously pleased to form an attachment for my mother and an interest in my approaching advent was visiting.

Very early, I began to associate aristocracy with flat-heeled, square-toed shoes, in a day when most children's stubby feet were being sacrificed to the false grace of a pointed toe and ordinary shops refused to display even small children's boots without heels; with short white socks when a mistaken modesty bade mothers cover their small daughters' legs in long, black stockings; clean finger-nails when it was the vogue to cry "let children be children" (meaning let them be pigs); glistening teeth, free from food and film before the alarming days of "one in every five will have it"; loosely hanging, unberibboned locks when two or four tight braids, according to the texture of the hair, flamboyantly decorated with huge, bright-colored bows at the nape of the neck were the vogue; and severely tailored outer play garments, mostly dark blue, when little girls self-consciously appeared on sleds or skates bedecked in last year's finery, and bearskin, crushed plush and velvet betokened the style.

Looking at the children thus accoutred and then examining myself by careful scrutiny, I perceived a striking similarity. So elated was I by this discovery of homogeneity that I entirely forgot to note the difference in the color of our skins. I was so happy in just being a little girl of the sort I admired I neglected to remember that I was colored.

Something happened to me then,—something so deeply satisfying, so limitless in its beneficence, so far-reaching in its results, that I set down details here cognizant of hazarding charges of snobbery. It was as if I had been slipped for all times into an impregnable suit of armor with which to shut in after years all subsequent buffetings of the world. No curious stares, no disapproving comments, nor the starkest criticism in my presence of my wise

mother's extraordinary taste could shake my equanimity or self-satisfaction. The claim is made, I know, that we see life in retrospect through rose-colored glass, but the actual unembellished fact is that I,—a Negro by birth,—a very small girl by years,—began my battle with a hostile, Caucasian-dominated life outside the home-nest, as a happy, self-assured, young being.

Later years soon dimmed the illusion that the symbol of aristocracy is outward dress and appearance—that it is even that soft-mannered or arrogant veneer which so often deceives,—in fact that it is anything but the serenity and strength of mind which come from a consciousness of clear vision, straight thinking and a right evaluation of every detail of life's complexity—not blue-blood but a sterling heritage,—a taste for the fine and the beautiful,—courage and fineness; not wealth in dollars and cents, though to keep high our self-set standards today, we must have money and plenty of it or trail in the dust of unfulfillment a goodly portion of our splendid desires,—not money,—but riches,—a keen and open mind,—a fertile brain, a hungry intellect,—a sane and wholesome outlook on life,—joy in little things,—the gift to love and love abundantly;—not suavity,—correct manners, soft-voiced covering of an empty or dishonest heart, nor yet hauteur,—smug self-esteem through bending heads which might look up in competition—but gentility,—that kindness, consideration, forbearance, tolerance, magnanimity and helpfulness to every living thing which betoken true refinement,—but my firmly established belief that I could measure with earth's elite never vanished.

As a Negro, I came to learn that I belonged to a despised group,—a group hailed everywhere by every ordinary white child as "niggers" or "darkies" —a practice much more common during my childhood even in the north than it is today slightly south of the Mason-Dixon line; that I must suffer impertinent and malicious stares at school every time "Old Black Joe" or "Swanee River" were sung unless I happened to be in the class of a child-lover,—and thank God there were a number to whom I now offer gratitude, who smilingly chose the morning songs themselves and never seemed to remember the existence of those tunes; that I must hand over the set of tea-dishes fallen to my lot as an impartial or blind Santa Claus's gift from a Caucasian Baptist Sunday School Christmas tree because a white infant objected to "that little colored girl" having dishes while she had only a book; that I must play better basket-ball than any other member

153

of the team to keep my place on it as representative of my high school; that I must always be in company with a certain lovely Caucasian in order to drink soda or eat luncheon in certain exclusive shops or bathe at certain beaches; that the privilege of touring the beautiful southern part of "the land of the free and home of the brave" must be foregone because of the insufferable inconveniences maintained by discrimination; that colleges catered to prejudice, and all learned people were not cultured; that some were cats and brutes and boors; that men and women, too, of warped mind and narrow sympathies often dominated the earth,—at least a considerable portion of it, and bent to their evil wills their brothers less fortunate because cursed with a black skin; that my people were burned alive and seldom a voice raised in protest, yet gladly saluted the flag which refused them protection, and in time of war, laid down their lives for a country in which they had lived on sufferance; that "might is often right" so far as exploitation of black men is concerned, and that justice is the white man's meed alone. I could not help it. It was life.

Yet, for every ill, life offers compensation. Being a Negro is sweet at times. It carries with it privileges which cannot but warm the heart of the most cynical and callous. The bitter may denounce friendly overtures as patronage, asking only a fair chance to make their mark according to their abilities, but this is a very partial old world after all,—a world in which the scales for reward and punishment are seldom equal. We rise,—too often, perhaps,—on personal favor,—not only Negroes, but all people. Since we are of this world, if not with it, it seems sensible to rejoice in the kind offices of our well-wishers. "Look not a gift horse in the mouth."

I soon learned that although a representative number of patched up and hungry-looking little plebeians liked to call "Nigger, nigger, never die, black face and shiny eye," and a few sturdy, rosy-cheeked ones, too, every time I passed by, the majority of the children who came from big, comfortable-looking homes,—even elegant houses on quiet streets—(for I went to the public school in a day when intelligent and far-sighted parents had not yet felt the "menace of socialization" or doubted the efficacy of mass training for the individual, and the earlier popularity of the private school and private tutor was on the wane)—were forever seeking me out to make up their ring or complete their team or play their games, and were constantly inviting me home to luncheon "because I want Mama to see you," (Mama being one of those "wholesale-generalizationed" tongued ladies who had pronounced sentence on all colored children as being rough, dirty, and foul-minded).

Remember, please, that I was very young and very human. I enjoyed it all. Preening myself on my desirability as "such a *lovely* little colored girl," I soon let it be known in certain "white trash" enemy groups that I was not allowed to associate with common children! And when I went home at his invitation with my first beau,—an adorable eight-year-old named Leslie, who I might wish even now could read these lines,—and his family, all gathered on the large veranda of his home to receive his fair lady burst into laughter and gurgled, "Why she's *colored*," I thought they were delighted to find me different!

Little prig—little fool! What does it matter,—which or both—so I was happy. Is it not every child's right to be happy? I was happy.

Again, the earmarks of my Negro blood won me a coveted position as alto in a duet with a beautiful little Jewish soprano who has since become nationally known. Nearly all the class entered the competition, but when, by elimination, only three candidates were left, there was such bitterness and weeping and wailing between the two little white girls desirous of singing "The Miller of the Dee" with this exquisite, divine-voiced doll, that the teachers cut short all controversy with the naïve announcement, "If we let the little colored girl win, the others won't feel so badly." "Beauty and the Jacobin!" How times have changed!

My high school career was practically free of all race consciousness, due, I am now positive to the absolute impartiality and unbiased principles of the head, a man of genial character but inflexible rule, and a corps of, for the most part, broad-minded, tolerant teachers who very adroitly never permitted the question of color and race superiority or inferiority to crop up. I was just one of the many, a single pupil in a classical school ministering to a heterogeneous group of hundreds of raw young people, making my mark and claiming notice according to my special talents, solely. Only when I made the basket-ball team was I conscious that my efforts alone had been superior to every other member's and yet I was last to be recognized. But who shall say the extra endeavor a Negro must always put forth in competition with white men does not rebound to his own benefit and credit? Was I not the better player on the court because of longer and more skillful practice before making the team?

Quite apart, however, from my school affiliations, there was another larger and more beautiful life opened to me, solely because I was a Negro. I may or may not have had an arresting personality, I may or may not have been well-bred, well-dressed, generally well-appearing. The fact remains that had I not been distinctly a member of my own racial group, I should never have become a quasi-protegée of an exquisite woman on whom the Gods had smiled in every way at her birth and on through life,—who was graciously pleased to entertain me in her home, introduce me to her friends and take me about everywhere,—not as her hired companion nor the daughter or granddaughter of some faithful retainer in her father's or mother's ménage, but as an interesting little colored girl who deserved to see the best that life offered, and who because of the barrier of a brown skin must otherwise be denied anything but occasional tempting glimpses.

Through her generosity, I tasted a life utterly beyond the reach of most Caucasians, tasted it under the pleasantest auspices, and therefore came to set store on being a Negro as something rare and precious.

The college years did not dispel this assumption. Rather, they tended to heighten it. The disappointments and heart-aches, which every normal teen age girl away from home experiences, were not due to color prejudice. At my college, Wellesley, in my day,—not so very long ago either—the authorities permitted no discrimination. The student body, consequently, taking their cue from their elders and betters as they always do, consciously or unconsciously even today, engaged in no wholesale active hostilities.

There were girls, of course, who tried to be mean and hateful,—usually from small towns in the north and west,—the southern girls, it is my joy to relate, with one lamentable exception—and that from the Nation's capital—were all ladies, and though their faces sometimes flamed with protest at the new order of relationships they were forced to endure, their good breeding never failed and, in time they came to be pleasantly civil outside the classroom as well as within, some of them even achieving a friendliness in senior year and a cordiality at reunions that was not to have been dreamed of in Freshman days, but for the most part, everybody wanted to do something kind for the one little black girl,—alien in a lively, callous, young world of fourteen hundred Caucasians, even the villagers to whom intimate contact with a Negro, not a hairdresser or laundress, was a privilege.

Again, it was always those choice spirits who roam the world and tread the high places of life unfettered by the bonds of public opinion,—either the very, very wealthy or the very blue-blooded, or the jealous devotee of the true principles of democracy, eager to put into practice her newly-conned theories, who were most generous in their friendliness and delightful in their overtures. Sadly must I observe that it was seldom the orthodox Christian recognized by her piety in repeating the prayer for all sorts and conditions of men and her lip-service to "God created of one blood all nations for to dwell upon the face of the earth" who stepped aside from her own interests or widened her circle to include me, but then,—she was not missed.

It was delightful—being a Negro at college. She who would decry the kind of satisfaction derived therefrom must indeed be a hypocrite or else abnormal. Let her consider the creature who walks alone through life, white or black,—friendless, unnoticed, uncherished, and reflect that it is a normal human being's craving to be liked. If, for wholesome reasons, and certainly there is nothing un-

wholesome in being a Negro, except in the eyes of certain vicious Nordics who seek to make it appear so, a person is liked,—what matters all the rest?

Even today, at a time when the entire attention of the white world at large is focused upon the Negro, with what intent or ultimate purpose it is difficult to forecast; when lynching is increasing, prejudice growing, the right to discriminate sustained on questions of civil right, north and west, as well as south, and unfair competition against the Negro threatening his economic existence except as a peon or pauper,—there is a zest in being a Negro.

Read the recent editorial comment on a dainty brown-skinned, bird-throated comedienne, Florence Mills, and take thought of the homage an intelligent world pays to art irrespective of race or color. Sit in capacity-jammed Carnegie Hall and hear the delicate exquisite music made by Roland Hayes, and know him judged a supreme artist, not of his race but of the world. Then consider. Have I not cause for pride of race?

There is honey as well as hemlock in the cup of every Negro,—sunlight as well as shadow.

. . . .

But as a woman, what did I learn? That the sun shines on the just and the unjust,—that the mountains clap their hands and the morning stars sing together? That the glory of the sunset fades into the exquisite dusk of twilight and the mid-darkness of night bursts into the glory of the dawn? That the green of the tree-leaf turns to a magic red and gold and when winter comes, spring is not far behind?

Did I learn this as a woman? Ah, yes, and more besides,—that the peace and the beauty of earth,—fulfillment,—lie within the mind, embedded and enshrouded in an elusive quantity called soul, —whose entity now men doubt. Bend the body to the rack, confine the intellect to the torture of eternal limitations, the soul is away and free,— ranging the hills,—roaming the fields, winging on the breeze to an elysium which only God can withdraw. The majesty of mountains, the loveliness of twilight, the ineffable beauty of sunsets, the rush of sparkling waters, the pure calm of the deep woods, the mystery of oceans,—starlight, moonlight,—sunlight,—vast spaces under the infinite sky are mine, —mine because I am a woman,—a human being,— one of God's great family for whom He created the world and all that therein is. Smiling eyes of children,—blue eyes under golden curls as well as black eyes in tawny faces are turned toward me. Work, play, and that highest opportunity, the opportunity to help and to give, to mother and to heal,—are mine. "Non ministrari sed ministrare" is the radiance of existence. And can I not keep company with the greatest minds of the earth for all times in my books?

Life is rich and beautiful to a woman.

I am a Negro—yes—but I am also a woman.

"Two men looked out from the prison bars,
One saw the mud, the other, the stars."

A Glorious Company

By Allison Davis

HERE is an old Negro song in which the band of those destined for Heaven, with the prophets and King Jesus, are safely transported thither aboard a train! This journey by train to their last, long station is but an accentuated expression of the fascination and mystery which trains hold for Negroes of the south. I have often thought that the Negro farmhand would lose heart once for all, were it not for the daily encouragement he takes from the whistle of his favorite locomotives. Tied to his plow, under the red, burning sun, or aching with the loneliness of the sterile night, he can find all his desire for escape, all the courage he lacks in the face of the unknown, mingled with his inescapable hopelessness, in the deep-throated, prolonged blast of the express-train, like a challenge to un-travelled lands, a terrifying cry to his petty township.

A journey by train for no more than three or five miles fills the poor Negroes of the south with confidence and elation. They are not only holiday-makers; they are seekers and adventurers. With all their children and world's gear about them, they leave nothing more precious than a squalid, smoke-painted shanty, with its empty pig-sty; who knows, then, if perchance they may not find a changed life in the next town or county, and never return? It is pitiable they should not yet have learned they have no fair country, and that oppression rides with them. Yet, no one who has not had his world bounded into less clean and metaphorical limits than those of a nut-shell can understand the hope which these, who journey from home, feel at the possibility of escape.

To them, the mere fact of motion suggests new independence, and incites their trammeled spirits with unbounded enthusiasm. They are rolling, in a rolling world, and at every local station exhort their friends, from the windows, to join the band.

"Git on boa'd, little children,
 Dere's room for many a mo'."

is the spirit, if not the letter, of their greeting.

Aboard, they are all friends, drawn by their common adventure. A gambler and bully-boy lavishes his famed courtliness on a withered, old sister, brave in her antebellum finery, and falls at length into her "revival" plans. I have often noticed a fine-looking type of old gentleman, whose rich, brown skin, and soft, curly hair lend him a gentility the Jewish patriarchs lacked. He seems destined to encounter some buxom, dark-skinned "fancy woman," who cleverly leads him into his favorite discourses on the virtues of renunciation and purity. Trained in flattery by her mode of life, she sits like a rapt student at her master's feet. And if, by unlucky goodness of heart, she offers him a pint of her own home-made "sperrits," knowing the indigence of the pure in heart, he will feel the simple testimony, and forgive.

There will be also the irreconcilables, like this white-skinned lady from the north. She feels only the indignity of the segregated train, and suffers from a kind of hyperaesthesia in this crude gathering of her own people. The odors from their full meal of fried chicken—I have seen even the delectable cabbage in lunch-boxes—arouse in her a genuine hatred of the whole clan; and she would enjoy lynching those wayworn sisters who unshoe their tortured feet. These black folk from whom she shrinks, however, are incorrigibly gentle and courteous, and seek by persistent attentions to make her comfortable,—even to talk with her like a fellow-being in a world of trouble. But her thoughts are fixed, with bitter longing, on the parlor car.

And yet, among the Florida tourists, from the observation car through the dining and lounging cars, down to this truncated segment of the baggage car, she would find no wit and smiles to put zest in the journey, like these about her. Starvation, one's own ignorance, persecution, hard luck, and the way of woman, all are turned into laughter, now reckless, and now ultimately philosophic. A jet-black woman is laughed at by her equally dark escort for spending time and effort to rouge and powder;—and she sees the ridiculous futility of her vanity, and laughs more heartily than he! A consumptive of huge frame jokingly threatens the young porter for treading on his feet, and cannot laugh without pain. And in one corner, in spite of the scowls of the conductor, a one-legged miner sings rich harmonies to his guitar, strumming with fervent sympathy, *Wonder Where's Dem Hebrew Children?* That *he* should look to Palestine two thousand years ago for homeless ones to pity!

More animated and cheerful is the story-teller, touched by just enough of the grape,—turned corn now in this makeshift world—to inspire him to a longer tale of his wanderings. He knows himself a romantic protagonist for this young college-boy who listens, and carries his adventures farther into the hero-world. There, sweet brown girls cherish him, or "evil womans" betray him, according to the powers of the grape. For the most part, he has had Herculean jobs in the mines or on the docks, and harder luck with his women than Samson; but now that he's once again "railroading, behind an eight-driving engine, with the rails ringing," his confidence returns. Tomorrow, nay tonight at the end of his fare, he may be hungry and in the park; but as he talks now, homelessness and starvation are dangers in romance, no more fatal than the wounds of the archangels, which bleed ichor, and heal forthwith!

So it is with them all, escaping the weight of hardship and persecution by some exhilaration of the moment. In an hour now, many will be left at their lonely, country station, while the great engine burns its fiery trail across the black sky, driving on into other lands with happier children. But now they are still in a band and confident. Their pride and courage are fortified by the swaggers of the porter, for he is one of their own; they feel it a strange and hopeful dispensation that he should be here to guide them safely in. So they roll on into a mystery.

In the great, city station, this sense of mystery becomes at once awful and exhilarating. They give porters tips of five cents in a beautiful trance of lavishness. The marble under their feet is turned to buoyant ether, and the great dome above draws their spirits in prayers and hallelujahs. And their exhilaration is the keener because against this brilliant spectacle, they can see in their mind's eye the alley-shack where they will come into the city's life. Now they feel only that here is a journey finished in a new and better land, full of light and splendor.

They have not gone this journey of physical hardship and spiritual cramping without the strength of hope and faith. This faith they will not lose in the newer lands to which they must eventually come, for it is revived daily by the barest victory over disease and poverty, and these will travel with them, to chasten. They go also with humility, which we will not think meanness of spirit, until we have known the daily bitterness of being forced to resign hope and manhood. And if they are humble, having faith in their journey, and courage still to face it with laughter and friendliness, perhaps they may be allowed to go in their stocking-feet, at ease over their dinner of cabbage, until they shall understand the ways of our fine lady, and some day, perchance, even of the Florida tourists.

A STUDENT I KNOW
By Jonathan H. Brooks

He mocks the God invisible
  To whom his mother prays;
"What stands on faith for proof is built
  On shifting sands," he says.

To him life is a heartless game:
  "I grapple, fight, defy,"
He says: "the world is his who wins;
  The losers, let them die."

Ah, greenhorn-pilgrim, duped by thieves
  And left to writhe in dirt
Beside the way to Jericho—
Wounded, robbed—and hurt!

— AND I PASSED BY

By Joseph Maree Andrew

I USED to take so much of Life for granted. Enough to eat—enough sleep—enough rest—not too much to do—the schools I wanted—the things I wanted—friends with the things they wanted.

I had even been pit-pat too. Took the Natural-Trickery-of-the-White-man to be an indelible streak in the breed. An indelible streak that only called for enough distrust on my own part to get along.

I used to take so much of Life for granted. But once the Wing—the WING of Death—swept across my home. Swept across my home twice in two short years.

It swept twice. It made sure that all of my heart was beneath the two pieces of the World that men call graves.

I used to take so much of Life for granted. When the Wing had swept clean the halls of my home, people came and talked. Came to talk, to tell me how to face two spaces that were empty forever. Empty spaces that ached. Then the talk and the people flowed back around me like blood from around a wound.

The Empty Spaces ached. I was the flesh around the wound—the Empty Spaces, the wound.

I cried to high Heaven—"Is God really good—?"

But I should have bowed and cried low—"Yet-somehow—God is really good."

I had taken too much for granted, you see. The Wing swept clean. It swept away the scales from my eyes, too. I began to soften.

—Soft, you will see what I mean.

The scales left my eyes. I decided I could again see and talk once more without dropping out of things into my own abyss.

Thus I set out on a winter's evening with a friend to dinner. Cold air pooled around us as we stepped out of the door.

I took a deep sniff—drew in as much as I could—pressed my cheeks deeper in the fur around me—appreciated my friend's well clad appearance—sniffed her perfume—and let my pulse race ahead to the click of our heels on the pavement.

Nothing troubled us. Absolutely nothing at all. School and its work lay behind us. A home we could really enjoy lay ahead.

We pattered. Light talk pattered with our heels.

"Let's walk all the way." I had to skip a step as I said. It was so good to be freely alive.

"I want to walk for once," replied the girl beside me.

The hill mounted. Our blood pounded. Our heels clicked. Our tongues raced —I could breathe deeply and I could only know it was cold by the whiffs of the air across my nose (which is strangely tender in winter).

The hill veered sharply. We would either have to prolong the jaunt or take a short cut.

"Are you afraid to cut through—Street? asked my companion. She mentioned a street that is not supposed to be safe after dark.

It has sad houses, sad stores in every available space, and people, white and colored. up and down it. It is sad. The white and colored people fight pitched battles and hate each other as if each blamed the other for being there.

"No! of course I am not afraid." My pulse made me say that.

We struck out. I really was a bit afraid. That made my pulses race harder. We crossed an intersection. I stumbled over the car tracks and hopped the curb. Then I turned to look back.

"Not buttered fingers but buttered toes," I explained.

The other girl did not answer. She looked beyond me. I turned the other way to look too.

Something soft brushed against me. A girl—slender, dead-white—in a light blue dress with a low round neck—and with bed-room slippers on her feet—staggered against me.

I welched away. She fell in a sort of confusion against the building behind us. The street light lay full in her face. Her eyes were half closed, her mouth slightly opened.

Something made me catch hold of my throat. The girl staggered and stumbled. She went around the corner.

"Oh—." It sounded futile even to me, but I said it. We both stared at one another. I rambled on: "She did not have a coat!" I started toward the corner. "She is sick!"

"You'd better let that cracker alone! You do not know this place! This is—Street!" cried the girl with me.

I wavered. This was —Street.

That sent us on up the hill. A weight fell on me. The sidewalk made me stumble. I felt burdened. I was stumbling.

I sat at the table. Food, talk, good fellowship flowed around me, bathed me about.

"Come to and answer my question!" some one said beside me.

"Mustn't let yourself worry, my dear," the hostess whispered in the kindly warmth of motherly middle age.

Tears wavered in my eyes. She thought I was rooting back.

Digging beneath my wound. . Filling my Empty Spaces with dreams that hurt. But—

—Cold. A blue voile dress. Bed room slippers. Eyes half-opened. But she was white. She would have pushed me away if I had touched her and she had seen my brown flesh.

What did I have to do with it? She would have spat in my face.

Still a white face swam before me. It swam between me and my plate. A pale blue voile dress. I only knew it was cold by the touch of wind across my face.—

I tried to blot it out then. I tasted food. Tasted ideas. Talked. Listened. Gave in talk. Shut it out.

—Shut out the cry within me. Shut out the cry—What had I to do with it? What had I to do with it?

Played. Played the piano to shut it out.

"You always play so beautifully for me!" the hostess purred.

Beautifully for her! I was trying to send out the warmth my fingers should have had to a thin pale body in a blue voile dress. Trying to make myself hard. Playing down the fight that was within me.

—You should have gone back!

What had I to do with the—

With thee! Jesus of Nazareth—

I was too soft. It was the Empty Spaces that made me soft. People forget things that have nothing to do with them, why could not I? Why could I not let it alone? Empty Spaces. She was sick. The dress was blue voile.—

A room full of warmth and easy pleasant lovable folk.

The room was warm—bare arms—Empty Spaces. She would leave a space empty. Someone else would become the Flesh-Around—the Wound. Aching around an Empty Space. Empty. Aching.—

And I had gone up the hill.

Jesus of Nazareth! What had I to do with Thee?—

I took my hands off the keys and laid one quickly over my lips.

"Does your tooth ache?" someone queried behind me.

I had to leave then.

Someone else was talking in the room next to me as I put on my hat. "She takes her sorrow too hard. She must give them up!"

I knew they meant me—that was it. I thought of myself so much—so much for granted—that everyone knew I only thought of Things as they related to me.

—Always me. I had not gone back. She hated my kind. I would not let her "Spit in my face." Me.—

Sometimes I think I see her white face and feel her brush by me.

What had I to do with Thee, Jesus of Nazareth?

God forgive me. Forgive me for letting You stumble by me—alone.— In a thin white body this time; into the dark—in a dress that was no dress—no shoes—into the dark of a winter night.

Forgive me for letting hate send me up the hill while You went down. I wonder where You went then?

I do not know why I did not go back to You. Today I cannot say why. Someday, though, God, I shall have to tell You why.

WHO'S WHO

AARON DOUGLAS is one of the most original of Negro artists; he was one of the sixty-five American artists selected for exhibition with The Society of Graphic Arts; now on art fellowship at the Barnes Foundation. *Arthur Fauset* won the **OPPORTUNITY** first prize with his short story "Symphonesque," reprinted in O'Brien's and the O'Henry Memorial Awards volumes, author of "For Freedom." *Paul Green,* professor of philosophy at the University of North Carolina has written many plays of Negro life. His "In Abraham's Bosom," was awarded last year's Pulitzer Prize. *John Matheus* is a professor of Romance Languages at West Virginia Collegiate Institute and an **OPPORTUNITY** and Crisis short story prize winner.

Countee Cullen has published two volumes of his own poems "Color" and "Copper Sun" and an anthology of the younger Negro poets—"Caroling Dusk." *Charles Cullen* is an artist who has recently found a new enthusiasm in drawings of Negro characters—he illustrated "Copper Sun" and "The Ballad of the Brown Girl." *Julia Peterkin* is the author of "Green Thursday" and "Black April," two of the foremost books about Negroes. *Zora Neale Hurston* has written short stories and plays and more recently has turned to the study of Negro folklore. *Guy B. Johnson* is a co-author of "The Negro and His Songs." He is at the University of North Carolina. *John Davis* took his Master's Degree at Harvard last year and is now publicity director for Fisk University. *Gwendolyn Bennett* has taught art at Howard, and is now on an art fellowship at the Barnes Foundation and a columnist for **OPPORTUNITY**. *Nathan Ben Young* is an attorney in St. Louis. He once lived in Birmingham. *Edna Worthley Underwood* is a poet, novelist and translator of international reputation, author of *The Passion Flower, The Pageant Maker* and other volumes.

Arthur A. Schomburg is perhaps the greatest of Negro bibliophiles. His collection of rare books was recently turned over to the N. Y. Public Library. *Dorothy Scarborough* is author of "On the Trail of Negro Folk Songs." She is a professor of English at Columbia and has written two novels. *Phillis Wheatley* was the first Negro poet (1753-1784). *Dorothy Peterson* is a teacher of Spanish in the New York Public Schools. *Professor Ellsworth Faris* is the head of the Department of Sociology at the University of Chicago and *Eugene Kinckle Jones* is Executive Secretary of the National Urban League. *Dr. E. B. Reuter* is professor of Sociology at the University of Iowa. *William Pickens* is Field Secretary of the National Association for the Advancement of Colored People. *Alain Locke* is editor of the *New Negro*. *E. Franklin Frazier* is a young sociologist now preparing for his degree of Doctor of Philosophy at the University of Chicago and a frequent contributor to magazines. *George Schuyler* is on the staff of the *Messenger* and the *Pittsburgh Courier* and a contributor to magazines. *Theophilus Lewis* is dramatic critic for the *Messenger*. *Abram L. Harris* is a professor of Economics at Howard University. *T. Arnold Hill* is director of the Department of the Industrial Relations of the National Urban League, formerly Executive Secretary of the Chicago Urban League. *Richard Bruce* is a young artist and poet. He is at present filling a role in *Porgy. Ira Reid* is Industrial Secretary of the N. Y. Urban League. *W. P. Dabney* is author of *Cincinnati's Colored Citizens* and editor of the Cincinnati Union a free lance newspaper. *Francis Holbrook* is an artist who has contributed frequently to Opportunity. He lives in Brooklyn.

Brenda Moryck is an **OPPORTUNITY** and Crisis prize winner for essays and short stories. She teaches school in Washington. *W. E. Braxton* is an artist. He won the gold and silver medals offered by Adelphia College, Brooklyn.

THE NATIONAL URBAN LEAGUE

Organized 1910 ❦ ❦ ❦ ❦ ❦ *Incorporated 1913*

17 MADISON AVENUE
NEW YORK CITY

THE NATIONAL URBAN LEAGUE is an organization which seeks to improve the relations between the races in America. It strives to improve the living and working conditions of the Negro.

Its special field of operation embraces cities where Negroes reside in large numbers.

The Executive Boards of the national and of the forty local organizations are made up of white and colored people who have caught the vision of social work and believe in justice and fair play in the dealings of men with each other.

The Leagues Program

It maintains a Department of Research and Investigations with Charles S. Johnson as Director, who also edits "OPPORTUNITY" magazine—the official organ of the League. This Department makes thorough investigations of social conditions in cities as bases for the League's practical work.

As rapidly as practicable committees are organized to further the recommendations growing out of such studies and especially to stimulate existing social welfare agencies to take on work for Negroes or to enlarge their activities in behalf of their Negro constituents. Occasionally special work for Negroes is organized where existing agencies are not willing to assume work for Negroes, or where there are no available facilities for meeting these needs.

The League furthers the training of colored social workers through providing fellowships for colored students at schools of social work and providing apprenticeships in the League's field activities for prospective social workers.

It conducts programs of education among colored and white people for the purpose of stimulating greater interest on the part of the general public in social work for colored people.

The League has a Department of Industrial Relations with T. Arnold Hill as Director. This Department seeks:

1. To standardize and coordinate the local employment agencies of the League so that exchange of information and more regular correspondence between them can assure applicants for work more efficient and helpful service and employers of labor a more efficient group of employees;

2. To work directly with large industrial plants both in cities where the League is established and in communities removed from such centers to procure larger opportunity for work and for advancement on the job for Negro workers and to stimulate Negro workers to a fresh determination to "make good" on the job so that their future place in industry may be assured;

3. To help through available channels of information to ascertain points at which there is need of Negro labor and points at which there is an oversupply of Negro labor and to use existing agencies of publicity and placement to direct Negro labor to those points where they are most needed and where their families will more easily become adjusted.
   This Department seeks to promote better relations between white and colored workers not through activities involving force, but through the orderly development of a feeling of good-will and comradeship. This accomplished would mean the removal of barriers against Negro membership in organized labor.

Officers:

L. HOLLINGSWORTH WOOD, President EUGENE KINCKLE JONES, Executive Secretary
LLOYD GARRISON, Treasurer

Contributions in aid of the League may be made direct to the National Office.

LIST OF AFFILIATED BRANCHES OF THE NATIONAL URBAN LEAGUE

❧

AKRON, OHIO
Association for Colored Community Work
493 Perkins Street
MR. GEORGE W. THOMPSON

ATLANTA, GEORGIA
Southern Field Secretary
239 Auburn Avenue
JESSE O. THOMAS

ATLANTA, GEORGIA
Atlanta Urban League
239 Auburn Avenue
JOHN W. CRAWFORD, *Exec. Secy.*

BALTIMORE, MARYLAND
Baltimore Urban League
521 McMechen Street
R. M. MOSS, *Exec. Secy.*

BOSTON, MASSACHUSETTS
Boston Urban League
119 Camden Street
SAMUEL A. ALLEN, *Exec. Secy.*

BROOKLYN, NEW YORK
Brooklyn Urban League
105 Fleet Place
ROBERT J. ELZY, *Exec. Secy.*

BUFFALO, NEW YORK
Urban League of Buffalo
357 William Street
WILLIAM L. EVANS, *Exec. Secy.*

CANTON, OHIO
Canton Urban League
819 Liberty Avenue, S. E.
GERALD E. ALLEN, *Exec. Secy.*

CHICAGO, ILLINOIS
Chicago Urban League
3032 South Wabash Avenue
A. L. FOSTER, *Exec. Secy.*

CLEVELAND, OHIO
The Negro Welfare Association
2554 East 40th Street
WILLIAM R. CONNERS, *Exec. Secy.*

COLUMBUS, OHIO
Columbus Urban League
681 East Long Street
N. B. ALLEN, *Exec. Secy.*

DETROIT, MICHIGAN
Detroit Urban League
1911 St. Antoine Street
JOHN C. DANCY, *Exec. Secy.*

ENGLEWOOD, NEW JERSEY
*Englewood League for Social Service
Among Colored People*
71 Englewood Avenue
LOUIS S. PIERCE, *Exec. Secy.*

KANSAS CITY, MISSOURI
Community Service Urban League
1731 Lydia Avenue
EDWARD S. LEWIS, *Exec. Secy.*

LOS ANGELES, CALIFORNIA
Los Angeles Urban League
1325 Central Avenue
MRS. KATHERINE J. BARR, *Exec. Secy.*

LOUISVILLE, KENTUCKY
Louisville Urban League
615 W. Walnut Street
J. M. RAGLAND, *Exec. Secy.*

MILWAUKEE, WIS.
Milwaukee Urban League
631 Vliet Street
JAMES H. KERNS, *Exec. Secy.*

MINNEAPOLIS, MINN.
Minneapolis Urban League
71 West 7th Street
St. Paul, Minn.

MORRISTOWN, NEW JERSEY
85 Spring Street
MISS ALICE WHITE

(OVER)

LIST OF AFFILIATED BRANCHES OF THE
NATIONAL URBAN LEAGUE

NEW YORK CITY
New York Urban League
202 West 136th Street
JAMES H. HUBERT, *Exec. Secy.*

NASHVILLE, TENNESSEE
The Public Welfare League
708 Cedar Street
PAUL F. MOWBRAY, *Exec. Secy.*

NEWARK, NEW JERSEY
New Jersey Urban League
212 Bank Street
THOMAS L. PURYEAR, *Exec. Secy.*

PHILADELPHIA, PENNSYLVANIA
Armstrong Association of Philadelphia
1434 Lombard Street
WAYNE L. HOPKINS, *Exec. Secy.*

PLAINFIELD, NEW JERSEY
Plainfield Urban League
1226 Arlington Street
MRS. EVA KNIGHT, *President*

PITTSBURGH, PENNSYLVANIA
Pittsburgh Urban League
518 Wylie Avenue
ALONZO C. THAYER, *Exec. Secy.*

RICHMOND, VIRGINIA
Richmond Urban League
2 West Marshall Street
C. L. WINFREE, *Exec. Secy.*

SPRINGFIELD, MASSACHUSETTS
St. John's Institutional Activities
643 Union Street
DR. WILLIAM N. DEBERRY, *Exec. Secy.*

SPRINGFIELD, ILLINOIS
Springfield Urban League
1610 East Jackson Street
SAMUEL B. DANLEY, JR., *Exec. Secy.*

ST. PAUL, MINNESOTA
St. Paul Urban League
71 West 7th Street
ELMER A. CARTER, *Exec. Secy.*

ST. LOUIS, MISSOURI
Urban League of St. Louis
615 North Jefferson Avenue
JOHN T. CLARK, *Exec. Secy.*

TAMPA, FLORIDA
Tampa Urban League
1310 Marion Street
MR. B. E. MAYS, *Exec. Secy.*

WATERBURY, CONNECTICUT
Interdenominational Committee
81 Pearl Street
MRS. LEILA T. ALEXANDER

WESTFIELD, NEW JERSEY
Westfield Urban League
417 West Broad Street
MISS IRENE SUMERSET, *Exec. Secy.*

HARTFORD, CONNECTICUT
22 Avon Street

YOUNGSTOWN, OHIO
Booker T. Washington Settlement
962 Federal Street
SULLY JOHNSON, *Exec. Secy.*